To Paul

You're a stand up
guy. Thank you
for the recommendations

Vince

12.10.03

INVINCEABLE
PRINCIPLES

INVINCEABLE PRINCIPLES

Essential Tools for Life Mastery

Vince Poscente

Resources for Life Mastery

INVINCEABILITY SERIES
2528 ELM STREET, SUITE 200
DALLAS, TEXAS 75226 USA
PHONE: 800-791-2078
WEBSITE: www.invinceability.com
EMAIL: vince@invinceability.com

PRINTED IN THE UNITED STATES OF AMERICA

BOOK PRODUCTION BY PHELPS & ASSOCIATES, LLC, LANCASTER, OH
COVER DESIGN BY JON BENSON
COVER PHOTOGRAPHY BY LESLIE BAKER
"Creation of Adam" by Michelangelo Buonarroti: Sistine Chapel, Vatican, Rome, Italy / SuperStock

Cataloging-in-Publication Data
(prepared by Quality Books, Inc.)
Poscente, Vince.
 Invinceable principles : essential tools for life mastery /
Vince Poscente. -- 1st ed.
 p. cm. -- (Invinceability series)
LCCN: 99-94555

 ISBN: 1-893430-00-6 (hardcover)
 ISBN: 1-893430-07-3 (pbk.)

 1. Success. 2. Self-acutalization (Psychology)
I. Title.

BF637.S8P67 1999   158
                  QBI99-697

This book is dedicated to my children, Max and Alexia.
As I wrote the following pages I asked myself,
"Would they be proud of what their father wrote?"
Children learn by the example they have. So, with my kids in mind,
I offer you, the reader, the twelve "Invinceable Principles."
May we all lead by the best example possible.

TABLE OF CONTENTS

F OREWORD BY ALAN HOBSON

Mount Everest Climber and Summiteer, author of From Everest to Enlightenment—An Adventure of the Soul

It took me thirty-nine years, ten expeditions to high altitude, and three trips to Mount Everest to finally reach the top of the world. When I stood at last in the rarefied air at 29,028 feet on May 23, 1997, with the world at my feet, the feeling was one of elation and anxiety. I was thrilled to be there, but concerned that I still had to make it down safely from the peak.

About 40 percent of those who die on Everest die on summit day, descending from the summit. Having expended too much energy on the way up, they do not have enough metaphorical gasoline in their gas tank to make the round trip, and they perish on the descent. Experienced Himalayan climbers celebrate when they are safely back in base camp, and not a second before.

My descent from the top of the world became a descent from hell. Exhausted, my legs to the point where they were almost collapsing underneath me, the only thing that kept me going was a trick I had learned from Vince Poscente.

"CAN, WILL," I repeated to myself over and over again, one word for each step ... "CAN climb Everest, WILL climb Everest," just like I had repeated tens of thousands of times in training.

During the descent to our high camp at twenty-six thousand feet, I lost bladder control. I was too tired to fumble with zippers so I went in my climbing suit. It felt good not to have to fight any more. I let go of my ego and resigned myself to taking thirty more steps. Then, I sat down in the snow for a rest, got up, and took thirty more painstaking steps. This went on for five and a half hours. They were the longest five and a half hours of my life.

When I eventually returned safely to base camp a few days later, what struck me most was not the sheer physical discomfort of what I had had to endure to achieve my dream. What hit me then, and which continues to amaze me now, was how profoundly important my mind had been to my effort—and to my very survival. I was astounded to discover that even with an objective as apparently physical as ascending more than five and a half miles above sea level, it was my mind more than anything that had driven me onward.

Invinceable Principles is about the power of the mind, and the spirit. It is written by a man who has discovered first-hand what the mind can do.

In 1988, Vince Poscente was a recreational skier. Four years later, he was in the Olympic finals in speed skiing, and his nation's fastest man on skis. His record was faster than the terminal velocity parachutists achieve during free fall.

I have practiced Vince's techniques and used them in the most rigorous environmental conditions on Earth. He is a man from whom the world can learn much, and he has much to give. I give thanks for his presence on the planet. He helped save my life. There can be no greater testament to the power of what you are about to read. If you apply only one of his principles, it could have a profound effect on your life. If you apply them all, you will never be the same again, nor will the world.

ACKNOWLEDGMENTS

Imagine a piece of paper where you may see a collection of dots in random order. Connect the dots in a certain way, and it all makes perfect sense—a pattern is revealed. Life is the same way. Seemingly random people and events ultimately reveal a pattern more profound than any scripted effort. Such is the genesis of this book. As I list the acknowledgments for this book, each person may be randomly named but they have contributed to a fabric of experiences for which I am eternally grateful. The following people each have played a valuable role within the context of these pages.

I often tell people that I over-married. My wife Michelle (whose nickname is Missy) is my friend, business partner, mother of our children, entrepreneurial marvel and super-woman all wrapped into one. She defines caring! Her love and support helped me dedicate the time required to meet the demands necessary to write a book of this magnitude. As you will read, I referred to some of her experiences as notable examples. She is a fascinating and engaging human being. I learn from her how to leave this world just a little bit better each day.

Secondly, my parents and family have contributed a great deal. With an Italian father and Irish mother how could I help but learn about the importance of family? My father, deceased at fifty-nine, lived with the utmost of integrity. Every ethical or crucial decision I make in my life is gauged with what I believe my father would have done. In addition, my mother taught me the importance of being a seeker. It is her example that molded me into a person of relentless curiosity and wonder. This book is a testimony to the profound influence that both my father and mother had in my life. To my brother Steven, sister Christa and their respective spouses, Patrice and Ken. Thank you. I look back and realize how many times I could have been a model big brother and wasn't. But you loved me anyway. You are living examples of the importance of family. I would be remiss if I did not single out two cousins who have become more than family—they have become true friends. Jay and Kai are two people whom I hold in high esteem and fond regard. Also, a special thank you to LaDell Lemmons (mother-in-law extraordinaire).

There is the family at home and the extended family at work. Each new day I think of how fortunate I am to be surrounded by astute, loyal, dedicated, tenacious and fun-loving people. Specifically, Jane Atkinson and Leslie Baker have helped build Vince Poscente International into the company it is today. Thanks also to Dillon Boyd and Forrest Jackson for their enthusiasm and expertise. In addition, I would like to thank the staff at International Speakers Bureau for their continued support: Neal Shiller, Jay Kemp, Tipton Crews, Jere Davis, Darrin Powell, Linda Perez, Christa Haberstock, Dan LaBroad, Julie Driver-Grau, Renee Bromfield, Suzanne Pharr, Jennifer Meehan, Leslie Wheiler, Annmarie Marek and Debbie Berren ... thank you for everything!

Friends come and go. When I left Calgary to live in Dallas I thought I was leaving behind friendships—friendships that I held very dear. In fact, the following people have stayed as constant as the Northern Star. Dale Leicht is a valued and treasured friend and together we have spent countless hours trying to figure out life and something even more perplexing ... the opposite sex. (Perhaps enough material there for another book ...) Sean and Debbie Cochlan are always a joy to be with. Grant and Joan Carlson make hanging-out an art form. Bryce and Kelly Medd always make me smile, and John and Christine Malyk have been steady friends throughout the years. I will always treasure Patrick Walsh and Cattis Hackman. Alan Hobson is another friend where with all the ups and downs (mostly ups) we could fill a novel. Jamie Clarke is a friend who should have "Fun" for a middle name. Dave and George Bamber supported me through thick and thin and deserve the highest praise for their loyalty and friendship. Liz Garland is the epitome of "special." She is a friend, mentor and counselor all wrapped up in one.

Since I am new to Dallas, my local friendships are still developing. The best just seems to surface. I can't think of better people in a city of over 3 million people than the following friends. In no particular order I appreciate and value, Gail and Kelly Davis, Mike and Michelle Weiner, Steve and Pam Straus, Dennis and Niki McCuistion, J.B. Smith, Marc Schwartz, Mo Monaghan, Randy Wallace, Fred Seipp, Larry Foster, Joe Foster, Jeff

Conley, Marcia Zidle, Julie Alexander and James Huggins.

In the speaking industry I have developed friendships and mentorships that transcend business. To people like Art Berg, David Rich, Shep Hyken, Dale Irvin, Joe Calloway, Ian Percy, Lou Heckler, Mark Sanborn, Connie Podesta, Randy Pennington, Les Brown, Larry Winget, Jeff Slutzky, George Campbell, Dave Gordon, Jeff Blackman, Dr. Lee Pulos, Terry Brock, Tal Stokes, Nando Parrado, Sugar Ray Leonard, Floyd Wickman, Rosita Perez, Brian Tracy and John Gray—thank you for your support. A special thank you also goes to all the speaker bureau representatives that I have had the privilege of working with. Bureaus in North America play a valuable role in providing professional services to meeting planners across Canada, America, Mexico and around the world. With bureau partners, businesses and associations are the clear benefactors.

Speaking of business, to each and every member of the Young Entrepreneur's Organization and the Young Presidents Organization whom I have had the good fortune to meet, you are an amazing bunch of people. Recently, Jim Reep, an incredible leader passed away from cancer. Jim taught me important lessons in the new age of leadership. I would like to acknowledge the friendships of Billy Weisman and his family, Roy Terracina, Michael Osterman, Frank Argenbright, Karen Behnke, Gerard Cappello, Howard Lauria, Keith Alper, Milledge Hart, Joey Lane, Murray Smith, Rick Sapio, Rand Stagen, Bill Loughborough, Brady Wood, Joseph Rende, Jame Fierro, Seth Davidow, Bill Kimberlin, Brad Berkley, Jill Clouston, Maria Cintron, Sean McGinnis, Gord and Lisa Mawhinney, Kevin and Katie Wilson. Plus, a special thank you to Glenn Solomon whose St. Francisville retreat provided a valuable place of inspiration for writing the first draft.

Fellow authors, many of whom I never met, gave me the opportunity to leverage their vast knowledge. Thanks specifically to all the authors who are noted in the bibliography. If you like books, you will love every single work listed. Also, I would like to thank Sam Horn and the Maui Writer's Conference for an unforgettable experience and unbelievable inspiration. Thanks to Dianna Booher and Dan Poynter for the extra attention to a first-time author.

Looking back at the collection of people who belong in this acknowledgment section are my Poscente and Craig relatives, the entire Lemmons family, the Lewis clan, Doug Young, Mertie and Dale Wood, U. Gary Charlwood, Max Gibb, Diane Jones Konihowski, Carol Anne Letheren, Peirre Jury, John Raftery, Ken Read, Jim Hunter, Dave Irwin, Brock Usborne, Eric Hards, Laurent Marechal, Bill Sannich, Peter Workum, Tye and Carrie Fields, C.J. Mueller, Kenny Dale, Phillipe Goetschel, Jeff Hamilton, Camilla Hackman, Tarja Mulari, Laurent Sistack, Warren Finlay, Brett Finlay, Michelle Gibson, Tricia Ewert, Liz Garland, Val Majeau, Kathy Kerr, Rose Anne Kerr, Ray Cote, Mara Vizzutti, Peggy Merlin, Al Dyer, Jaine Fraser, Gene Edworthy, Tom West, Cathy Glover, Charlotte McNaughton, Reid Morrison, Alice Humeny, Catherine Humeny, Catherine Broomfield, Michelle Platt, Wendy Walker, Ben Morin, Carla Anderson, Lucie Thibault, Bill Warren, Roger Jackson, Trinity Bushner, Randy Best, Bob Gasper, Doug Hansen, Danielle Nadeau, Dave McMillan, Richard Way, Bob Roth, Stu Penny and J.R. Shaw and his family.

A very special thank you goes to Janice Phelps for her editing and publishing skills. Her quiet confidence, exceptional professionalism and tenacious persistence were very much appreciated. In addition, Jon Benson's amazing skills with graphic arts continue to impress me beyond measure. Both Janice and Jon are simply the best at what they do.

Finally, thanks to you the reader. It is a humbling experience to put words to paper and have them read by thousands. I trust you will enjoy what you read and learn what you might.

INTRODUCTION

Tell me: what were the best five years of your life? The ideal answer is—the last five. This book will take you on an in-depth exploration of Invinceable Principles, general truths that if internalized and used on a daily basis will create the pathway to life mastery.

Writing a collection of principles that promises such a lofty goal is a daunting task. Yet, my life has been a series of events taking me assuredly and confidently to this point. Writing it took considerable effort, but getting here was an interesting journey—a lifetime of experiences in a relatively short period of time.

The book, *The Alchemist,* is an inspiring collection of experiences by a young seeker who looks for his fortune and finds himself along the way. Prevalent in the book is the importance of signs and omens that should be paid attention to. With that in mind, I look back to the time when I just graduated from high school. I had finished a summer job working on a ranch and was preparing for my first year of college.

It was an unseasonably cool fall evening and the sky was filled with millions of crystal clear stars. I was inside and, as it was my habit, I had gravitated to the fridge to see what there was to eat. Out of the corner of my eye, I noticed in the window light dancing on the horizon. It was the Northern Lights, the Aurora Borealis.

The Aurora Borealis is a phenomenon of ions in the atmosphere that react to sun flares. The undulating river of light appears to be thousands of slivers of light clashing and shimmying to put on a different show every time they appear. Its displays are never the same time, never the same place, and never expected. They are nature's nocturnal gift to anyone who happens to look up for the brief moment they appear. Growing up in Canada, I would often see the Northern Lights as a youth and imagine it was a reflection of the sun bouncing off the polar ice cap—the dancing lights a result of the floating ice where the polar bears lived.

Living in Sherwood Park in northern Canada was an ideal community. It was a private hamlet of just over thirty thousand people, yet it was close enough to enjoy all the conveniences of a larger city, Edmonton. On this particular night, there was zero humidity and any city lights that shone went directly into the heavens.

I dashed outside, not hesitating to grab a jacket since I had no idea when "the show" had begun nor when it would end. Cranking my head back, the lights were more vibrant than I had ever seen before. Despite the street light fifty yards to the north, I could easily make out the bright band of lights undulating like a snake. It was as if an impressionistic painter had found paints of light-colored white, yellow and glow-in-the-dark green. It moved and shifted, shooting off strands from one horizon to the next.

Its magnitude grew and it seemed as though it was gearing up for something big. Then in an instant everything changed. The colors of red, purple and magenta added to the existing lights and flashed into a spiral directly overhead. It was as if I was looking at a satellite picture of an instantly forming hurricane created by the dancing strands of the northern lights.

The strands themselves changed from a two-dimensional up-and-down to a three-dimensional in-and-out. Imagine millions of fine, ubiquitous, undefined strands of angel hair bobbing in and out of the atmosphere. Like a sea of light beams floating on a swirling ocean. It was awe-inspiring!

The vortex of light began to wind up tight directly overhead. Then, just as quickly as it appeared, it changed again. Now the swirl appeared to spin downward directly down on me. A spiraling tunnel of light started to descend over head. My *Star Trek* infested imagination entertained the thought of being beamed up. I was frozen in place. I couldn't believe what I was seeing—what I was experiencing.

Then the tornado-like funnel stopped descending. It paused, and time seemed to grind to a halt. I held my breath. There was no sound.

A moment later the light danced all around, in all directions. The vortex of light dissipated into a cacophony of light across the whole sky. Like the ending to Beethoven's *1812 Overture*, the heavens danced and the show was over with a dramatic flash. The experience left me vibrating. I just stood there trying to make sense of what had happened.

Then that voice—the one we all have—spoke to me. (The voice that is in the background of your thoughts. The voice that if you listen carefully right now, is speaking to you as you read this book.) It said, "The future is yours to do special things."

I never forgot that moment, and my life has been an effort to meet that challenge.

As you read, you will find a collection of research and personal experiences. I have been fortunate to stand on the shoulders of giants and integrate their research with mine. This book is intended to touch you logically and emotionally. It is meant to spark a long-lost thought. It is designed to fire a desire within you to change in bigger and better ways.

Like you, I am a work in progress. Probably the best time to write this book would have been fifty or so years from now. That way you would have gotten a collection of thoughts and research with a broader background. But the next best time to write these twelve Invinceable Principles is right now. Take what you want, learn what you can and apply what inspires you. Most of all ... act.

This book will cover two areas ... you and other people.

If you are an incorrigible non-conformist, you can go to the chapter you are most curious about. But, for you linear types, each chapter is designed specifically to build a foundation for the next and later chapters. Enjoy your discovery or rediscovery of the Invinceable Principles.

PRINCIPLE **1** ... PERSONIFY PROACTIVITY

"We cannot become what we need to be by remaining what we are."
—*Max DePree*

Be a seeker. Leading a life of total dedication to the truth—this makes you a seeker, a person of curiosity and wonder, a person of hope and ever-increasing levels of wisdom. Yet "truth" is an interesting word.

A truth is simply *your* truth. Learning about the way others perceive truth is another perspective to behold. Your perspective is your reality, and reality is the truth of the individual. Seeking to truly appreciate life unfolds the answers—and reveals even more questions. In turn, the more you learn, the more you shift from being a purveyor of truth to a quiet (but still quite active) seeker. Remember ... still waters run deep.

Seeking includes both self-examination and studying the ever-changing environment. By proactively learning, you discover that which was not clear before. Socrates said, "An unexamined life is not worth living." Harsh; but if so, let's start living...

OPEN TO CHALLENGES

There are challenges and problems in both positive and negative situations. As a seeker, you treat these as opportunities. By learning, you will open yourself to challenges in a way that welcomes change. But we naturally avoid challenges. Thus we must find ways to make the unnatural natural. Our instincts will tend to direct us to safety. We naturally choose to limit our growth and give in to security. It is there we stay, and it is there we begin to disintegrate.

In the words of T. Alan Armstrong, "If you are not getting better, you are getting left behind." By growing through a dedication to truth and openness to challenge, you will consistently find ways to improve yourself. Clearly this is one of the reasons you are reading this book.

The future is yours to do special things.

This chapter, Personify Proactivity, is a critical starting point for the twelve Invinceable Principles. You will learn the whys and hows of creating the journey toward life mastery. You will discover that Personify Proactivity is a philosophy of how you approach life. In turn, the results and rewards you get will be in direct proportion to the degree that you actually personify proactivity.

The Japanese have a single word to define this approach. It is *kaizen*.

KAIZEN

Mr. Masaaki Imai was the first person to introduce the word kaizen to the world beyond Japan. He is the author of *KAIZEN, The Key to Japan's Competitive Success*. By bringing a single word to the forefront of personal and corporate development, he succeeded in hitting a nerve. Individuals and organizations realized that the advantages the Japanese brought to international marketplaces were founded in kaizen.

Mr. Imai writes that "the essence of kaizen is simple and straightforward: Kaizen means improvement... The kaizen philosophy assumes that our way of life deserves to be constantly improved."

According to the NASA Langley Research Center, "Kaizen means continuous improvement in personal life, home life, social life, and working life as a whole."

Since people naturally seek higher ground, kaizen, when framed properly, is natural to the individual. Pushing through fears and self-doubt, backed by a kaizen approach, we discover that all circumstances are opportunities for constant improvement. In order to embrace this philosophy and make it our own, let's explore how we grow and why.

ENTROPY VS. GROWTH

Entropy is a component of the Second Law of Thermodynamics, which states that there is a general tendency of all observed systems to go from order to disorder. This law was developed in the context of 19th century studies of steam engines. It was learned that energy spent is energy lost. Any and all energy that is used must come from somewhere. The net result is energy gets used up until there is none.

Taken to the extreme, in billions of years, the universe will simply disintegrate into a mass of nothingness. Obviously, this is not something to look forward to.

Growth, on the other hand, is the force of life. In many ways it seems to contradict the force of entropy. However, life stands out as a wanton exception to the Second Law of Thermodynamics.

FLOW OF ENTROPY VERSUS FLOW OF HUMANITY

Humanity is made up of individuals. We evolve as individuals and thereby evolve as a society. Through our recorded history and evolutionary past, uncovered from the Earth, humanity has arguably improved and grown. We know more than generations past. We live longer and "better" lives along the way. Where, then, does entropy fit into the picture? Philosophers, scientists and theologians have yet to agree on an answer to this question. I, for one, will not spend the next two hundred pages giving you my perspective. Suffice to say—we tend toward higher ground.

Individually, we aspire to ascend Maslow's hierarchy of needs from food and shelter to self-actualization. Ultimately, this ascension will only happen through the choices we make. Proactivity over passivity will deliver us to that higher ground we seek.

There are times when we follow the flow of entropy. One classic example of this is by becoming a victim of a situation or circumstance. As "victims" we are stuck. In victim lies chaos. Victim follows the entropic flow.

But if we take responsibility, or as Stephen Covey calls it, "the ability to respond," we will then act from a place of accountability, a place of choice, power and self-determination. We then personify proactivity.

> **Personifying Proactivity is a philosophy— a method of approaching life.**

G ENTROPY

The modern Olympic games were revived in 1896, by the French aristocrat Baron Pierre de Coubertin. As a philosopher and academician, de Coubertin led a group of colleagues to found guiding principles for the Olympic Games. They set the standard with three Latin words: *citius, altius, fortius*—swifter, higher, stronger.

They purposefully did not use the words swiftest, highest, strongest. The pursuit of excellence involved personal bests, peak performance within the individual and on the sports field. De Coubertin and his colleagues ensured that the foundation of the Olympic movement mirrored the ever-present potential for humanity's quest for excellence—not perfection. With sport as the backdrop, *citius, altius* and *fortius* celebrated humankind's potential.

In my own journey to become an Olympic athlete, I carried this philosophy through every day of training and each ski race I entered. In fact, I added another tongue-in-cheek term to *citius, altius, fortius:* It was "smartius." I knew that in a competitive environment, personifying proactivity included ways to find the most intelligent path from Point "A" to Point "B."

To grow, you have the option to find ways to live smarter and wiser. By doing this, you redefine winning. Winning then becomes a process of being more than just "Number One."

Over one hundred years ago, no one understood this better than Pierre de Coubertin. In fact, he authored the Olympic Creed, which states, "The most important thing in the Olympic games is not to win but to take part, just as the most important thing in life is not the triumph but the struggle. The essential thing is not to have conquered, but to have fought well."

Olympians do not have the exclusivity on excellence. *Citius, altius, fortius* (and even smartius) are principles that everyone can follow. We can phys-ically learn to quicken our reflexes, reach new heights and strengthen our bodies. We can learn and grow in many ways.

Then what must we do? Simple! Choose to do one hundred things one per-

Citius, altius, fortius and smartius

cent better, rather than one thing 100 percent better. Personify proactivity in all things that you do. Do not look for leaps of excellence. Instead, apply excellence to everything. You will then discover that your path to excellence is the way you will embody the philosophy of kaizen. Kaizen works both personally and professionally. The growth of individual employees leads to corporate growth.

Despite the implosion of Japanese banks, the downward spiral of the Nikkei stock market and the beating the world markets have inflicted on most Japanese businesses, the Japanese remain steadfast to kaizen.

Matsushita-Panasonic has 6 million staff suggestions a year. Ninety percent are put into action by a company-wide day-by-day approach toward continuously improving results.

Toyota Motor has a system whereby 1.5 million suggestions are processed each year and 95 percent of them are put into practical use.

Nissan management seriously considers even the smallest detail. "Any suggestion that saves at least 0.6 seconds—the time it takes a worker to stretch out his hand or walk half a step" is reviewed and integrated into operations.

HIGH-PERFORMING MENTALITY

The highest performing athletes I witnessed in sports had what I call the "high-performing mentality." Instead of going to the coach and asking, "What do I do next?" the high performers would partner with the coach in learning and growing. The same can be said for players in corporate North America.

Top-down initiatives permeate our corporate culture. Mechanisms for input come from management at the top, and (at best) set the tone for loosely arranged contributions from the lower ranks. The competitive markets of today demand that the individual take more responsibility for action. In the past, leaders often gave lip service to the idea of an entrepreneurial mind-set from their employees.

Today, at an increasing rate, individuals are determining markets. The Internet allows people to vote their decisions on-line. The flow of money is increasingly an individual vote, not an organizational one. No longer do corporations and governments have exclusivity on future outcomes. More than ever, power lies in the hands of the individual. One click of the mouse in this interactive world and the future is further defined. Like a school of fish, the pack moves like a unit responding to the opportunities (eating) or dangers (being eaten). The personification of proactivity must come from the individual.

Harry Dent, author of *The Great Boom Ahead,* draws the analogy of the whale and a school of minnows. Companies like General Electric are the whales. People with access to the Internet are the minnows. With opportunities everywhere, some of the best ones take a bit of finesse to reach. For example, on the other side of a barrier there is some food. To get to the food, there is a hole. The whale could never get to the food, but the school of minnows shaped like a whale can reduce down, swim through the hole and reassemble on the other side of the barrier. Dent's metaphor is clear. Organizations are being motivated to find ways to be more flexible and nimble. If not, they will be pushed aside.

Tom Peters, co-author of *In Search of Excellence* and *The Pursuit of WOW,* lauds the courage of Bill Gates, but not for his empire building of Microsoft. Instead, Peters notes Gates' delayed realization of the potential of the Internet, and the almost overnight, company-wide decision to change the direction of Microsoft's focus from producing software programs to channeling its resources to gain control of the Internet functionality market share. In the snap of a finger, Gates had a new direction and "the school of minnows" was forced to figure out "Now what?" Is Microsoft perfect? Far from it. But it responded in a way completely unlike a traditional corporate "whale." The converse is still going on, even in Internet companies.

A friend of mine called America Online to rectify a billing problem she had with the service. After what seemed like an eternity of touch-tone options and remaining on hold, she finally reached an AOL representative. After explaining the problem, my friend was told that AOL was not going to do anything about her situation. Understandably, she became irate. The response she got from AOL customer service personnel was, "We have 15 million clients, and I personally don't need any more problems ... if it is that big of a deal to you, go to another Internet service provider."

Initiatives must come from the individual. The dance of high-performing organizations has the leaders *and* the lower-ranks waltzing to the same tune.

Finally, high-performing mentality will change governments. Personally, I am tired of whining, sniveling crybabies who accuse the government for the wrongs in this world. Improvements by individuals (not just a select few, but you and me and everyone else with the power to choose their future) will improve corporations. Then, improved corporations will lead and governments will follow. Do not expect government to lead. Oddly enough, they follow. Sound idealistic? Not if you consider the option.

So, now what do you do?

SELF-MOTIVATION

First, there is a big misunderstanding of the Nike slogan "Just Do It." This slogan implies that one is sufficiently motivated to take action and has some sort of plan predetermined.

Coupled with the notion of kaizen, "Just Do It" has a better, more intelligent ring to it. With this approach in mind, Mr. Masaaki Imai has ten basic tips for kaizen activities. Combine these with a way to personify proactivity, and you have the makings of a "Just Do It" strategy.

Tip #1: Discard conventional fixed ideas. Move forward to definable goals. Do not focus as much on the path to get there. New opportunities and new directions may occur to you along the way.

Tip #2: Think of *how* to do it, not why it *cannot* be done. "Realistic" is a dangerous word. Instead, by knowing that the outcome would be desirable, hypothesize methods to accomplish this goal.

Tip #3: Do not make excuses. Start by questioning current practices. Again, focus on the outcome. Excuses will not take you there, but acting on the means to the end will. Do not be afraid to make mistakes. You will learn more by failing.

Tip #4: Do not seek perfection. Do it right away even if for only 50 percent of the target. For example, four months after having the idea to write this book, it was done. I did not wait to start. I did not wait at each stage. Of course I would like this book to be perfect, but it will never be so. Along the way, implement tip #5.

Tip #5: If you make a mistake, correct it right away. My children are both under the age of two. They have a bib that they wear once in a while. It says "Spit Happens." Mistakes happen. High-performing people correct their mistakes immediately, especially when those mistakes involve other people. "Hey, I made a mistake. I have an idea of what we can do about it."

Tip #6: Do not spend money for kaizen; use your wisdom. How much do you know about the way your car is repaired when you take it to a mechanic? Chances are, nothing! When you seek to personify proactivity for your own pursuits, then you must be proactive. Remember, however, some of the best solutions happen when you pause, stand back and think. "Just Do It" is *not* about blindly charging ahead. Plan. Take ownership and move yourself through the process.

Tip #7: Wisdom is born out when people are faced with hardship. Welcome problems as opportunities to learn. Think of a hardship that you have experienced in the past. Now ask yourself, would you change anything about that experience? Most often, the answer is "No, otherwise, I wouldn't have learned what I know now."

Tip #8: Ask "Why?" five times and seek root causes. Each time you ask why, come up with a new answer. Go deeper with each answer. You will surprise yourself.

Tip #9: Seek the wisdom of ten people rather than the knowledge of one. Remember how this chapter started. A person's perspective is their truth. You will learn ten truths versus just one.

Tip #10: Kaizen ideas are infinite. You never "arrive." You are in a process of learning and growing. Always seek higher ground.

Ten great tips, but a waste of ink until you understand where your motivation for action comes from. Entropy remains a universal and powerful force. You have your own weapon that can combat the flow of entropy, coordinate the high-performing mentality and facilitate unlimited self-motivation. It is a tool that is more powerful than all the computers at IBM; the tool is—your brain.

How the mind works

The brain is a complex and powerful tool. To best explore the potential of the brain, let's first study its evolution, properties and characteristics.

The brain

As far as evolutionary scientists know, the human brain evolved in three main stages. First, the Reptilian brain, at the innermost core, is the most ancient and primitive. It is located at the brainstem, near the top of your neck. It controls many of your body's instinctive functions, such as breathing. Next evolved the Mammalian brain with new functions and ways to control the body. It also controls your emotions, your sexuality and is a key component to memory. Then evolved the neocortex, the gray matter, as the third part of the brain. You use this portion for talking, seeing, hearing, thinking and creating. This "human" brain is the bulk of the whole and has two symmetrical hemispheres which communicate. These three brains interconnect and determine human behavior.

The left and right hemispheres are often talked about, but rarely fully understood. The detail-oriented, verbal and sorting side of the brain is on the left. The intuitive, spatial, non-verbal side of the brain is the right. To best remember this, learn that left is logical and right is creative. Both sides are connected by the corpus callosum and this is the actual pathway or switching system for information exchange between the two hemispheres. When these different aspects of the brain integrate, learning is much more profound.

Within the brain there are six intelligence centers, each having different functions and interrelating in thousands of ways on a constant basis.

1. **The Prefrontal Cortex:** thinking

2. **The Motor Cortex:** activity

3. **The Temporal Cortex:** speech center

4. **The Parietal Lobe:** spatial ability

5. **The Occipital Lobe:** visual center

6. **The Cerebellum:** "little brain," balance and posture (handy when learning a skill like riding a bicycle or playing a musical instrument)

Finally, there are three key relay points that are often referred to as the three gatekeepers.

1. The Amygdala: relays the instinctual fight-or-flight reaction to various parts and organs in the body

2. The Hippocampus: relays information to other parts of the brain

3. The Caudate Nucleus: also a relay of information to parts of the brain

THE ELECTRICAL INFORMATION NETWORK BETWEEN YOUR EARS

At birth we are born with between 100 and 120 billion *glial* (the Greek word for glue) cells or active neurons in the brain. In fact, you could put thirty thousand neurons on the head of a pin, and they would not touch. Around the turn of the twentieth century, William James discoverd that we lose the use of roughly 90 percent of our active neurons. This natural process, called pruning, actually strengthens the neuronal connections by reducing the interference and leaves us with 10 billion neurons, which are more than sufficient. This fact is responsible for the general consensus that humans only use 10 percent of the brain.

Nature's way of improving the efficiency of the brain is to refine thought processes. This is the reason for the profound importance of childhood experiences. A majority of the pathways and connections are sculpted in the early years. It is understood that by the age of six much of the way we think and will learn is firmly established.

Each active neuron in the brain has up to twenty thousand different connections (dendrites) with other cells. In his book, *The Amazing Brain*, Stanford University professor Robert Ornstein says that the number of connections is probably more than the number of atoms in the universe. I repeat, *more than the number of atoms in the universe.* Sound incredible? Think of it this way (as described in the book *The Learning Revolution*, by Gordon Dryden and Dr. Jeannette Vos):

> Consider what happens if you took only ten everyday items—like the first ten things you did this morning—and combined them in every possible sequence. The result would be 3,628,800 different combinations. Take eleven items, connect them, and the number combinations is (ten-fold) 39,916,800! So now try combining 10 billion cells in every possible way—when each one can make up to 20,000 different connections—and you get some idea of the creative capacity of your own brain.

THE ANT VERSUS THE ELEPHANT

You have one mind, but it is separated into two distinct functions—the objective and the subjective mind. In other words, the conscious and the subconscious act as the waking and the sleeping mind, the voluntary and the involuntary mind, respectively.

The primary use of the conscious mind is what you currently, logically embrace as your thinking mind. The subconscious is actually the engine, drive train and central computer system running the whole thing. Moreover, the conscious mind knows what is real and what is not. The subconscious mind, on the other hand, takes in information as fact. It does not know the difference between real and surreal.

Research by Dr. Lee Pulos from Vancouver, Canada, has uncovered that in one second the subconscious mind uses 4 billion neurons all at once. In that same second the conscious mind uses a paltry two thousand neurons. That is a massive difference.

Imagine a tiny fire ant on the back of an African elephant. The ant would be the conscious mind. The elephant would be the subconscious mind. As you read this book, you are reading these words with your conscious mind. You are processing the meaning and storing it with your conscious mind directing this informational traffic. Yet your unconscious mind in the very same second is guiding all bodily functions, keeping your balance, monitoring your body temperature, processing things that happened in your life, repairing a bruise, fighting a virus, thinking about tomorrow and the list goes on. If at any given time you think that you are in control, think again.

Let's say you look in the bathroom mirror and decide (with your conscious mind) to go on a diet. Meanwhile the subconscious mind might be programmed very differently. In fact, you may have a myriad of subconscious reasons why going on a diet is a bad idea.

Think of the ant walking on the back of the elephant. The ant is walking north saying "I am going this way, in the direction of a diet."

Ant = conscious mind
Elephant = subconscious mind

Meanwhile, the subconscious mind (the elephant) is walking south saying, *"I don't think so.* I like that food. I'll start another time. I don't deserve to feel good about myself. I need to eat to feel better. I can't control my urges, etc., etc." Which way is the ant really going? South!

Here is another example. A sales person decides to make more money. A year later, she looks at her commissions and sees the same production as the last two years. She wonders why. It is likely that she made a conscious decision to make more money. The ant, still on the back of the elephant, walks in the direction of "more money." Meanwhile the elephant thinks, "Hey, I got into sales because I wanted more free time. By making more money I would have less time with my family. Plus, more money would certainly bring more taxes, problems and decisions. Then there are the negative perceptions around money to contend with. Moreover, I grew up knowing that money is the 'root of all evil' and people that have money are 'filthy rich.' Oh, and by the way, I'm not worthy of success. So I'll just stay right where I am and not go the direction the ant is going."

When you can get the ant and the elephant to go in the same direction, the result is success—success that is often beyond your expectations. In some cases, the subconscious mind knows exactly how to set things right.

FINDING A WAY

Brain-damaged individuals or patients who undergo some form of brain surgery must undergo the re-education of these pathways. In fact, the brain will attempt to find new neuronal connections (previously unused). Think of a downtown street that has been closed to traffic and opened as a pedestrian walkway. At the same time, other streets have been changed to a complex system of one-way avenues. As a driver, your usual route was changed, and you creatively find the most efficient and effective way to get you and your car to your destination.

Until recently, it was thought that we were all born with a set number of brain cells. Studies have now found that DNA in the neurons is active, thus leading to different conclusions. In addition, advances in research lead neurologists to doubt that the brain is losing a million neurons per year. In fact the large neurons do not die but appear to simply shrink. Robert Terry, a neuroscientist at the University of California in San Diego concludes that there is "no significant decline in neuron density in the three important areas of the brain." Any decrease in large neurons appears to be offset by an increase in smaller ones.

The brain appears to keep a reserve of dormant cells. University of Calgary neuroscientists Brent Reynolds and Sam Weiss discovered a way to stimulate dormant brain cells into "active duty." With a chemical called Epidermal Growth Factor, Reynolds and Weiss were able to take cultured mouse neurons and cause inactive, immature brain cells to divide and form mature ones. The future of brain research will uncover new frontiers, to "boldly go where no man has gone before," to ... pardon me, my subconscious mind just took over. Where was I?

STREET SMARTS

With the immense potential of the brain, our potential in life is boundless. In his outstanding book, *Emotional Intelligence,* Daniel Goleman builds a solid case for why some people with high IQs do not reach their full potential and why others with average IQs excel. Goleman contends that emotional intelligence, unlike IQ, is not fixed at birth. It is an intelligence that can be built upon and strengthened (a sort of "street smarts"). It is through emotional intelligence that we can grow and counteract entropy.

Actually, we can grow our street smarts through a strategic one-two-three punch that holds exceptional potential. The ancient Greeks espoused the virtue of three key areas: mind, body and spirit.

The mind is where you grow intellectually. You feed the mind with knowledge and experiences. By personifying proactivity you expand your awareness and broaden your wisdom. Meanwhile, you nurture your body by eating healthy foods, exercising and stretching. Your energy is boosted, and your mind is sharpened through activity. It is in a better position to take care of your body. Finally, spiritual growth rounds off the package. You balance your life mentally, physically and spiritually.

As powerful as the mind is, we are held back by self-limiting beliefs. Because the subconscious mind takes the lead role in producing our ultimate results, we then have the difficult challenge of changing behavior governed by attitudes and beliefs that we are not conscious of. There are various ways we, in effect, get in our own way.

UNDERSTANDING THE COMFORT ZONE

You have heard the term before ... the comfort zone. It is commonly known as the areas in your life most familiar to you. You tend to stay within these areas and avoid the unknown. The comfort zone can also be defined as the familiar zone.

You gravitate to people and situations that are familiar to you. You are comfortable with familiarity. At parties you hang out with people whom you know. You fold your arms the same way each time. You start brushing your teeth at the same place. You drive to work the same way. You ingrain patterns in all areas. We are all truly "creatures of habit." In most cases these patterns serve us well. But they can limit your individual growth in a variety of ways. John Stuart Mill stated, "The perpetual obstacle to human advancement is custom."

What would be different in your life if you ventured outside your comfort zone? Who would you meet? What opportunities would present themselves?

In fact, think of a time, accomplishment, or event when you really felt proud of yourself. What led up to this point? Who was there when you first got the idea? I am willing to bet that you were in a situation (or with someone) that you were unfamiliar with. It was there that the journey toward your accomplishment was born.

A few years ago, before we were married, my wife Michelle organized a surprise going-away party with friends, colleagues and neighbors of mine in Calgary. I was moving to Dallas and had built quite a network of people in my twelve years as a resident of Calgary. Michelle coordinated the whole party from Dallas, managing to get key people from each area of my life.

The stage was set. I was told that I was going to speak at a cellular phone company sales rally. When I walked in the door with my speech notes in hand, I stood, open-mouthed, as I first wondered why my college friend, Sean, was in the room with all these cellular phone salespeople. Then I saw Patrick and Cattis, friends and real estate clients. Why were they there? Then I saw my neighbors. Teammates from my hockey team. Realtors I used to work with. Employees from my present job. Relatives. Then, Michelle—whom I thought was in Dallas—appeared before my eyes.

> # How would your life be different
> # if you ventured beyond
> # your comfort zone more often?

It was a huge surprise!

Later on, I was amazed at how people stuck to their own groups. There was very little mixing of people from the various areas of my past. It was an odd collection of cliques that refused to mingle. They had fun. I had fun. But I often think of how the party would have been different had people walked outside their comfort zone and met other people from other groups. Moreover, how would their lives have been different had they done this? Who knows?

THE TALE OF MBI

Once upon a time there was a huge multinational corporation called MBI. MBI stood for Mucho Business International, and every employee at the company followed a dress code. They were to wear green suits, green ties and white shirts. Green was the color of money and money was the name of the game!

One day, management sat around a table and wondered how they could make more money. Then, one of the "thinkers" in the group who had been doodling on a pad popped up exclaiming, "I have a great idea!" All the managers gathered around the chalkboard while the thinker drew his idea for all to see.

"The way I figure it," he said, "if we take all the high-producing people in this area and swap them with the low-producing people in the other area, we will make more money." He continued his idea, "The high producers will get into the low-producing areas and find ways to build sales. Meanwhile, the low producers will already have the momentum built from the high producers, and they will simply maintain status quo. The bottom line is—" he said as he turned to the group, "we will make more money."

All the managers in their green suits, green ties and white shirts, of course, sang the company theme song while jumping up and down. It was a great idea.

Sure enough. When the high producers went into the low-producing areas, they found ways to make more money for themselves and MBI. What the managers didn't expect was what happened to the low producers.

These people started off okay, but then slowly but surely lost sales, market share and the green, green money, to the competition.

MBI hired consultants with Ph.D.s from the Havlots Business School (that's the college where they talk about money a lot). They reviewed the statistics and explained what had happened to the MBI bottom line.

It turns out the consultants, those savvy Ph.D.s, uncovered the age-old nemesis of businesses everywhere… the comfort zone was up to its old tricks again.

The high producers were put into a financial situation that was below their comfort zone. As a result, they did a number of things to get back to their own level of comfort. They would get to work a little earlier. Make that extra call. Give that extra special customer service and go the extra mile. They slowly, but surely, raised their sales and made what they used to make.

The low producers were the exact opposite. They started to make more money than they ever made before in their lives. They loved it. They partied all the time and spent money on lots of extras. They bought even more things on credit. Then, slowly but surely, they sabotaged their sales. They showed up for work late. They missed meetings. They got distracted easily. They procrastinated and they daydreamed at work. Their sales went down, back to exactly what they were making before. They, too, were back in their comfort zone around money.

In the end, MBI still couldn't figure out how to change the comfort zones of low producers. The company made about the same as they used to make except they had a huge consulting bill. (By the way…the consultants lived happily ever after.)

LEVELS OF DESERVABILITY

Another way to frame the comfort zone is with a person's upper and lower levels of deservability. People have proven out the theory time and again:

levels of deservability will keep people in the zone where they subconsciously feel they belong.

Lotto winners, sales people, inheritance recipients more often than not, manage to find themselves back where they were within two or three years of their windfalls.

We all have levels of deservability around relationships, as well. This is one of the key reasons why some relationships are doomed from the start. If one person goes into a relationship with a solid family upbringing, where his self-esteem was nurtured and his self-confidence was strengthened, his level of deservability is probably reasonably high. But what if he's matched with a partner who has a shaky self-esteem? Perhaps she comes from a broken home where she was taught to distrust people and protect herself from pain. Her programming is likely to result in a lower level of deservability. The end result is a man and a woman with completely different levels of deservability around love.

Whether you call it a comfort zone, familiar zone or levels of deservability, the net effect is limiting the growth and potential that you have within your reach. The chances of personifying proactivity would diminish greatly, and you would be left wondering why you don't have the life you really want.

To proactively stretch your comfort zone and raise your level of deservability, you will need to step out and take risks a little more often. It is here that you create opportunities.

CREATING OPPORTUNITIES

RISK

Take more risks. Visit the great unknown more often, but remember: I am not talking about taking earthshaking risks or being rash. Like a prospector who pans for gold, you don't find gold back in the saloon. You pack the mule with supplies, a tent, a map and a large pan.

So far in my life I have:
- skydived,
- luged,
- flown a hang glider,

- flown a sailplane,
- bungee jumped,
- scuba dived with sharks and
- skied at 135 miles per hour in the Olympic games.

Each and every one of these sports involved certain degrees of risk. Each and every time I approached the task by applying the same strategy: "All risk must be minimized and reasonably manageable." Simple due diligence was the credo. I would study, analyze and research. I would take slow and methodical steps before I ever took that first leap, flight or run. There was and still is absolutely no substitute for preparation. Yet, ultimately there comes a time where you evaluate the immutable qualities at hand and you decide, "it's time."

Herodutus, an ancient Greek historian, said, "Great deeds are usually wrought with great risk." If you want to accomplish great things or you aspire for great rewards (i.e., a ton of money, fame, happiness, a promotion, a new business) then what great risks are you preparing to take? Take the example of Mary Kay, Inc.

In 1963, Mary Kay Ash had an idea to sell beauty products at home showings. With a background in direct sales. Mary Kay originally never intended to start her own business. In fact, she began writing a book for women in business to compete in a male-dominated workforce. In listing ideas that work and ideas that don't, her idea to sell beauty products at home showings took form. She knew it would work and charged ahead with her plan. She decided to take a risk.

Her first sale amounted to a $1.50 profit. She realized she needed to up the ante before she would reap the rewards. She changed her selling techniques and took $5,000, which was the total of her life savings, and revised the packaging. With her twenty-year-old son she modified the sales presentation and took another leap. One sale lead to others. She turned a $34,000 profit her first year (not bad for 1963 dollars, but just the beginning of an amazing growth curve). Now Mary Kay, Inc. has grown to

Step out and risk a little more often.

over $2 billion in retail sales from over 500,000 independent beauty consultants in twenty-seven countries. In 1998, *Fortune* magazine rated Mary Kay, Inc. as one of the top one hundred companies to work for in America.

What did Mary Kay Ash have that others didn't? Well, money actually, but I am talking about in 1963. She had the courage to act and the curiosity to explore. Will Rogers once said, "You've got to go out on a limb sometimes, because that's where the fruit is." Risk is risk. There is no way around it. Plus, ask yourself what is the price you will pay if you don't take the risk?

Peter Drucker says, "People who don't take risks generally make about two big mistakes a year. People who do take risks generally make about two big mistakes a year." The issue, then, is: what risks are you not taking at this moment? What risks could you take, while still remaining relatively safe and stretch your comfort zone at the same time? The next step is actually subtler, but no less important.

THE ALLOW APPROACH

Once you have taken the risk, what is next? All the pushing is best complemented with an approach at just allowing. Your actions communicate to your environment your intentions. You have given notice of the direction you are taking. God wants you to succeed. The universe wants you to succeed and other people want you to succeed (with the exception of people who can't stand to see others get what they want).

It is here that you eliminate wanting and expectation. You will always gravitate toward your current dominant thought, points out Earl Nightingale. If your dominant thought is wanting, you will create more wanting. Then, you will not *have*, you will remain in the state of *want*. If you stay in expectation and that is your primary focus, you will create even more expectation. You set the target, act and then allow the results to follow.

The Chinese have a saying, "Don't push the river." It means to understand the flow and work with it. It does not mean to be a cork in the river. Whatever you have risked is at stake. Know your destination, use the flow that surrounds you and maximize its usefulness.

Put another way, there is a story from the writings of Chuang-tse that supports allowing and eliminates expectation and want:

One day, K'ung Fu-tse and his disciples were within eyeshot of the waterfall at the Lu Gorge. The spray from the water could be seen for miles and the base of the falls ended in a violent and turbulent pool. As they gazed at the beauty and the power they noticed an old man seemingly fall into the dangerous water. They witnessed him being tossed about in the turbulent pool. They immediately rushed to aid the old man.

As they came around the bend they found the old man had climbed up on the bank and was walking along the path humming a tune. K'ung Fu-tse asked the old man how he could survive what was certain death. He asked what special powers the old man possessed.

"Nothing special," the old man replied. "I learned while quite young and practiced it over the years. Now I am certain of success. I go down with the water, and I come up with the water. I follow it and forget myself. I survive because I don't struggle against the water's superior power. That's all."

My Irish grandma often said, "Put your weak hand in the strong hand of the Lord." What she meant is abundantly clear. There is a superior power that knows what is right. There is flow of life that can be trusted. Your choice is to either trust what you cannot see or to fight and resist it.

ACTION = CHANGE

Earth-shaking action is sometimes required, but is often not the way. The way to make change fun is to simplify the action. Make certain actions routine and matter of course. Simple, methodical actions will shift change from an event to a comfortable process.

For example, leading up to the Olympic games I had every intention of winning the gold. I wanted to be a *Cinderella* story, and I knew that with a gold medal in hand I would be vaulted onto the speaking circuit and fulfill my burning desire to make a difference in the world. At the Olympic games I placed fifteenth and was vaulted into nowhere. There is zero demand in the speaking circuit for Olympic athletes who don't win in the Olympics. But, a good idea will not go away. I continued with my real estate sales and became increasingly dissatisfied. I could not stop thinking about speaking professionally.

I had just experienced the largest personal sacrifice I had ever gone through. I was spent. I had reached physical, emotional and financial limits that most people would gladly avoid. The sacrifice was huge, and I did not want to go back. On top of all this, I was in an extremely unhealthy marriage, and I did not know how to fix it.

Still, the idea of becoming a professional speaker did not go away. Then, five months after the Olympics, with a marriage in shambles, I was asked to speak to ninety people at a networking breakfast. I said yes and gave the presentation a month later.

The response was phenomenal. The group loved it. They laughed, cried, were moved, inspired and gave a long, heartfelt standing ovation at the end. Then one person walked up to me at the end and said, "Vince, you have got to do this for a living." He did not know that I had given up on that thought a long time ago. Then, independent of the first person, another member of the audience said, "You have got to do this for a living." When one person says something, I listen. When two people say the same thing, I notice. When a third and fourth person volunteered the same advice, I had no choice but to pay attention. I was being given a message and it was too profound to ignore.

I pushed the thought aside for a couple more months, but the idea was now like an echo in my brain. I couldn't ignore it any longer. So, like my skiing experience, I ventured into the unknown. Maybe there could be a demand for an Olympic athlete with a unique story, even if he didn't win.

Today I speak to over eighty groups a year. I get paid more than I ever dreamed I would make, and I am having a ball. How did this all happen?

I took methodical, measured steps. I took a stride outside my comfort zone and learned what I could. Then another step, followed by another. I did not take giant leaps. I simply explored.

Now it's your turn. There is something you're holding back from doing. The voice of self-doubt has gotten your ear and you are deafened by disbelief. What is it? If you did take just one step, what would it be? How difficult would that step be? How small of a sacrifice would that small step result in?

If you are still searching and don't have a clue what it is you might be doing, do not despair. It is okay not knowing. Some of the most interesting people I know are forty-five years old and still don't know what they want to do with their lives. If so, follow the advice of Mark Twain, the great American wordsmith and master of the obvious, "Do something every day that you don't want to do." This will ultimately "pop" you out of your familiar zone and consistently make the zone wider and higher.

You have risked, allowed and acted to create change. Now it is time to massage your perspective.

PERSPECTIVE

Remember, your perspective is your truth. Possibly your truth has not been serving you as well as it could. It's time to broaden your perspective. Gaining a comprehensive perspective expands that which you perceive to be true. If so, bring it on. Where are the best places to gain perspective?

Go to the places where others have perspective. This may strike you as an oversimplified statement. Yet, in all my research, many people prove it out time and again; they will never seek to put themselves in this kind of situation. They would sooner stay put than learn more and risk having put themselves in the position where they have a choice to make.

The flip side is also true. I have witnessed people go to church and realize what was missing. They have gone to a conference and experienced an epiphany. They have visited a business and it has changed their life. All because they went to gain perspective.

After that agonizing decision to pursue the speaking business, I asked a number of professional speakers if they had any advice. They all said, without exception, to attend the National Speakers Association convention. I did and the perspective I attained changed my life.

In the last four years I have spoken to over 150,000 people. Time and again, people have asked if I had a book. "No, I'm not a writer," was my response. Then I realized I needed to take my own advice. It was as if I was running around saying, "Take my advice, I'm not using it." Soon after, I sought advice from a number of authors. The vast majority recommended that I attend the Maui Writer's Conference. I did and immediately thereafter, I began writing this book.

Perspective goes hand-in-hand with learning.

Go to places where others have a better perspective than you.

LOVE OF LEARNING

Embrace this philosophy: maintain a love of learning. We were all born with this love. But, over time we lose it. I remember loving kindergarten and then first grade. But in second grade, I had a teacher who scolded me constantly for daydreaming. It got to the point where, if I ever did do something right, my teacher would put my desk at the front of the class and embarrass me when I was just trying to fit in. I retreated mentally. My teacher was then overheard telling other teachers I was "borderline retarded." It took my parents years to build up my self-esteem. I hated academics and it was a slow process to turn things around.

What memories do you have of school? For most of us we were brought up to think of class as a punishment of sorts. Let go of the old paradigms that were programmed in when you were in school. In class you were extrinsically motivated to learn. If you did not learn, you were punished by poor grades. To many graduates, the last day of school is the first day of freedom. Change your mind about learning. Help others do the same.

We learn two ways. First, we learn reactively. We learn the most when pushed outside our comfort zone. We learn from trial and error, traumatic experiences, chaos and—everyone's favorite—relationships. Secondly, we learn proactively. This is where you choose to learn. Learning from night classes, mentor meetings, books, tapes, courses and therapy (which is usually inspired by confusing relationships). Where are you right now? Proactive or reactive or a combination of both?

If you are generally proactive, the chances are you're actively learning ways to regain comfort. You may be reading this book to gain a better perspective. The actions you take to learn will lead you through future risks you will undoubtedly encounter.

If you are mostly reactive, just wait, the surprise is on its way. That is when you will be blind-sided when you least expect it. Clearly the choice is yours. But, remember the words of John F. Kennedy when he said, "The best time to fix a leaky roof is when the sun is shining."

Reinforce the merits of the high-performing mentality. The love of wisdom is one trait of a peak performer. Charles Garfield, author of *Peak Performers*, says it best:

Searching for the peak performer within yourself has a basic meaning: You recognize yourself as a person who was born not as a peak performer but as a learner. With the capacity to grow, change, and reach for the highest possibilities of human nature, you regard yourself as a person in process. Not perfect, but a person who keeps asking: What more can I be? What else can I achieve that will benefit me and my company? That will contribute to my family and my community?

One of the measures of success that we have in society is wealth. Another measure of a successful person is attaining a position of leadership. A third measure of success is demonstrating exceptional wisdom. What do these people all have in common? Books. Think of the last time you visited a person with any or all of these three characteristics. Did he (or she) have a library or an extensive collection of books? Yes. A recent Gallup poll concluded that people with high incomes read an average of nineteen books per year.

GETTING UN-STUCK

You have experienced, or may be currently feeling "stuck" where you are in life. This common state produces an odd feeling. The burning question is often: "How did I get here and why am I still stuck?" The answer would be easy, if the path to the solution was through the conscious decisions (remember the ant) you could make. But through the subconscious (the elephant), you will find the way to getting "un-stuck."

THE PITTER PATTERNS OF LITTLE DEFEATS

Over the years you and your environment have been programming the conscious and subconscious mind. You have succeeded in ingraining both patterns that serve you well and others that limit your effectiveness. Each part of the brain works in harmony to protect and guide you through life. The primary source of undesirable situations is born out of patterns you hold unconsciously.

You "max-out" your Visa card and wonder how you got there again. You get in a familiar argument with your spouse, and he says this, and you say that. He gets you back and you press his buttons. It goes back and forth until you end up in that familiar and uncomfortable place where neither of you is talking and you wonder, "How did we get here again?"

Even though we are gifted with the power of choice, we often are beings of conditioned reflexes. We are vessels of Pavlovian conditioning where a repeated stimulus will create a pattern of predictable responses. We each have four ways to change patterns:

1. Instantly. This is usually associated with hitting rock bottom. (This is a common approach with alcoholics and/or substance abusers.) He loses his house, his family has walked out, he has been fired from his job and he is left penniless. Then, the alcoholic says, "Oh, I get it. I have to stop drinking." Boom! The pattern is changed, but the price of change this way was far too painful.

2. Through trial and error. This is where a vast majority of people can be found. It is not bad. It simply follows our natural tendency to learn by doing. We try, make mistakes and move forward.

3. The proactive approach. Learning this way can be accelerated by reading, tapes, courses and mentor meetings.

4. Acting strategically. This method is the single greatest way to heighten your comfort zone, efficiently and effectively. Through a step-by-step process that you have strategically laid out, you change patterns. By applying subtle yet constant and repetitive pressure, you will notch up your capabilities. Old patterns will simply disintegrate and disappear. Ultimately, it comes down not to how much you do, but how often you do it. Bishop Gore said, "God does not want us to do extraordinary things; he wants us to do ordinary things extraordinarily well."

Any of these four methods do change patterns. To better understand how the strategic method works, let's take a minute and draw a metaphor for change.

Imagine you are going to build a house on the sunny side of a mountain. You know that you will need water from the river, but it flows on the dark side of the mountain. You notice that at a certain point where the river approaches the mountain, it veers off to the valley on the dark side. You conclude that if you dam the water in a certain way, you will redirect the flow to the sunny side.

The river is a deep, well-established pattern. It has been there for many, many years. Your patterns are the same. How you change a pattern is best done strategically. So, you take a rock and put it at the key point in the river.

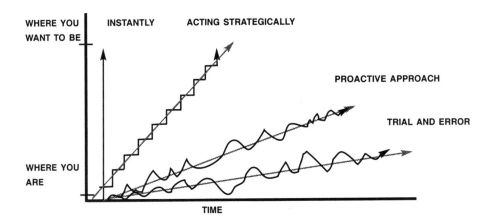

Nothing happens. The river is altered slightly but the pattern still carries on.

Each time you pass by the river (the pattern) you toss another rock in the river. Each time you slightly change the river until one day, you notice a trickle of water start to flow toward the sunny side. Given enough tenacious effort, you eventually change the pattern completely and the old pattern no longer exists.

The sunny side of the mountain is the place we all seek. Where, through our commitments, we will find the happiness that we have earned.

BALANCE

Balance is the Holy Grail of the '90s and the new millennium. Balance is a funny thing though. You find people talking about wanting it, yet it is only a place we get to visit. The goal is to visit it more often. Think of a pendulum that has large swings and short swings. The large swings are the chaotic times. You may be the kind of person who thrives on chaos. If that is what "floats your boat," go for it. It works for you and that's all that matters.

The short swings are a little easier to deal with, but you often don't experience too much excitement. If that is your deal, go for that. As you can see, there is no "right" way. Your journey is a life-long process toward life mastery.

The Greek word *sophrosyne* means a care and intelligence in conducting one's life; a tempered balance and wisdom. This is the moving target ... the balance we seek.

Chaos is entropy; therefore, orderliness opposes entropy. On the flip side, a life of stagnation falls prey to entropy, as well. So you, the seeker, are challenged to find the ever-changing balance.

THE BALANCE FORMULA

To find more balance, follow the four recommendations offered by Dr. Deepak Chopra:

1. Moderation. Avoid the extremes. Too much of anything is bad and unhealthy.

2. Regularity. The seasons balance each other. Tides ebb and flow. Take lessons from nature. Add regularity to moderation because we are the only creature on this planet gifted with thought, intention and choice. We can make the decision of regularity and visit balance more often.

3. Rest. Give yourself time to rest. Couch potatoes have taken this to the extreme. This is not balance. Add rest to moderation and regularity.

4. Activity. Activity (balanced with rest, regularity and moderation) goes a long way to maintaining a sane existence. You can also fall into the habit of taking activity to the extreme.

How you live determines the outcomes you enjoy or suffer. A balanced lifestyle will determine your fate. From 1965 to 1971 the research team of Lester Breslow and Nadia Belloc did an extensive study on aging patterns using seven thousand subjects. Within a detailed questionnaire on health and lifestyle, they uncovered habits that were generally consistent toward creating a balanced lifestyle.

- Never smoke

- Regular form of exercise or activity

- Moderation of alcoholic intake (no more than two per day)

- Seven to eight hours of sleep per night

- Breakfast every day

- Around the ideal weight for height (no more than 5 percent under and 20 percent over the ideal)

BALANCE WHEEL

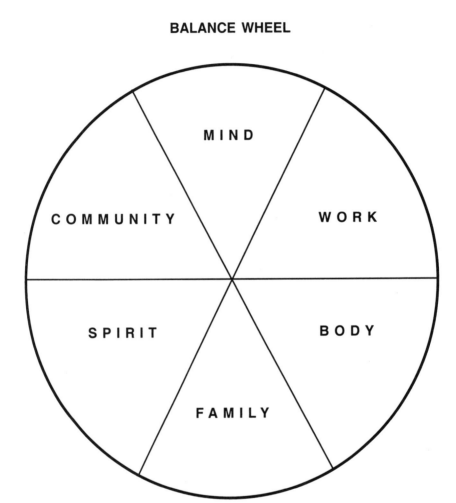

• No eating between meals

IMBALANCE

If you find yourself out of balance, ask yourself three questions:

1. Are you eating right? Nutritionists, doctors, Ayurvedic specialists and even your mother will ask you this question. Take care of the body and you will feel better physically. Eat a balanced diet that is rich in nutrients.

2. Is your mind at ease? Strengthen your emotional and psychological foundation. Disease is dis-ease. Learn and grow. Explore and probe. Seek the answers to the questions that echo in your mind. Gautama Buddha believed, "Pain is inevitable, suffering is optional." Difficulties will strengthen you and teach you.

3. Do you feel safe? Take inventory of your surroundings. Is your home a haven? Do you have financial reserves protecting you from unforeseen circumstances? Is your workplace a source of anxiety? Daniel Goleman adds that, "The goal is balance, not emotional suppression: every feeling has value and significance." In other words, judge nothing as negative. Choose to gain value from your discontent.

Seeking the answers to these questions will help you arrange your life where you will always return to balance.

BALANCE WHEEL

In life there are six components that must generally balance each other in order for you to thrive. These six components are categorized under two areas—intrinsic (1 to 3) and extrinsic (4 to 6). Finally, each one requires both active and passive attention.

1. Mind. Through learning and meditation, you develop the mind.

2. Body. By being active and resting frequently, you rejuvenate the body.

3. Spirit. By praying or attending church you feed the spirit. Balance this with the allow approach, too. Sometimes it's best just to let go and have faith.

4. Family. Pursuing family activities (along with simple "hang-time") contributes to a healthy family life.

5. Work. Balance your ambition to accomplish goals with acceptance of the present.

6. Community. Give your time and your money to your community.

Do not get trapped into believing that the balance wheel means you have to spend equal amounts of time in each area. In fact, this wheel has been around the training and development circles for years. The biggest mistake trainers make is to get participants to grade the amount of time they spend on each area by marking a dot close to the center if it is a little and toward the outside if it is a lot. Then after instructing the student to draw a line from each point to the next, the trainer points out how "unbalanced" the wheel is. "It would be like trying to roll down the road with an odd-shaped tire." Wrong! Nobody has perfect balance in all these areas. But it is entirely possible to spend some time in all areas, every day.

What works best is placing the wheel in front of you every day. Could you put a check mark under each category? Your sanity would benefit greatly. You are the best judge of what is appropriate for you, your family, your work and your community. Some days one area would clearly outweigh others. Fine. Deal with it and move on. Again, it is not how much you do, it is how often you do it.

IN SUMMARY

The ten areas to personify proactivity are:

1. Be a seeker who is open to challenge and following kaizen.
2. Defeat entropy through a high-performing mentality and self-motivation.
3. Understand how your mind works and the awesome power of your subconscious mind.
4. Develop your street smarts.
5. Expand your comfort zone and raise your level of deservability.
6. Take risks and use the allow approach.
7. Take actions that are measured and methodical.
8. Gain perspective and reestablish your love of learning.
9. Change your patterns and you will get "un-stuck."

10. Seek ways to balance your life in the areas of Mind, Body, Spirit, Family, Work and Community.

Each of these twelve chapters contributes to your action plan where you can personify proactivity. Robert Browning once wrote, "My business is not to remake myself, but to make the absolute best of what God made." How do you improve and make the best of yourself? What consistent approach will you take? What are the ongoing steps to get there? The single greatest method that I know is to develop and apply a consistent strategy.

PRINCIPLE 2 ... APPLY CONSISTENT STRATEGIES

"Luck is a matter of preparation meeting opportunity."
–Oprah Winfrey

Three *very* **important words.** I once spoke to a group of salespeople who worked for Cowan Financial Services in New York. The night before the presentation, I sat around the table with some of the key employees and we discussed strategies for success. One person, spoke of a time when the owner of the company, Howard Cowan, asked people to finish the sentence: "Successful people are..."

Each person around the table proceeded to give their contribution to the sentence. One said, "committed." Another said "happy." Another said "rich." Yet another said "opportunists." When it came to be my turn, five words fell out of my mouth, and I realize now that they are the backbone of any message I deliver to groups when I speak. My answer was, "Successful people apply consistent strategies." Each word supports the other. Together they produce results in life—far beyond your wildest expectations.

As I look back on my Olympic experience, the single greatest reason for my success was due to an approach that applied consistent strategies.

In *Coming into Harmony,* Ilse Klipper writes:

> No accomplishments in life come without our steady effort and endurance. An athlete cannot win a competition without regular practice; similarly, personal transformation is not achieved without perseverance. The process of changing deeply ingrained thought patterns requires daily practice. Persistence and repetition are essential if we wish to transform old habits of the mind and body.

GOOD INTENTIONS

Growing up in western Canada, I managed to see my Irish grandmother, who lived in Toronto, about once a year. Each and every visit was memorable. She was the kind of person who managed to see things from a different perspective. Best of all, she had a great sense of humor and a loving way. She was strong, and I admired her a great deal.

I remember her amazing ability to recite sayings and quotes. One of her favorites was: "The road to hell is paved with good intentions." As a child, it took me a long time to actually figure out what that meant. In a way, I am still learning the wisdom of this statement. In effect, it means to go beyond intention to application. You can have all the good intentions in the world, but, without action, they are useless.

Jim Rohn, a master communicator and author, states that, "Affirmation without discipline is the beginning of delusion." Given the power of suggestion, you can affirm a great number of things. Yet, your results will be a product of your actions.

PRAXIS

Take the example of musicians or athletes. They know in theory how to do it. Through application they truly learn it. The Greek word *praxis* means to "learn by doing." There is no replacement for first-hand experience.

Let's say you were going to learn how to swim. You could go to a class and hear a speaker talk about swimming and how it is done. You might learn a little.

You would learn more if the speaker brought along videos or actually demonstrated how to do it in the water. You would learn a little more.

With praxis, you would be put in the shallow end where you are taught how to float and then stand up. You learn how to hold your breath and resurface. You then learn the basics of swimming by trying it out for yourself. Clearly, *praxis*, learning through first-hand knowledge, is the best method.

Taking steps into the unknown or known are basic to achievement. Should you apply consistent strategies, your achievements are improved. Maybe taking action is not an issue for you. Possibly, your frustrations lie in how to get others to act. Possibly they are your employees or your children or your spouse. Take the following lessons learned by Coca-Cola.

Make your personal and professional statement tangible.

PAINT THE PICTURE

Capture people's imagination. Paint a picture for them and they will know how they fit into the ultimate goal. Set goals for others without connecting with their imagination and your consequences will be in peril.

Jim Crupi, a Dallas-based strategy consultant, tells a story of how Coca-Cola, Inc. attempted to raise the commitment level of its employees. When they revisited their original mission statement, Coca-Cola, Inc. had something along the lines of being the premier soft drink provider with exceptional quality, service and profit for shareholders. Anyone who read the mission statement did not connect with it. Moreover, you would have been hard pressed to find anyone who even remembered what it said.

As a result, a task group at Coca-Cola revised their guiding statement. Their mission changed to a vision statement. They knew they had to get something that painted a picture—something that instilled a sense of purpose and meaning and that each and every Coke employee could relate to and remember. The end result was magical.

The new Coca-Cola, Inc. vision statement was "To put a Coke within reach of every human being on the planet." *Wow!* You can easily see a stock boy relate to that statement along with everyone in the whole chain of operations. This vision statement paints a picture that you can see. You can almost hear the sound of a cap being popped off a bottle and taste the syrupy bubbles in your mouth.

Take the lesson from Coca-Cola and apply it to your life. Write your own personal and professional vision statement. Make it tangible and identifiable. Give it a sense of purpose and wonder. Your approach to an application of a consistent strategy will become easier.

If you are an entrepreneur or run your own business, the same techniques apply. If you have employees, get them to contribute to the vision statement that you have.

My wife Michelle owns a company called International Speakers Bureau. Each year she takes her staff on a planning retreat designed to set the tone for the upcoming year. At the first retreat, the group went through and identified their strengths and weaknesses. From this, they brainstormed what their values were for the company. Each employee agreed on the top five core values and then decided on a vision statement.

Their contributions led to a strong vision statement that painted a picture. Much like Coca-Cola's vision, the employees came up with: "Anytime, anyone, anywhere on the planet needs an education or entertainment resource, they contact International Speakers Bureau." The aftermath of the retreat was amazing. Each employee walked away feeling that they were part of something. They felt that they had contributed to the foundation of something important and their levels of commitment went up.

The lesson is clear. Give people the opportunity to design their vision statement and their level of ownership goes up.

The same can be said for salespeople. If you are a salesperson, design your own vision statement. Identify the ways and means that your information, service and products make a difference in the lives of others. Think of a grander purpose for your role in sales. What connection do you feel to this role? Paint a picture in your mind.

ADD VARIETY AND FLEXIBILITY

So far, we have covered how to apply consistent strategies. The power in your approach will be from how much variety and flexibility you build in. It almost sounds like an attempt to be spontaneous at a certain time each day. No.

Relax the structure of your plan. Apply your consistent strategy with variety. Be flexible if opportunities present themselves. Find a way to balance drive with acceptance. This is more like the art of excellence through the example of the Chinese symbol of yin and yang.

YIN AND YANG

The concept of yin and yang considers an apparent contradiction of forces. It is the Chinese dualistic philosophy where things exist in a harmonious

YIN & YANG

YIN	**YANG**
Night	Day
Female	Male
Water	Fire
Heavy	Light
Inward	Outward
Earth	Heaven
Moon	Sun
Winter	Summer
Calm	Agitated
Downward	Upward

paradox. It is beyond balance, which implies 50/50 or meeting halfway. It simply is a mutual coexistence of two opposites.

The concept of yin and yang is amazingly useful. As we mature, we become more comfortable with life's paradoxes. We learn to embrace the whole, even where some ambiguities could naturally lead to conflict. We accept irony with gracious understanding and perhaps even humor.

For example, when children love their parents and idolize them, they view their parents as "good." Then, when the children are disciplined, the parents become "bad." It takes maturity to embrace opposites.

IN RELATIONSHIPS

You fall in love and notice that cute way your girlfriend snorts when she laughs. Then, after a year or two, what once seemed cute fades into a silly, annoying habit. It's embarrassing. It's bad. It may eventually become unbearable and the focus of your negative feelings toward her. Then, depending on your maturity level, you accept her for who she is, and it simply "just is."

F. Scott Fitzgerald said, "The test of a first-rate intelligence is the ability to hold two opposed ideas in the mind at the same time, and still retain the ability to function."

YIN AND YANG IN BUSINESS

In the business book *Built to Last,* authors James C. Collins and Jerry I. Porras describe visionary companies as being capable of dealing with a series of paradoxes. Collins and Porras clearly prove that in corporate life instead of having yin *or* yang, it is possible to have yin *and* yang and function successfully.

For example, visionary companies were, and continue to be, able to have corporate purposes completely separate from any profit orientation and a strategic and efficient pursuit of profit. Or, companies could have clear direction and dedication to flexibility and experimentation.

PROCESS IS THE GOAL

As we mature from the experiences we collect, we learn more about how we think, feel and act. For the most part, setting a goal and striving toward it is the acceptable means to an end. In the 1980s we had targets, to-do lists, time management techniques, goal setting seminars and competition in climbing the corporate ladder.

In the meantime, we have climbed into rarified air. It is as if we are above the tree line and the achievement became more important than the journey. I lived that lesson in my pursuit to reach the Olympic games. Once I qualified to compete in the Olympics, I set a new goal... to win the gold medal! The first goal came true, why not the second? I drove hard and came close. Going into the final run I was in sixth place. But in the final run I made a mistake and dropped down to fifteenth place. My goal to win was lost. I felt like I lost. I wanted to win and I didn't.

Today, I use the same strategies in building my speaking, writing and tools for life mastery business that I used to get to the Olympics... with one important difference. I changed from a fixation on the goal to a fixation on the process. It is ultimately the yin and yang of achievement. It is as if instead of just focusing on eating the plate of food I have in front of me, I make time to enjoy it. I pause here and there noticing the different tastes and textures the food has on my tongue. The act of eating becomes an experience. The result of a finished plate will come soon enough.

How do you reach your goals? Do you push through? What is the price that you and those in your life pay to be part of your drive and determination? Change your mind from using a process to *acquire* a quality goal to the understanding that a quality process *is* the goal. Know that the results take care of themselves. Your focus on the process blends like yin to the focus on the yang of your results.

"I'LL BE HAPPY WHEN..."

It's easy to get caught in the "I'll be happy when..." mentality. "I'll be happy when I get a bigger house." "I'll be happy when I get a smaller place."

"I'll be happy when I get a promotion." "I'll be happy when I get a new job."

"I'll be happy when I get in a long-term relationship." "I'll be happy when I get rid of this long-term relationship."

It never ends.

You may recall the expression, "Success is a journey, not a destination." Chances are you agree with it. But do you truly understand it? Do you live by principles where you are more focused on the journey than the destination?

THE PAST IS THE PAST

Fixating on the future isn't healthy. Neither is being obsessed with the past. The past is the past.

It is a good teacher but nothing more. The past serves your future, but really has very little to do with your present choices. You choose what you want. The past is the past.

David Viscott, in his book *Emotionally Free*, states, "You can speculate, you can lament, but much as you may wish to return and round off your emotional experience, you can never go home again. Your real home is in this place, at this time. The present is for action, for doing, for becoming, and for growing."

In essence, we need to refer to the future, acknowledge the past and focus on the present. Embrace the moment and only then will you know peace.

ROUTINE IS NATURAL

Applying consistent strategies seems like such an obvious way to accomplish anything, but it is easier said than done. Applying all the requirements to consistently follow a diet is easy. Following a consistent workout schedule is a piece of cake. Cold calling thirty prospects every day is a snap. Studying every day during a university course is simple … right? Not for us regular human-folk. Routine is often difficult, yet routine is actually quite natural.

Night follows day, the Canadian goose flies south in the fall, and my mother will always call me on my birthday and tell me what she said the day I was born.

Why then do people rebel from some habits? Most of the reasons are unconscious. There are various ways that we get in our own way. Without the luxury of changing our mind, the next best way is to apply a consistent strategy to create a habit.

Probably the most famous strategy was initiated by Alcoholics Anonymous and has become a general rule of thumb. It takes twenty-one days to create a habit. As a part of the twelve-step program, recovering alcoholics are supported to break through the twenty-one day mark. There is no conclusive data to support that twenty-one is a magical number, but it is a milestone for the subconscious mind to believe in. The more you believe in the twenty-one day rule the more the subconscious gears up to embrace twenty-one days as a turning point. It is as if the routine is fixed at twenty-one days.

EXAGGERATE TO IMPRINT

Whenever I teach someone how to ski, the single glaring mistake I notice in all students is where they put their hands. Since balance is the foundation of good skiing, the hand placement sets the tone for how the rest of the body aligns itself over the skis. By teaching people to exaggerate an action, they are then more inclined to imprint their motor skills with the proper form.

People naturally put their hands down and often to the back when skiing. The steeper the slope, the further the hands drop back. Despite the angle of the slope, the body must be over the skis to maintain control of turning and speed. By putting the hands out front and facing down the slope, the balance is maintained. The problem exists when the student feels he or she is leaning downhill and will pick up speed as a result.

In order to overcome this tendency, I instruct the students to exaggerate an action to imprint a new habit. I ask them to put their hands way out, as if they are driving a big bus. Putting the hands out on an imaginary big wheel forces the body over the skis and, thereby, control is maintained. It is amazing to watch students who think that they are putting their arms too far out front, in this exaggerated fashion, when in reality their arms are just barely out front. The more a skill is exaggerated, the more it is imprinted on the subconscious mind. Eventually the students are ingrained with the habit of keeping their hands out front. Balancing on the skis, on most any run, becomes second nature.

MANIACAL OBSESSION

Another way to create a habit, one that I particularly like, I learned from an experience I had with Alan Hobson, a mountain climber and adventurer. In 1997 he went to Mount Everest for a third time in an effort to reach the summit and return home safely. Alan and I have been friends since 1985, and despite my move to Dallas we remained in touch. Leading up to his third climb, he happened to visit me in 1996, midst his training and work schedule.

I picked Alan up from the airport and it was about dinnertime. I planned for us to visit and have some Tex-Mex food. When I mentioned my plan to Alan he said, "No, I have to work out. Then we can eat." I was hungry and knew Alan well enough to veto his request.

"Alan, I'm hungry and we have to eat."

"Well, then you eat. I am going to work out."

"Alan, come on. Let's eat and…"

> **The more a skill is exaggerated, the more it is imprinted on the subconscious mind.**

"Stop the car," he interrupted, grabbing my attention.

"What?" I wondered if the plane ride hadn't depressurized his brain.

"Listen, Vince, I am going to Everest in a year. Working out is my insurance policy. I will not make any exceptions to my training routine." Alan seemed maniacally obsessed. His workouts were non-negotiable. Needless to say, Alan got his way. (The next year he and his long time-partner Jamie Clark reached the summit of Mount Everest.)

After the Olympic games I faced my own challenges with training and working out. Only once did I get back into a routine, when I trained for a marathon. Outside of that, I could not seem to get myself motivated to train. My weight and fitness fluctuated to the point of frustration.

My experience with Alan taught me the power of a maniacal obsession, of making no exceptions. Zero tolerance sets the stage for routine to take hold. The application of a consistent strategy with regards to your health is non-negotiable.

If you find yourself vacillating on a proper routine that you would like to do, try applying a maniacal obsession. It works.

WALK YOUR TALK

Some parents are amazed that they can't seem to get their children to do their homework. Yet, what example do the parents give their kids? Do the parents dedicate themselves to a self-help or workout routine? Walking your talk is a great way to motivate yourself. No one likes to live a lie. Be honest with yourself, and you will find the motivation to do what you advise others to do.

The speaking business is an interesting industry. The vast majority of speakers I know walk their talk. For me, I talk about peak performance, strategy and having fun along the way. If I spoke and I wasn't having fun, I would look (and feel) the fool.

Wayne Dyer talks about balance and living fully. He runs ten miles per day, every day. Part of his motivation undoubtedly comes from a place of integrity. Why would he recommend an active lifestyle if he didn't live one himself?

WHAT IS THE COST TO YOU?

Striving toward a benefit is a "no-brainer." If you sell more, you will make more money. If you smile more, you will get more smiles back. If you shower more than once a week, you'll smell better. All kidding aside, you may be aware of the benefits, but you are still not properly motivated to take action. Try turning the tables. Ask what the cost would be to you.

If you did not brush your teeth for six weeks on end, there would be a cost to the health of your gums and teeth. If you did not find the time to show affection to your spouse each day, there would be a negative impact on your relationship. If you don't regularly show affection and support to your children, what will the results be? If you don't give value for the job you do, how much longer will you be employed?

Knowing the cost to you will give you a choice. Knowing the pain of tooth decay and how unattractive a toothless grin is, it is easy to justify and ingrain a routine to brush your teeth twice a day. Living in an unhealthy relationship is *hell*. Children who are a problem or self-destructive are agony. Getting fired sucks! These are negative implications of not applying a consistent strategy. Hey, if it works, use it.

CURSILLO

In order to apply a consistent strategy, you will need to prepare and focus before you can act. The preparation is a journey in itself. The word for preparation for a journey is *cursillo* taken from the Spanish language. *Cursillo* is a common word in Spain and is derived from *curso*, which means "little course." In the context of the Roman Catholic church in the early 1940s in Spain, the *cursillo* was to last just a few days with the idea of intensity, of doing a great deal in a short period of time. Their design was formed by the leaders of the Catholic Action group in response to a movement toward an independent laity. The term *cursillo* was chosen because it did not essentially have a religious undertone and the courses were designed not to be overly pious.

Pursuing your own *cursillo* will pay dividends when you are asked to perform or do well. This became abundantly clear the second time I went parachuting—and my parachute did not open.

JUMPING OUT OF A PERFECTLY GOOD PLANE

In 1982, I visited Australia and met the Australian national parachute champion Graham Windsor. Graham lived in Canberra and invited me down to try it out. During the ground course, he laboriously covered all the equipment details and emergency procedures. The part I remember that was most annoying was how he made us put a demonstration pack on and practice the technique of deploying the reserve chute, in case the main chute did not open. He made us do it over and over and over again. It was a simple process using the "Piggy Back" chute where both the main and reserve chute were on the back. It required you to put your right thumb through a red ring, pull out the rope attached to the ring by extending the right arm, and then you had to grab the rope with the left hand and further extend the rope. This two-step process first jettisoned the malfunctioning main chute and then deployed the reserve chute.

The first jump was great. It involved dangling from the wing support strut and waiting for the jumpmaster to say, "Ready… jump." Because we were each attached to a static line, the main chute would immediately deploy, and in three seconds we would be floating on air under a big, beautiful nylon chute.

I don't remember much about the three-second fall, but when the chute opened, the body and leg harness gave a violent yank where it lifts and separates (if you know what I mean). The trip down was an adrenaline rush, combined with a perspective on the world one rarely sees. I couldn't wait to take another jump!

As I wrestled with the special attachments on the harness, I was wearing coveralls and the Australia sun was beating down making preparations fairly uncomfortable. Finally, I went over to Graham and said that I was ready. His first response was "Why did you take that chute?"

"I don't know," I replied, "I just picked up the first one I saw."

"Well, don't take that one, mate, take that blue one laying over there."

"Why?" I asked in a hot-and-bothered tone.

"I packed the blue one. I don't know who packed the one you are wearing," he said as he went back to his duties.

I paused, blinked and then immediately started undoing the clips that held the parachute pack on. By the time I had the blue chute on I was last on the plane. I kept hearing a little voice in my head say, "Don't do this."

With the plane completely full of skydivers scrunched up sitting on its floor and me being last in, I was going to be the first out. Plus, there was no option to not jump. There was simply no room to do anything.

As the plane spiraled up to altitude, the little voice got louder: "Don't do this." Pretty soon Graham, the jumpmaster, signaled to the pilot to "power off." The engines were shut and I had to expeditiously get out and hang from the wing's strut support. There was no turning back.

Now the voice was screaming, "DON'T DO THIS!"

"Ready?" Graham said, through the wind noise.

"What?" I asked to vainly stall for time.

Amused, he looked at me and asked with a smile... "Are you ready?"

"Yeah, I guess so," I said, as I continued my white-knuckle grip on the strut.

"Jump," he shouted.

"What?" I said, desperate for a different word. Any word other than jump.

"Let go!" he said, still smiling.

"Just do it," I thought to myself, "It's just nerves."

I let go and counted the required, "ONE THOUSAND, TWO THOUSAND, THREE THOUSAND," and then it happened.

I felt a slight yank and then heard a deafening roar. I looked up, and my chute was all tangled in the ropes. I tried to shake the chute open by pulling apart the risers but it wouldn't budge. I distinctly remember looking straight ahead and experiencing a succession of thoughts. "I've got a malfunction. I wonder how quickly I'm coming at the ground? Don't look down. PULL THE RED RING. THE RED RING."

The next couple of seconds seemed to last an eternity. As I pulled the ring by extending my right arm, I briefly went back into free fall. The lapse between jettisonning the main chute and the opening of the reserve chute was unnerving. It was then that my life literally flashed before my eyes. A dozen experiences from childhood on upward, then the roar began again.

This time it was the reserve chute opening up and working quite well, I might add. The adrenaline rush was amazing. Adrenaline coursed through my veins to the tips of my fingers. It was an incredible feeling!

A couple of days later I started to think about what if the reserve chute didn't open. What would it have felt like to fall to my death? I will now never parachute again. But, there was a "silver lining" to that experience.

First, I learned first-hand that we humans are capable of dealing with more pressure than is imaginable. Secondly, the *cursillo* approach to any activity will pay off. Take deliberate and determined action to learn more.

WHEN YOUR NECK IS ON THE LINE

For any situation where your neck is on the line and your peak performance is required there are three basic steps.

1. Prepare. Note the words of Robert Schuller, "Spectacular achievement is always preceded by unspectacular preparation." Had I not repeatedly prepared and practiced the emergency exercise, I may not have seen my twenty-second birthday. Sometimes mistakes are cheap. Sometimes they are costly. Either way, you pay a price for mistakes that could have been avoided.

2. Focus on the solution (don't look down). I have a friend who is a goaltender in a men's over-thirty hockey league. He once had a chance to spend time with Wayne Gretzky. In their conversation, my friend asked Gretzky what kind of equipment a certain NHL goalie wore. Gretzky's comment was classic: "I have no idea, I actually only see the net when I'm playing." The solution is not found in the obstacle. Focus on the opening, the solutions, and outcomes you desire and for heaven's sake, don't look down.

3. Act quickly and deliberately. With the speed of change today and increasing competition everywhere you look, you must act quickly, yet deliberately. Learning from preparation will put you ahead of the competition. Preparing and focusing on the solution will give you an advantage when you are faced with the need for quick action. Being deliberate means you know what you are doing or you are applying reasonably good judgment. With this preparation and focus you will confidently succeed more often.

PATIENCE, PATIENCE, PATIENCE

At the ancient city of Delphi in Greece, an inscription in marble contains advice from the oracle, "Know thyself." Two thousand five hundred years have passed, and still the mission we face remains the same: Know yourself, and you'll know your next step. Each step we take is an exercise in patience and understanding. Reaching a goal in a heartbeat would be convenient, but is scarcely the way. The consistency, the application and the strategy all hinge on how patient you are with your persistence.

THE CACTUS AND THE ROSE

Imagine that you have two seeds. One is a rose seed and the other a cactus. Your approach to grow both plants will require patience. The rose will need active patience, while the other needs a more passive patience.

Applying consistent strategies is either active or passive, yet both need patience. The hard-driving type of individual can attempt to force his way to success, but nature's way will always win.

Planting ideas in the subconscious is like planting cactus seeds or rose seeds. Some ideas need consistent, active nurturing (like changing a pattern, or creating a new habit or shifting your comfort zone). Other ideas need passive and patient attention to anyone or anything that is on its own schedule—like people, committees and due processes.

I have a good friend who is a hard driver. Anything he gets involved in is won through sheer determination. The one area he has faltered in consistently is his relationships. One day he confided in me a conversation he had with his best friend.

In describing his frustration with his current girlfriend, he hypothesized how a different strategy could be applied to his relationship. His friend gently reminded him that relationships are like growing plants. They don't grow quicker by pulling them up. They require patience and nurturing.

In another situation, I had learned of a Young Presidents Organization (YPO) conference that would be held in New Zealand. As a speaker, I wanted to be invited to speak there, but there was no process to apply. The organizers were in New Zealand, Australia and the U.S. Plus, the YPO headquarters was staffed with people who also helped out with the agenda.

Application of consistent strategies hinges on how patient you are with your persistence.

Getting this engagement was remote, but at a Vince Poscente International staff meeting, we put a sign on the bookings board that said "YPO New Zealand." Every day we passed by the sign to the point when it no longer registered consciously. Six months later we got a call inquiring whether I would like to speak for this YPO event.

In this case, like many others, we simply envisioned the goal (like planting a seed) then gave in to passive patience.

Zorba the Greek relates his own learning around patience:

> I remember one morning when I discovered a cocoon in the bark of a tree just as the butterfly was making a hole in its case and preparing to come out. I waited awhile but it was too long appearing and I was impatient. I bent over it and breathed on it to warm it. I warmed it as quickly as I could and the miracle began to happen before my eyes. Faster than life. The case opened, the butterfly started slowly crawling out, and I shall never forget my horror when I saw how its wings were folded back and crumpled; the wretched butterfly tried with its whole trembling body to unfold them. Bending over it, I tried to help it with my breath—in vain. It needed to be hatched out patiently and the unfolding of the wings needed to be a gradual process in the sun. Now it was too late. My breath had forced the butterfly to appear, all crumpled, before its time. It struggled desperately and, a few seconds later, died in the palm of my hand.

That which you resist, persists. This goes for patience as well. If you resist patience, you will continue to be frustrated. In addition to patience is a keen understanding of the forces at work. People, especially, have their own agendas. Their own perspectives. Their own truths. Much like pushing a cork under water, it will bounce back. Hit it hard and it will bounce back harder. Without expending any energy the cork will effortlessly wear you out. Here you learn the ways of the cork, and you learn how to conserve energy for positive purposes.

Patience, like action, is a skill. Learning to balance the two is the yin and yang of applying a consistent strategy. The more you practice the better you get. Practicing patience, that is applying a consistent strategy to learn patience, will help you succeed. The opportunity you have is to find out how, when and under what circumstances. The more you explore this, the more you will learn about it.

In Summary

The ten ways to apply consistent strategies are:

1. Turn your intentions into actions.
2. You learn best by doing while remaining flexible.
3. Paint the picture for yourself and others.
4. Apply the yin and yang to your efforts.
5. The process is the goal. The goal is the process.
6. Develop routines any way you can.
7. Prepare yourself to act quickly, while remaining focused on the solution.
8. Be patient in your quest.
9. Patience is a skill; practice it and you will get better at it.
10. Balance your actions with passive patience.

Ultimately, you can apply consistent strategies with the finest of finesse and ability. But, when other people come into the picture, everything can get messed up. This is where you learn to nurture respect for others.

PRINCIPLE 3 ... NURTURE YOUR RESPECT OF OTHERS

"I still get no respect. Siskel and Ebert caught my act, and they gave me one finger up."–Rodney Dangerfield

Nurturing the respect of others would not be possible without a reasonably good foundation of self-respect. Following the guidelines from the first two chapters would definitely give you a great head start. Plus, by nurturing the respect of others you would feed your self-respect naturally. You get what you give, but you cannot give what you do not have.

RESPECT IS NOT A DECISION

You don't purposely respect someone. You either respect them or you don't. You may choose to disrespect parts of a person's personality and tend to focus on other parts that you do respect, but respect is not a decision.

The only thing you can control is the commitments you bring to a relationship. Ending a relationship because you don't respect someone essentially means you are no longer committed to making it work. Blaming something that you do not have control over is the easy way out. The whole basis of this chapter is founded in the commitments you bring to the table. If you agree or are skeptical, read on. If you completely disagree, then don't waste your time. Skip this chapter and go work on your commitment issues.

In 1993, I went through a divorce. She had her issues—I had mine. It would be easy for me to say that she was not committed, but I ultimately quit, too. In the end, my commitment disintegrated because I didn't want to pay the price. Having tried every available option I was aware of, it became hopeless. "At what price?" was the question that decided the outcome.

When I asked my ex-wife the ultimate reason why we divorced, her response floored me. She said she didn't respect me. This feedback expe-

---

Empathy grows and evolves from a feeling to a logical understanding.

---

rience gave me a lot to think about. This chapter contains the principle I've learned about respect over the last few years. Seek to find where respect comes from, how it is enhanced, and the powerful tools to strengthen it.

EMPATHY

Respect comes from empathy. From the Greek, *empathiea*, meaning "feeling into," empathy is our understanding, awareness and sensitivity to the feelings or experiences of others. We more or less feel empathy and would be hard pressed to describe how it is we actually know. We are born with an innate ability to be empathetic. Over time, this ability matures.

KIDS AT A YOUNG AGE HAVE EMPATHY

When our second child, Alexia, was born, our first born Max was thirteen months old. His reaction to our new arrival was fun to watch. At first Max seemed to wonder when this nineteen-inch visitor would go away, back to wherever it came from. It was especially fascinating to watch when Alexia would cry, how Max would get a sincere look of concern on his face. He would always try to reach out and pat Alexia on the head. Three months later, when Max would cry, Alexia would furrow her brow and look in the direction of Max, clearly sensitive to his feelings as well.

At first, humans have empathetic capabilities solely on the feeling level. At a core level, infants seem to understand when something is wrong with another person. Over time, empathy matures. The empathy grows and evolves from a feeling to a logical understanding.

Developmental psychologist Martin L. Hoffman, at New York University, researched the capabilities for empathy of infants and toddlers. In one case, a one-year-old attempted to comfort a crying friend by bringing over his own mother, despite the fact that the friend's mother was in the room, too.

Harvard psychologist, Robert Rosenthal, and his students devised what is regarded as one of the largest studies on the topic of empathy. It was named the Profile of Nonverbal Sensitivity, and defines a person's ability to read non-verbal messages. With tests on over seven thousand Americans and people from eighteen other countries, subjects reviewed a videotape of a young woman expressing a full range of emotions. In one scene there would be motherly love, in another scene jealous rage. Other scenes depicted seduction to revulsion, forgiveness to rejection. Each scene was carefully edited to conceal one or more nonverbal cues along with muffled sound. For example, in one scene all the cues but the facial expressions were blanked out. In another, only certain body movements were recognizable, thereby leaving it up to the viewer to interpret the non-verbal cues.

The studies found that subjects who were better able to interpret nonverbal cues were better adjusted, more socially adept, and, of course, more sensitive. Not surprisingly, women were more empathic than men and there were signs that over the forty-five minute test empathic skills could be improved (there is hope for men yet).

In a modified Profile of Nonverbal Sensitivity given to over one thousand children, results showed that highly empathic students were also the most emotionally stable and popular among their peers. They also had higher grades in spite of generally having lower IQ scores than their counterparts with high IQs but low empathic scores.

Since empathy can be learned, respect can be nurtured irrespective of the situation or the "wrongs" that you perceived.

EMPATHY IS THE GATEWAY TO RESPECT

For most of us empathy is natural and easy to understand. For example, you can look in the Bible and draw from the Ten Commandments certain rules that simply make sense. They don't require any profound logic. More than anything, you just know they are right. Do not steal. Do not murder. Do not testify falsely against your neighbor. Do not commit adultery.

Along with Christianity, Judaism, Hinduism, Buddhism and Islam all espouse a moral creed and ethical conduct.

The entire Jewish faith, for example, has its basis in ethical conduct. Some of the Buddhist precepts are for a person to refrain from:

- killing and harming living beings
- stealing and taking that which is not yours
- causing harm through sexual misconduct
- false speech, harmful speech, gossip, and slander

Overall, they have guidelines for one to live without bringing harm to another. We connect with these rules in a fundamental way through empathy.

THOSE VOID OF EMPATHY

It baffles most of us when we hear the horrific stories of child molesters, rapists and other violent people. How could these people not know the wrong they do? It is an unfortunate reality that some people are incapable of empathy or, at best, have selective empathy.

On the CBS show *60 Minutes* an infamous Mafia mobster was interviewed. When the mobster was asked about how he felt about killing over twenty people, his affect was blank. He shrugged his shoulders and said, "They had it coming to them." Then, the mobster was shown family photos of one of his "hits" and he still had no sign of empathy for the family members left behind or the lives of the two fathers he murdered.

Later in the interview, the hit man described how the government reneged on their agreement for leniency in return for informing on the mob he used to work for. As he talked about the raw deal he felt the victim of, he brought up how his daughter warned him, and he didn't listen to her. Now he feared for her life. He got emotional when expressing concern for his family.

The interviewer clarified that he felt concern for his family. He said, "Yes." The interviewer pointed out that the mobster would be devastated if anyone in his family was hurt, and he said, "Yes." Then the interviewer reminded the mobster about the family members of the men he murdered. "What about them?"

The mobster's expression instantly changed. He looked back at the interviewer and said blankly, "What do you mean?"

"Don't you feel what you did hurt their family deeply?" asked the interviewer.

"I don't know about that," he said as flatly and as void of any empathy as you could imagine. "Those guys had it coming to them."

People, like this mobster, subvert empathic wisdom and are able to rationalize any situation.

Rapists do not understand the pain of their victims, rationalizing the act as "she is just playing hard to get" or "she deserves it" for whatever reason.

In perspective-taking therapy developed by William Pithers, a prison psychologist in Vermont provided promising results. Sex offenders (primarily rapists) were brought through a series of exercises meant to make tangible the victims' perspective. The offenders watched interviews of emotional recounts of sexual assaults. This was followed with written perspectives from the victim's point of view and then a presentation to the group. Meanwhile, the offender answered probing questions about the experience. Finally, the offenders reenacted the crime, all the while playing the role of the victim.

Pithers' therapy has produced a 50 percent reduction in repeat cases, compared to offenders who did not receive the perspective-taking therapy.

Child molesters are a different beast. They convince themselves in some bizarre way that they are only "showing love to the child" or "just this once is okay." Therapy with these molesters is largely ineffective. The statistics on recidivism of child molesters is still practically 100 percent. These repeat offenders are nearly impossible to rehabilitate and incarceration is society's best defense.

SOCIETY WITH ITS SELF-ABSORBED MENTALITY

Recently I was asked what two words would describe society today. Immediately, my answer was, "Self-absorbed."

You see it everywhere. On a small scale, you walk behind someone in a mall, and they just stop to make up their mind where they really want to go. They effectively stop you in your tracks and block your way. They are completely oblivious to you and everyone else. It would stand to reason that based on the fact that there are other people shopping, too—somebody just might be behind them. Oh, and my pet peeve: people who stop at the bottom of stairs and talk to other people they just met. Wake up, people!

We are sharing these stairs with you, too. You see it on the highways, too. When merging into traffic, some people would rather have you fit somewhere behind them, than in front. Despite the opening, they will speed ahead and leave you trying to merge back where you are no concern of theirs.

You also see the self-absorbed mentality taken to a more extreme level. The '90s has proved to be a gruesome decade for child violence.

In 1993, three-year-old Jamie Bulger was kidnapped from a British shopping mall by a couple of eleven-year-old boys. They forced him to walk two miles and then they brutally murdered the helpless toddler.

In 1996, fourteen-year-old Barry Loukaitis, from Moses Lake, Washington, entered a math class carrying an assault rifle. He killed his teacher and a boy who reportedly had teased him earlier. Loukaitis also stood over another student while this dying classmate choked to death on his own blood. In a later confession his excuse was offered in a bewildered state, "I guess reflex just took over."

On March 24, 1998, Andrew Golden, eleven, and Mitchell Johnson, thirteen, stole nine guns from Andrew's grandfather's home, went to school, and methodically proceeded to follow a plan to murder their classmates. The two boys pulled the fire alarm then waited outside to massacre whomever they could. This bloodbath resulted in the deaths of four students and a teacher along with severe wounds to eleven others.

On May 20, 1998, fifteen-year-old Kip Kinkel shot his parents, killing them both, and then proceeded to Thurston High School where he killed two students and injured twenty-two more.

From mid-1997 to 1998, four incidents of child violence accounted for fifteen dead and forty-two wounded.

Just a few weeks before *Invinceable Principles* went to press, Eric Harris, eighteen, and Dylan Klebold, seventeen, planted dozens of bombs and terrorized Columbine High School's students and teachers in Littleton, Colorado. The pair killed twelve students, one teacher, and wounded several others, many seriously. Then they shot themselves.

The common aftermath has communities joining for candlelight vigils, all asking the same question, "Why?"

MANY BLAME THE VIOLENT MOVIES

In 1995 and 1996, the movie industry was aggressively accused and politically attacked for gratuitous violence allegedly accounting for the rise in violent acts in North America. The industry countered that it is not their fault since, "everyone knows that the movies are just fantasy."

Refer to the example in Principle 1 where the conscious mind (the ant) knows it is fantasy, but the subconscious (the elephant) experiences it as reality. Yes, when people go to a movie they know it's fantasy. But, that is with the conscious mind. The more a person is drawn into an experience, the more the subconscious mind takes in information as reality. In one second of violence in a movie, the conscious mind processes that information with a couple of thousand neurons. At the same time, the subconscious mind processes it with billions of neurons. The same goes for the next second and every second of time thereafter.

Repeated enough times, the movie-goer eventually becomes desensitized to violence. The empathy is numbed and the mind is reprogrammed. Go to movies such as *Pulp Fiction, Scream, Very Bad Things* and you will be shocked to hear masses of people laughing at the "funny way" a character was killed or mutilated.

Look at it this way. The cornerstone for my training program for getting to the Olympics was mental training through visualization and imagery. The best way to visualize and imprint the subconscious mind is to find a comfortable setting. Visualize in a dark, relaxed environment where you can lose yourself in your mental training. Create an experience for the mind. Imagine the details. The best visualizations also include emotions as well. Repeated enough times, the skill is ingrained into the mind as second nature. Given enough repetitions, the mind unconsciously believes that what was visualized really happened. Movie theaters accomplish the same environment for imprinting subconscious.

> ## Our subconscious is constantly bombarded with images and beliefs that ultimately stick.

OTHERS BLAME THE VIOLENT MUSIC

There is a Pearl Jam video where the main character, "Jeremy," shows a troubled youth how to get even. Jeremy fantasizes revenge against students who have teased him in class. Barry Loukaitis was reportedly obsessed with this video.

Bones Thugs-N-Harmony's "song," *Crept and We Came,* chimes the words, "Follow the murderous ways." This was reported as one of Mitchell Johnson's favorite songs.

Bands like these are criticized for the impact their music has on the youth of today. Yet the musicians counter they are just a reflection of contemporary society. They are "only entertainers and not engineers of societal belief systems."

Again, refer to the example, in Principle 1, where learning is accelerated using both the left and right sides of the brain. With the help of the corpus collosum, the right-brained music (creative) is connected to the left brain words (logic) to ingrain a truth into the subconscious mind (the elephant).

If you want to create a truth in the unconscious, then take the strategy of repetition, repetition, repetition.

STILL OTHERS BLAME THE VIDEO GAME INDUSTRY

Recently, my cousin Jay Poscente received a video catalog in the mail. He counted the number of violent video games in a catalog an inch thick and revealed that over 90 percent were violent in nature. There are "games" like "Postal Worker" where you pick your weapons and massacre people in various settings. This game is known for its graphic nature and realistic effects. The more you play this or any other game, the better you get at it.

"Doom" is a popular game where you choose weapons, get points for kills, and you are impervious to any return fire. There is apparently very little consequence for your actions.

"Rainbow Six" is a military-grade assassination simulator. It trains the subjects in tactics and strategies for murdering a pre-selected person.

Worst of all, many games like these are available on the Internet. Typically, the first four levels are free. With the seemingly endless supply of games, you could perfect your kill ratio on one game and move on to another, for years on end.

Mitchell Johnson's favorite video game was "Mortal Kombat," which has the aim to kill to win the game. The graphics of slashing, shooting and clubbing is state-of-the-art, three-dimensional animation with blood and gore for every kill.

The video game industry takes in $3 billion dollars every 365 days. That is close to $10 million dollars per day spent on this form of entertainment. It marches on despite the attempts by interest groups to eliminate its existence.

In Olympic training, repetition ingrained the skill in the subconscious mind. High performance visualization, repeated and compounded with an emotional attachment, increased the effectiveness of the mental training a hundred-fold. Again, the skill, repeated frequently in the mind's eye, became second nature.

When asked in the courtroom, teenage assassins cannot answer why they murdered, "I don't know. I just snapped, I guess."

Dr. Dorothy Otnow Lewis, a psychiatrist with twenty-five years of experience studying the motives of killers, believes that violence stems from a childhood of abuse and neglect. In her book *Guilty by Reason of Insanity*, she covers how, in many cases, the killer teenagers were victims of abuse or neglect, yet neither the parents nor the teen offer this information. Amazingly, they steadfastly remain silent on this detail.

Look at the divorce rates of today. Families are breaking down. In the families that remain intact or in combined families from remarried parents, double incomes are necessary. At best, in a bad situation, children are being neglected. The average North American child watches over three hours of television a day. They are bombarded with violent movies, music and video games.

The next time you're watching the news and see a candlelight vigil in the aftermath of a murderous rampage you will hear the words, "Why?"

Why, indeed.

TURNING THE TIDES

There is ample evidence that our society is going in the wrong direction. How do we turn the tides of this apparent self-absorbed mentality? Quite simply, it is you and I who will be part of the solution.

While on the Internet, I was sent a poem written by James Patrick Kenny, an Indianapolis High School student:

THE COLD WITHIN

Six humans trapped by happenstance, in bleak and bitter cold.

Each one possessed a stick of wood, or so the story's told. Their dying fire in need of logs, the first man held his back,

Four of the faces round the fire, he noticed one was black. The next man looking cross the way, saw one not of his church, and couldn't bring himself to give the fire his stick of birch.

The third one sat in tattered clothes; he gave his coat a hitch. Why should his log be put to use to warm the idle rich?

The rich man just sat back and thought of the wealth he had in store, and how to keep what he had earned from the lazy, shiftless poor.

The black man's face bespoke revenge as the fire passed from his sight. For all he saw in his stick of wood was a chance to spite the white.

The last man of this forlorn group did naught except for gain. Giving only to those who gave was how he played the game.

Those logs held tight in death's still hand was proof of human sin, they didn't die from the cold without—they died from the cold within.

What do we do? The answer is not just punishment to teach consequence. It is the investment of our most valuable resource, time. We must take time to educate ourselves and others. We must find ways to channel the creative energies of our youth and reverse the trends of neglect and even abuse. How much can we do? Remember: it is not how much you do, it is how often you do it.

In writing this book, I found writing at my downtown office was nearly impossible. So, I set up an area at home out in our guesthouse. This gave me a frequent chance to visit with my children during the day. Since it was fall, the weather was wonderful. Not too hot, and not too cold. At noon one day, I made a sandwich while my son, Max (one-and-one-half years old), was looking for some attention. I picked Max up and took him outside. We spent time on the bench swing under a large live oak. As we just sat and enjoyed each other's company, I realized how much differently Max must perceive the fifteen minutes we had on the swing than I did. Time is relative. To me, fifteen minutes was a fraction of the years I was on this planet. Max, on the other hand, had just eighteen months of earthly existence. Fifteen minutes to him was a much bigger deal.

Despite the demands to meet a deadline for this book, the fifteen minutes on the swing with Max could pay dividends toward the development of a healthy, stable child. Tomorrow and the days following I plan on giving Max and Alex quality "swing time" with their dad.

RESPECT PEOPLE'S TIME

If time really was money, if each second was a dollar, we would certainly spend it a little differently and respect the gift of another person's time in a new way. Giving of your time or saving someone else's time can be the greatest gift you can give. Time is our most valuable resource.

Peter Drucker, management and organizational guru says, "Time is the scarcest resource and, unless it is managed, nothing else can be managed."

Nurturing the respect of others must be measured with a respect of the time that belongs to other people. Find ways to respect another person's time. By respecting other people's time you open the door wide to receive the respect of others. This involves managing your time well and looking beyond yourself.

TWO TIME LINES

Tad James studies the language of the brain. His theories on Time Line Therapy outline two kinds of perceptions of time. Each one is so different that the understanding of the other is incomprehensible to most.

There are two truths to time ... "Through" Time and "In" Time.

The first kind of perception belongs to "Through Time" people. They perceive time as a measured, objective quantity. They are outside their time-line—understanding it as a continuum. Their reality is somewhat visual and they see time as an entity. They even look left to the past and right for the future when thinking of time.

The second perspective pertains to "In Time" people. Time is not remotely connected to a continuum. They think of time in terms of "now" or "not now." There is less of an understanding of consequence or impact. It simply exists. It is there when it's there. And not when it's not. In cultures like Jamaica, where the common slogan is "No problem," In Time people abound. Mexico is another generalization of the commonly used word *mañana*. It implies, "We'll do that tomorrow... or whenever."

I am a Through Time person. In fact, I am the poster boy for Through Time people. My wife is the lifetime, honorary member of the In Time club. How we manage to communicate is still beyond my comprehension. Whenever we have an event to go to, I give her reports on the time. I even go so far as doing the math for her.

"The dinner is at seven o'clock. It is six ten. It takes thirty minutes to get there. We have to be in the car in nineteen minutes."

"Okay, I'll be ready," she responds with a casual confidence.

I get the sinking feeling that all she registered was the seven o'clock.

Being on time for my wife is usually whenever she gets there. I know I am not alone facing this kind of frustrating reality of time. Dave Barry, the syndicated columnist, uses key jingling to signal to his wife that they are late. To him, it's a signal. To his wife, it's annoying.

Barry writes that his wife's definition of "on time for a plane" would be to drive to the airport just in time to race down the runway where the plane is taking off. As her car screeches to a halt at the end of the runway, a big hook comes out of the plane and snags his wife to put her on the plane.

The bottom line is there are two truths to time… Through Time and In Time. Both are right to each personality type. The challenge in relationships is to find ways to respect and allow each other's reality. The compounded issue is when you are late for people outside your primary relationships. What message do you send these people? The In Time people may not care, but the Through Time people get the message loud and clear that you do not respect their most valuable resource, time.

It is advisable to honor who you are and not change. Changing would be living outside of integrity. But, in situations where the message you send is important (like with children, clients, colleagues), valuing time sends a message that you are nurturing the respect of others.

LEAD BY EXAMPLE

Nothing you can do will send a stronger message than to lead by example. People may doubt what you say, but they will believe what you do. In all situations we must be the example we espouse. Each and every one of us takes on a leadership role when we nurture respect.

LEADERSHIP

In the Bible, Jesus is portrayed as leading by example. At one point he took off his garment and washed the feet of his companions. They protested that it should be the other way around. Jesus said, "I am doing this to set an example for you." For Christians, Jesus is the example of perfection.

You will notice that some people in public places will wear ID tags with the letters "WWJD" This is the acronym for What Would Jesus Do? If you look around, you will see WWJD on wristbands, key chains and stickers. It is a very good reminder—something to ask yourself when faced with a choice. Jesus set an example! It is up to you to do the same.

Walt Disney said, "People look at you and me to see what they are supposed to be. And, if we don't disappoint them, maybe, just maybe, they won't disappoint us." Getting people to live up to our expectations demands that we live up to our own expectations, too.

Avoid double standards at all costs. If you demand punctuality, you should be a shining example of punctuality. If you insist on honesty, you should personify honesty. If you expect fidelity, you should practice fidelity.

FAMILY FOUNDATIONS

No instruction manual comes with parenting. Although it would be nice, it actually is not necessary. The rules are simple, if you want respect, give it. If you expect love, offer it. If you desire your children to follow, then lead. Parenting is a leadership position, so lead!

Children learn by what they see, not by what they hear. While taking our fourteen-month-old son for his first haircut, my wife and I met a family that had a very negative energy. The father scowled constantly. He glared at his kids, wife and anyone else who might make eye contact. The mother was completely unenthusiastic about the whole experience. It was obvious she would have rather been somewhere else, with anyone else. Meanwhile the children were exploring the hair salon, seemingly oblivious to the parents' angry state. When Max was finished, the waiting parents went to get their three-year-old child. He went ballistic. He cried, complained and was clearly upset. As we were leaving the salon, we overheard the parents say, "What is wrong with you?" Children are the mirror image of what we show them to be.

WORK, PLACE OF WORSHIP, HOME, SCHOOL AND SOCIETY

Beyond the family, our actions have an impact on the people in our inner and outer circle. Gandhi once said, "We must be the change we wish to see in the world." To do nothing is to condone. Living the example is a choice you can make.

In ancient China, the ruler Chi K'ang asked Confucius what to do about all the thieves. The answer he received was not what he expected. Confucius had a way of telling the truth, regardless of whether it was diplomatic or not. "If only you were free from desire, they would not steal, even if you paid them to." Confucius suggested that, if the mighty ruler did not hoard his riches, he would naturally create an external shift by embracing an internal one. His subjects would follow his lead, thereby making stealing an unimaginable option. Typically, we try to change others by external forces, and we are likely to be frustrated by the results.

> # Leaders see themselves as responsible for the "family" they have built.

WORK

As I speak to organizations across North America, I witness both healthy and struggling organizations. Without an exception, I've found two things that contribute to the strongest companies.

First, there is a sense of family. Since I speak at conventions, many of the participants come from different corners of the continent and the rest of the world. The first and lasting impression I get from these corporations is that conventions are like family reunions. People are happy to see each other and there is an upbeat feeling in the air. Companies such as FedEx, Sprint, Long's Drugs, Express Personnel, Purolator Courier, Southwest Airlines, Shaw Communications and Amway are a few of the examples that come to mind.

For the most part, we spend more time at work than with our families. The willingness for businesses to include families as part of the corporate vision is starting to blur the lines between work and family. In many ways, our corporate culture is revealing itself as extended family.

The second and key ingredient of these strong groups is their style of leadership. Time and again, when I see a strong organization, excited about being together, I find a leader who cares—a person who manages by walking around. A person who is comfortable with people, not on a higher plain, removed from the masses. When you talk to employees there is a twinkle in their eyes when they discuss this leader. He or she is a leader who hugs people. Clearly they care for the person they haven't seen for a while. It is as if the leaders see themselves as responsible for the family they have built.

At work it is also the responsibility of the employee to lead by example. If you want loyalty from management, the best strategy is to be loyal. If you want security from your employer, the greatest demonstration you can make is to be counted on in any situation. Nurture the respect of your employer.

SPOUSES

Simple. You get what you give. Avoid any form of a double standard. Be the spouse you want them to be. The rest is up to the commitments you keep.

CHURCH

Our religious institutions have always been considered havens of what is right. Recent scandals involving sexual abuse of choirboys have rocked the foundations of the Roman Catholic Church. Despite the fact that the incidences are isolated and extremely infrequent, the coverage in the media naturally gives the perception that it is more common than it really is.

Still, the reason these events are exposed so widely is that the clergy are the perceived icons demonstrating the phrase "leading by example." These few "bad apples" have issues of self hate and lack of self respect, while trying to live up to a heavenly standard. It is a tough job and not everyone is cut out for it.

In my research for this book, I came across an interesting story about St. Francis of Assisi. One day he invited a young monk on a journey to a nearby village to preach. The young monk was excited and eager to learn some lessons on giving sermons from his mentor. All day long they walked the streets, tended to the needy and poor and literally were in contact with hundreds of people. On the way home the young monk was bothered and disappointed because Francis did not once gather an assembly of people and preach. He responded to the young monk's frustration by saying, "My son, we did preach. We were preaching while we were walking. We were watched by many and our behavior was closely observed. It is of no use to walk anywhere to preach unless we preach everywhere we walk."

SCHOOL

Think of your favorite teachers and your favorite classes. The teachers were passionate about what they were teaching and their jobs. As a student you could not help but gravitate to that passion.

Even if you are doing something you don't want to be doing, find what it is you love about it. I remember my high school chemistry teacher, Mr. Short.

He clearly loved teaching and he cared for his students. I never quite got the sense that he loved chemistry, but he always found interesting things to say about chemistry. Also, in high school, I had a physics teacher who made it clear that if he could do anything else, it would be to teach physical education and coach football. But, this teacher keyed in on things in physics he was fascinated by. Even though I was a pretty average student with reasonably good marks, I just loved physics. It was the way this teacher managed to focus on how physics explained the world we live in. His passion inspired others.

In college I took an accounting class from a professor who couldn't stomach using the standard accounting textbooks. He effectively made his own textbook out of hole-punched sheets and a three-ring binder. Every lesson had practical applications to real life. The book was designed to work with numbers that made sense to the students. His passion, to shift from just teaching to ensuring the students internalized the information, was infectious.

SOCIETY

Michael Jordan is widely considered to be one of America's most admired men, particularly among young people. When I went to the University of Alberta in the 1980s, a similar public figure was Wayne Gretzky. Both Jordan and Gretzky have two outstanding qualities. They have exceptional elegance with regard to their game, and they clearly understand the serious responsibility of being role models. Their example became clear to me when I placed second in a FIS (International Ski Federation) race at the Fortress Mountain Ski Resort in 1991.

I was regarded as the favorite to win the race. Prior to this race, Air Canada had managed to lose my racing skis for close to a week. I had to race on an old pair of training skis. Despite the equipment handicap, I was still on track to win in the final run. Out of the blue, an American racer beat my final run by a fraction of a kilometer per hour.

When I heard the news, I was off to the side where there were no people around, but I was within earshot and within view. Essentially, I threw a juvenile temper tantrum. I swore and kicked the snow with my ski boot.

Later, the race committee approached me with a formal caution. They had considered disqualifying me altogether but reconsidered and gave me a warning for unsportsmanlike conduct. They explained that "a number of people were watching my reaction and they expected more from the top Canadian racer."

I was embarrassed and disgusted with myself. But I learned a valuable lesson. People are watching. In fact, the higher profile you are, the higher the standard that is expected of you. Michael Jordan said, "The good part about being famous is being able to help people. The hard part is every day you have to be in a good mood, because that is what people expect. You learn to get good at it."

In the 1996 and 1997 seasons, the Dallas Cowboys had some serious public relations problems. There was one particular football star who had problems with the law, drug charges and associating with the "wrong crowd." He was virtually attacked by the media, and he fell victim to a virtual feeding frenzy of journalism sharks. When questioned on his responsibility as a role model, he eloquently said, "I never signed up to be no role model."

The net effect is the media and society build these multi-millionaire twenty-year-olds to godlike proportions. The public, especially children, idolize and mirror the behavior they witness—a baseball player whining over a contract that only offers $79 million when they say they are worth at least $90 million. A boxer who is convicted of rape, numerous accounts of misdemeanors and guilty of biting during a match is then deified with reinstatement and contracts larger than the GNP of some countries. (Hollywood action stars are paid in excess of $10 million or $20 million per movie to glorify killing and violence.) If they don't take the responsibility in society to lead by example, who will?

SELFISH — TOO MUCH, TOO LITTLE AND JUST RIGHT

Some kinds of selfish behavior are good examples for others to see. To follow your passion requires a degree of selfishness. During my training for skiing, I spent countless hours in the weight room and in training. Somehow, the solitary training didn't sit right with me. I wanted and needed to do things that make a difference in the lives of others. It wasn't until three months before the Olympics that I started to get feedback from people that I was an inspiration to them. Some people I barely knew came up to me and said that what I did gave them courage to pursue their goals.

How had they learned about me? I had no idea. But it made all the lonely hours of selfish training seem worthwhile.

Follow your passion and you will inspire others. Keeping selfish behavior in perspective is possible with a clever continuum designed by psychologist, Jaine Fraser, Ph.D.

Too little selfishness is unhealthy and a form of codependency. Too much selfish behavior is narcissistic and alienates others. Somewhere in the middle is a normal range, which is based on the average person.

I have a friend, George Fields, a seminary graduate, speaker and entertainer who describes selfish another way. "There's good selfish and there's bad selfish. A little more good selfish in this world won't hurt nobody."

Essentially, people will respect you if you live with integrity. Nurturing respect comes from within. It does not come from the environment.

WHEN RESPECT IS NOT RESPECT

Gangs proliferate in our urban cultures. They form and are propagated through a simple edict of respect. Respect is earned not through traditional leadership qualities but from fear tactics.

In the movie *Boyz in the Hood* a realistic scene shows one of the gang members holding up a gun and saying, "This is how I get respect." Honor, valor and sense of belonging feed the downward path of the gang members. Gangs seek only to exist in a perverse perspective on respect. They fight like rats in a cage. They exist to implode gradually and unceasingly into an abyss of right and wrong. Ultimately, they will never win. The respect they seek is temporary and fleeting, yet they seem to know no other way.

Education about the true definition of respect is the only way gang members will learn what is truly right and wrong.

FOCUS ON THE GOOD

It would be unrealistic to respect everyone all the time. Also, there are many opportunities to learn about *ourselves* as we react to the number of problematic people inevitably coming into our lives. Given that people will be different than we would expect from them, the best choice is to learn what we can and focus on the good qualities they have.

When I was racing in the World Cup, there was one individual who rubbed people the wrong way. He was different. Some of his qualities were flat-out unappealing. That is what others tended to focus on in him. On the other hand, this person had some other great qualities. He had moments when he had a huge heart. He was insightful and persistent. He showed tenacity and loyalty.

He and I ended up spending a fair amount of time together, and we learned a great deal from each other. Had the other members been exposed to this side of him, they would have had more to enjoy and less to complain about.

MICROCOSM OF FOLKLORE

Focusing on the good can create an opportunity for self-evaluation. By leveraging what you learn upon your own character, you can achieve a higher standard of self-respect. In turn you will create your own qualities that others will begin to admire in you. Ultimately, you can create something like a microcosm of folklore. The quality is noticed by many and you become known and respected for it.

For example, in 1985, I attended the Olympic Academy of Canada and met Lucy Thibault from Ottawa, Ontario. Toward the end of the academy, she offered to send me a study that was done on the Olympic movement. Because it was mentioned in passing and she would have to go out of her way to find it, I concluded the chances of receiving this report were slim.

Yet, two weeks later, I got a letter from her and even more information than I had expected. I was impressed. A couple of years passed and we stayed in contact. I always made it a rule that if anyone ever called me, I would call back. If I got a letter, I would write back. It seemed Lucy had the same rule.

One day, I had a meeting regarding the Alberta Youth Olympic Symposium and somehow Lucy's name came up. Each person at the table spontaneously had a positive thing to say about Lucy. One person said, "She always does what she says."

What would you want others to say about you?

"That's true," said another.

"You can always count on Lucy," said a third. I never forgot that moment. Best of all, Lucy had no idea it occurred. She had created a microcosm of folklore.

What would you want others to say about you? How would it be brought up? You'll never really know what others say about you, but a determination to create a microcosm of folklore is a fine start.

Find qualities that you like in others and model them. To earn respect from others, visualize how those admirable qualities should be exhibited in your life and of course, as you analyze, be specific.

BUILD IT AND THEY WILL COME

Build respect for others and they will become allies instead of adversaries. Here are a few ways that you can build respect:

WITH YOUR MATE

- Use empathy (especially you men reading this).
- Listen actively; attempt to understand.
- Don't give advice. Just listen.
- Accept who your mate is, and where he or she is coming from at that point.
- Key in on the positives and develop those as the qualities you respect.
- Trying to change that person is not your job, so don't try.

WITH YOUR BOSS

- Find out his or her objectives.
- Confirm that these are your objectives.
- Keep them in the loop with your actions ... find out the best way you can

communicate this to him or her.

- Action, action, action means results, results, results (pssst... that is what your boss is looking for...).
- Don't bring up problems without a solution in hand.
- Be on time, punctual.
- Communicate with confidence, look them in the eye, use open body language.
- Relax, show that you enjoy spending time with them ... walk the fine line between friendly, comfortable behavior and professionalism.
- Prove your indispensability.

WITH COWORKERS

- People don't care what you know until they know that you care.
- People give respect when they receive it ... give your time to them, and you will be amazed with the results.

WITH YOUR CHILDREN

Take the example from a hockey referee I know. He has a simple formula when dealing with an irate hockey player. If a player gets out of control the referee goes to the captain and makes it his problem. Then the player has the chance to skate away. If he persists or continues to lose control (especially in front of other players), the referee will give the player either a two-minute unsportsmanlike conduct, ten-minute misconduct or game misconduct depending on how badly the player disrespects the call he made. That way he gets the respect from the players and the guidelines are clarified.

The same goes for the coach. If he yells something out of line, the referee gives him a chance to repeat it. If he backs off, he lets it go. If he persists, it is a penalty, and one of his players must go to the penalty box to sit out the coach's mistake.

When dealing with your children, it's much like a hockey referee:

- Make sure they know and agree to the boundaries.

• Make sure they know the consequences or punishment for crossing the boundaries (make the consequences a removal of privileges they hold near and dear).

• Carry out the consequences or punishment if they do not do what they agreed to.

IN SUMMARY

The ten ways to nurture respect of others are:

1. You get what you give, but you cannot give what you do not have.
2. Respect is not a decision. Commitments are your only choice.
3. Empathy is the gateway to respect.
4. Avoid being part of the self-absorbed mentality.
5. Respect people's time. They may perceive time differently than you.
6. Lead by example everywhere you live and breathe.
7. Leadership starts with the family.
8. There's good selfish and bad selfish.
9. Focus on the good in others.
10. Earn your respect by building it.

Respect is a moving target. We can't control the respect we get. Plus, we cannot decide to respect others. You either have it or you don't. The single greatest tool you will ever need to nurture respect is a tool that erodes judgmentalism—the subject of Principle 4.

PRINCIPLE 4 ... ERODE JUDGMENTALISM

"What the world needs is more geniuses with humility.
There are so few of us left."–Oscar Levant

Human nature. Judging is as natural as breathing. We judge virtually everything we encounter. We judge whether something is safe or will cause us harm. We judge whether something is good or bad. We judge whether another thing is right or wrong. We judge other people. Yet, in some cases, our judgments do not serve us properly.

WHY WE JUDGE

Some judgments are necessary to evaluate and select appropriate actions. In fact, there are two processes necessary to decision-making—categorizing and judging.

If you go to pet a neighbor's cat and it claws at you, then you have the choice to judge all cats as dangerous and bad, or you categorize this cat as unfriendly at this time. You store this experience in your memory bank. Later you come across a different cat. If you followed your judgment that all cats are dangerous and bad, you would keep your distance. Or, if you categorized the last cat as unfriendly, you would leave the door open for the next cat to prove itself. It might nuzzle up and be affectionate.

Take this a step further. You go on a blind date with someone, and the date doesn't go well. The next time you have a chance to go on a blind date, you decline because of your previous experience. Based on one experience, you judge blind dates as undesirable and miss out on the opportunity to meet someone who could be nice.

Categorizing will serve you well. Judgmentalism will not. It's important to get away from labels, interpretations, evaluations and judgmentalism. Where do judgments come from? The answer is in the cognitive filter.

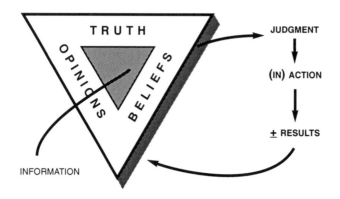

THE COGNITIVE FILTER

It stands to reason that your actions create your results. But where does the inspiration for the action come from? Our judgments lead our action. From where do the judgments originate? From the source of how we think. How we think is effectively like a filter for information. Information passes through our own individual cognitive filter and is then processed as a judgment. From that judgment we act or remain inactive. From our action or inaction we experience the results, which we perceive as positive or negative.

Our cognitive filter is our opinions and beliefs that make up our truth. This filter is uniquely our own. No one else perceives things exactly the way we do. Our perceptions are our truths. Our cognitive filter has been in the making our whole life. We take this filter everywhere we go. When we experience a situation we filter it, judge it and act on it. The results we enjoy or suffer are often in keeping with the truth we had in the first place. Note the arrow at the bottom of the diagram above. The common term for this loop effect is a "self-fulfilling prophecy."

Here is an example of how the cognitive filter works. Let's say your job is to interview a person for a sales position with your refrigerator company. You happen to pass by the front lobby of the office and notice a twenty-one-year-old man who has tattoos all over his arms. His nose is pierced and his hairstyle would rival that of any Rastafarian reggae singer in Jamaica. His clothes are reasonably professional, but you can't take your eyes off the snake tattoo that appears to start on one forearm and end on the other. You notice the boy take out the nose ring and put it in his pocket. He also rolls down his sleeves to hide his tattoos. You continue on your way through the lobby, when the receptionist stops you and says in a hushed tone, "He is your three o'clock appointment."

Your neighbor has a son about the same age as the interviewee. Her son also has tattoos and a nose ring. Plus, last night you saw a television documentary on Generation X. It showed how Gen' Xers were unmotivated, unwilling to work and got tattoos because they only understood instant gratification.

With this information at hand, you process it through your cognitive filter, causing you to instantly develop your "truth" about this individual. You then judge him as unworthy of the position. So, you take the appropriate action. You introduce yourself and ask if he has his resume with him. You explain that an unexpected meeting has come up, and that you cannot take time for him right now. You smile your best smile and promise that you will review his resume and call him if it looks like he might be a good fit for the job.

He walks out of the door, and you are relieved that you avoided any waste of your time.

Let's analyze the situation: You filtered what you saw. You saw what you thought to be a deadbeat. You judged him to be a poor fit for the refrigerator sales job and you got rid of him. But wait, there's more!

As you toss the resume into the wastebasket, you think about what a shame it is he is so unmotivated. He seemed like a nice enough guy. Then this voice inside you says, "You promised to read the resume." Being a person who keeps promises, you fish out the resume and you start to get a sinking feeling.

You read that the young man, while studying sociology, worked in Seattle for a competitor of yours. He was their number one sales person, four years in a row where he marketed to the student market. He sold a record ten thousand mini-fridges and enclosed a letter of recommendation from your competitor's president. It states how impressed he was with the young man who was able to graduate with honors and set sales records at the same time.

In a heartbeat, your cognitive filter changes. You know you goofed. He would be perfect for the college market you have been trying to break into for years. You rush back to the lobby. There, by the elevator, is the young man who you catch before he gets on the elevator.

What changed? Your judgment changed and you ended up with a new result. Remember: the result is often in keeping with your truth in the first place. Change your truth and you change your results. Change your truth, and you change your reality. In *Hamlet,* Shakespeare writes, "There is nothing good or bad but thinking makes it so." Your truth is your reality. How many times has your truth held you back from a better reality?

THREE TYPES OF JUDGMENT

For the balance of this chapter, we will cover the three judgments that can keep us from the results we might prefer: self-judgment, judging others, and judging situations. Please note that your mission is not to self-analyze to the point of being ridiculous. This would be going from "analysis to paralysis." Simply be aware of the opinions, beliefs and truths that prevent you from living a fulfilled life.

We all have suffered from the chains of constricting ideas. As we look at these three judgments remember: the single most satisfying journey is the journey within. By removing limitations imposed by judgmental thinking, you unlock your full potential—potential that is hindered when you literally stand in your own way.

SELF-JUDGMENT

Think of the world as a mirror. In a way it is a reflection of you. What you see is much of what you believe the world has to offer. You see what you look for. People will treat you as you expect to be treated. Much of these beliefs are subconscious. More importantly, if you don't like the reflection the mirror offers you, you have the power to change it. The viewpoints you choose to hold about the world are an expression of you. You will manifest in the world your subconscious beliefs.

Poor self-esteem is the largest inhibitor of what you would like to manifest. If you get out of your own way, you will be able to change your results. What does it mean: "to get out of your own way"?

> # Poor self-esteem is the largest inhibitor of what you would like to manifest.

That which is within you, your personal "truths," make up your judgments. You ultimately have judgments that work *for* you and judgments that work *against* you. These truths unconsciously protect you, but they can also get in your way.

GETTING IN YOUR OWN WAY

Below is a list of ways you hold yourself back. Check off the ones that you most often say to yourself.

____ I don't have enough money.

____ I don't have enough time.

____ I don't have enough energy.

____ I am not worthy.

____ I am not smart enough.

____ That is below me.

____ I will be rejected.

____ I'll be happy when I get in a relationship.

____ I'll be happy when I get out of this relationship.

____ Someone else will do it.

____ Someone else will take care of me.

____ I might look silly.

____ I am too old.

____ I am too young.

____ I might fail.

____ Commitments are smothering.

____ I am right.

____ I cannot forgive.

____ I cannot let go of the past.

____ I have no choice.

____ The grass is greener on the other side of the fence (a better job, a better spouse, a better place to live).

____ I know my job/spouse/environment will change.

____ This never worked before.

____ This will be too painful.

____ Hey, I'm the victim here!

____ This is not fair.

____ Things will never change.

____ There's too much risk.

____ I've paid enough dues.

____ The sacrifice is too great.

____ People and opportunities should just come to me.

Think of something you are pursuing and identify if you are getting the results you really want. Which of the judgments above applies to you? Take a moment and identify some judgments that are holding you back, but do not appear on the list above. Think of a time when you ended up with some very negative results. What truths and judgments got you into that situation in the first place?

A CASE STUDY OF A MARRIAGE GONE WRONG: ELAINE AND GERRY

This true story should give you an idea of what I mean. When Gerry was single, he was often frustrated and alone. He could never seem to get in a relationship that would last past three months. Every time it was the same: "I would fall in love, but three months later the girl would dump me and go back with her old boyfriend. Each time I was single again. I hated it. I wasn't happy, and I knew that I would be happy in a committed relationship."

Gerry finally met Elaine. They fell in love and things went great. "We knew it was right, so, before the three-month mark rolled around, I proposed." Soon after, Elaine admitted that she was still in love with her old boyfriend, Mark. Gerry gave her the option. "Forget about Mark or forget about me." Elaine picked Gerry, promised she would get over Mark, and so they got married. Soon after, she admitted that she couldn't actually forget about Mark and needed to spend time with him.

Gerry said, "I didn't like it, but what choice did I have? It made sense that if she resolved her past relationship, she could then move on with the present one." It was a difficult weekend for Gerry. She came back and said that she knew Mark wasn't right for her, and she renewed her commitment to their marriage.

Two months later Elaine announced she still was attracted to Mark and that she needed another weekend with him. This was very hard for Gerry to handle. Somehow he made it through another weekend, while his wife visited with Mark. When she returned, he asked, "Are we still married?"

Elaine responded with, "Do you expect me to decide this in one weekend?" They separated for the first time.

After a few months of trying to patch up their marriage while apart, they reunited. It was only a short while later they separated again when Gerry found out Mark was still in the picture. The marriage was in tatters.

Eventually, after two and a half years of trying to make it work, Gerry found a love letter to this same boyfriend. "I finally had to give up. I couldn't take it any longer and I don't think she could either. We separated again for the third and last time." This led to a divorce. A month after the third separation Elaine broke up with Mark and met another fellow.

"I realized Mark wasn't the reason for the problems; he was only a mechanism for Elaine to deal with the problem. Irrespective of her sabotage strategies, I had to come up with what I contributed to this unhealthy marriage. In fact, had I not proposed to her before three months, I would not have had to go through all that heartache."

What was Gerry doing in three months that was making these women check out? If Gerry didn't find the solution, he would be doomed for a lifetime of three-month relationships and a heap of frustration.

Then, in 1993, I met Gerry and gave him a list similar to the one a few pages back. The sentence that jumped out at Gerry was: "I'll be happy when I get in a relationship."

"All of a sudden it hit me like an avalanche of boulders," said Gerry. "If my happiness was dependent on this person, what unconscious message did my girlfriend receive loud and clear? My happiness depends on her!"

Who would want that kind of pressure? Plus, Gerry carried that same truth and judgment to every relationship he ever encountered. "I was a fun date until the pressure, which was never verbalized, became too great for her to handle."

Gerry decided immediately to find a way to be happy on his own. "It was as if I had had a piano tied to my rear end, and I was finally free from it. What a relief."

Six months later Gerry met Denise. She had an old boyfriend, too. This time was different. In fact, at three months nothing changed. No old boyfriend. No problems. Gerry was in uncharted territory. Two years later they got married and now have started a family.

THE MORAL OF THE STORY?

A simple change in your truth can dramatically change the results that you manifest. Gerry's truth was that his happiness was dependent on another person. Since this truth was unconscious, Gerry needed a great deal of introspection before he realized he was his own worst enemy. By changing his cognitive filter around relationships and happiness, Gerry changed his relationships for the better.

What "truth" is holding you back?

TAKE ACTION

Thoreau wrote:

> If one advances confidently in the direction of his dreams, and endeavors to live the life which he has imagined, he will meet with a success unexpected in common hours. He will put something behind, will pass an invisible boundary; new, universal, and more liberal laws will begin to establish themselves around and within him, or the old laws will be expanded and interpreted in his favor in a more liberal sense; and he will live with the license of a higher order of beings.

> # Slightly modifying your "truth"
> # will dramatically change your results.

Proactive self-examination is the only way to efficiently make any changes. Taking courses, going to counseling and reading self-help books (along with doing the homework) can accelerate this process. An Alcoholics Anonymous standard is: "If you always do what you've always done, you'll always get what you always got." When you put this book down, what do you expect to change with your life? If you want something different, what will you do that is different?

Change is a process that can lead to your becoming hard on yourself. When you start digging for what isn't working in your life, you might not like what you find. Don't beat yourself up. Remember: the past is past. In fact, you very well may catch yourself making a judgment. The key is not to get caught in the ironic loop of judging yourself poorly for judging. Instead, choose to learn how the next time a similar situation comes around, you will erode judgmentalism.

JUDGING OTHERS

> *"Human acceptance is the salvation of the world."*
> *–Barbara Aiello*

Judgmentalism assumes that you have the right to change someone else. Well, you don't. You only have the right to choose how *you* will change and behave. Trust others to make their own choices. Put the accountability for another's actions where it belongs, on the other person's shoulders.

Jesus said, "I do not judge you. Your own words judge you." He knew that judging others limited his capacity to realize change. The same issues exist today for leaders. The single greatest challenge in corporate North America today is to increase the sense of accountability of individuals and their contribution to the whole. The ideal situation would see leaders and subordinates marching together toward creation and restoration.

> # Living without judgment of others is not easy!

LIVING WITHOUT JUDGMENT OF OTHERS

A few years ago, I decided to create my own microcosm of folklore. The one quality that I didn't like about myself was how I constantly judged other people. I hated it and decided to change. It was extremely hard at first.

At the beginning, I tried to go a whole day without judging. I lasted all of two minutes. It was a deeply ingrained pattern. Persistently and methodically, I had to change the pattern, which was like putting a rock in the river to change the flow to the sunny side of the mountain.

Eventually, over time, I judged others less and less. It is now to a point where friends and peers have commented that "not judging" is one of my redeeming qualities.

Recently, I was asked to go to southern Oklahoma to be a judge in a beauty pageant. I said yes as a favor to a friend, Gail Davis, and didn't realize what I had gotten myself into until the first round of interviews. Since I was a close friend of Gail's, she knew me quite well. Between rounds, I announced to the other judges, "I don't like this; I don't like judging." It was too late. I was forced to give marks to each girl entered in the pageant. Most of it was agonizing, except for one time when I asked a girl what she wanted to do in the future. Her response was worth the trip:

"I want to be a brain surgeon," she announced. "But if that doesn't work out, I'll be a hair stylist."

As they say in the South… "Bless her heart."

IF YOU WALKED A MILE IN THEIR SHOES

It is far too easy to be frustrated with other people. Don't they understand? Is he stupid? Doesn't she see what she is doing wrong? Is that the best that you can do?

If you had even a glimpse of what that person has experienced in their life-time, you might have a clue why they are the way they are. None of us can ever appreciate the reasons for why some people do what they do. They have their own cognitive filters, made up of their own realities.

Everyone is acting from his own level of consciousness. This, in fact, is all we can ask of anyone or ourselves. Therefore, how could we logically ever judge another person to be wrong or bad? He is simply doing the best he can, given his unique cognitive filter.

Finding forgiveness can be difficult. First, recognize that you have been wronged at one time or another. You are also guilty of hurting others at times. No one is exempt. Second, forgiveness does not mean that you condone an action or behavior. Simply see yourself in that person. Third, there is a little child in each of us. Recognize the hurt of that little child. Your propensity to feel a deeper sense of empathy will increase dramat-ically.

Eliminate judgment and choose to relate to the pain, confusion or fear that person is experiencing. Seek the answer lovingly.

Another angle on walking a mile in their shoes could teach you about yourself. The next time you catch yourself disapproving of someone, you may be re-creating a pattern that pops up in many areas in your life. Digging deeper here may result in the realization that you have been your own worst enemy. Notice what you disapprove of and you will find the cognitive filter that creates your results.

Take for example a disapproval, like, "What he did is stupid." Your disap-proval may concur with an opinion or belief that "men are stupid." With that as your truth, you will manifest a number of judgments, actions and results in keeping with your original truth. This truth very well may be in the subconscious. If this all happens, you would find yourself baffled by issues you have with your husband or other men you have contact with at work or socially.

Therefore, analyze what things you disapprove of. Catch yourself disap-proving of something or someone, and work it backward from judgment. You will then be in the powerful position of making choices whether or not you want to create the same results.

DIFFERENTIATE BETWEEN A PERSON AND THEIR ACTIONS

Never look at someone else's *actions* and judge the *person* as being wrong or bad. Try not judging them at all. Notice the difference. Admit that you haven't walked a mile in their shoes.

Think of the last person who said something nasty to you. What did they say? How did it make you feel? What was your perception of that person?

Let's say a person at work said to you, "The market projections you submitted were useless and poorly thought out." Immediately, that would hurt. The next few weeks or months at work would be uncomfortable whenever you were around that person. Instead of judging the person as bad, take a step back. Find out what it is they don't like about the market projection report. Find out what stress they are under. Dig deep in an appropriate way and you'll discover an angry person is a hurting person. At best, you will find out why they attacked your work and they will, too. At worst, you will know that their actions may have been out of line, but that doesn't mean they are a bad person.

Another example could be with a child. Imagine you don't like the temper tantrum your daughter threw in the shopping mall. Disassociate the action from the person. You love your daughter. You don't approve of her actions. Send this message to your daughter and she will know she is loved, but her behavior was unacceptable.

This is why the language you use with a child is vitally important. Never say, "You are a bad boy." Instead, say, "What you did was extremely disappointing to me. I love you very much. Your actions were unacceptable."

There is even a positive judgment that has negative implications. For example, you could say, "Good girl," to a child. The message she hears is: "If you do this, I will love you." The love for the child becomes conditional. This could lead to all sorts of manipulative behavior. The best language to use with a child is, "You did that very well." The child hears approval for her action and does not tie it to any kind of conditional love.

JUDGING SITUATIONS (THIS INCLUDES MONEY!)

Similar to judging people, judging situations can limit your true potential.

A situation may seem bad, but it may just have some good in it. This is where the analogy for a glass as half-empty or half-full comes from.

GOOD OR BAD?

It's best in life to take the good with the bad because the bad might be *good,* and the good might be *bad,* or the bad might actually *be* bad, or the good could very well be good... Confused?

Let me explain.

I never would have gone to the Olympics if I had judged any of the following situations as being right or wrong, good or bad.

In 1983, I tried the sport of luge and fantasized about making the Olympic team one day. When I sat down with the national team coach, I asked her what my chances were. She said not very good at all. That was bad.

Wrong. Because I had just earned my degree in recreation administration and had experience in luge. I landed a job working in Calgary for the luge association leading up to the Olympic Winter Games. That was good.

Wrong. During the opening ceremonies I watched a luge buddy, Bob Gasper, walk in with the Olympic team. I quit, and he didn't. He was in the Olympics; I was in the stands. That was bad.

Wrong. Seeing Bob inspired me to try taking up speed skiing to see if I could do the same thing as Bob Gasper did in luge. That was good.

Wrong. I had never ski raced before and it was unrealistic to think I could be an Olympic athlete in a sport I had only tried once. That was bad.

Wrong. I practiced an intensive mental training program and speed skiing turned out to be my ticket to compete in the Olympic games. That was good.

Wrong. When I made the national team I had a legitimate shot at a medal in the Olympics. I knew if I took home some hardware, especially the gold, I would be able to follow my next passion, professional speaking. But I did not win. There I was, back selling real estate with no speaking requests. That was bad.

Wrong. I decided to develop a message around the journey instead of the end result. People loved it, and now I speak around the country with a fresh

You never know what is truly good or bad.

message on excellence. Winning is a journey of integrity. The great thing is I make more money and have more fun than ever before. That's good.

Sure, that's good. Why not?

The point of this whole story is you never know what is good or what is bad. In fact, it doesn't matter. If you believe that everything happens for a reason, you may be right. (Then again, you may be wrong, but it still doesn't matter). What is, is. You are in the process of life. It is a series of lessons and opportunities. Eroding judgmentalism of your self, people and situations will serve you greatly!

In the Bible, Paul said, "All things work together for the good of those who are called to God's purpose." If you label something as bad and stop there, what would you be cheating yourself of? What greater purpose of this perceived "bad" experience is there yet to unfold?

DON'T YOU JUST LOVE THAT FEELING?

When Greg Norman was learning to play golf he read books and information about Jack Nicklaus. At his first Masters tournament, Norman found himself matched with Nicklaus. As the two walked down the fairway after the first drive off the tee, Nicklaus asked Norman:

> "How did you feel off that first tee in your very first Masters? Did you feel excited? Did you feel nervous? Did you feel tight? How did you feel?"
>
> Norman responded by saying, "Jack, I was scared to death, my knees were shaking. I was nervous."
>
> Nicklaus said, "Don't you just love that feeling?"

It is a monumental shift from judging a situation as complete when you reach the result. Why not enjoy the moment? Think of a time when you fell in love with someone you just started to get to know. Remember the time you had when you weren't together and you longed to be with him or her? If you could re-live that moment, what would it have been like to revel in the moment of anticipation, regardless of the eventual reunion?

88

Here is that thought put another way. In A.A. Milne's book, *The House at Pooh Corner*, Christopher Robin is talking to Winnie the Pooh about what he likes best in the world:

> "Well," said Pooh, "what I like best..." and then he had to stop and think. Because although eating honey was a very good thing to do, there was a moment just before you began to eat it, which was better than when you were, but he didn't know what it was called.

Peggy Merlin is a friend who describes this enjoyment of anticipation another way. Years ago, Peggy developed what she called a "schoolgirlish" crush on the teacher of a certain personal development course. He was handsome and wise. He had a quiet energy that she loved. She found herself thinking about him a great deal. She even imagined what it would be like to go out with him. As time went on she finally built up the courage to let him know how she felt. With butterflies and nervous anticipation she approached him and said, "I have a crush on you."

"How nice for you to have that experience. Isn't it wonderful?" As he turned to walk away he said knowingly, "Enjoy the feeling."

Enjoy the feeling. It makes getting there more fun.

THE MONEY TRAP

"It is harder for a rich man to get into Heaven than it is for a camel to walk through the eye of a needle." This biblical expression has always confused me. There are a lot of wealthy people who do wonderful things in this world. In fact, there is nothing holy about being poor.

If money issues are nagging you right now, the best thing you can do is shake the negative notions you have with money terms like "filthy rich," "dirty money," or "stinking rich." These notions serve no good. They only promote negative judgments about money. Money is neither good, nor bad. It is what money can be used for that can be labeled as good or bad.

Your perceptions, your truths about money will ensure that you will never have any, have some, or have an abundance to serve your family, you and the world.

Detach money from people. Money provides good things. It pays the bills. When generated, it helps others. My wife and I have many people working for us at our two companies. The money we generate together helps families put food on their tables. It helps people achieve their dreams. The purpose of money is to help people. Generating more money means you can help more people.

Moreover, there is an endless supply of money. There is more than enough for everyone. Think of money as energy. Your job is simply to plug into it.

One time Maharishi Mahesh Yogi was discussing the ambitious growth of Transcendental Meditation with his colleagues. Finally, one person asked Maharishi, "Where will the money come from?"

Maharishi responded, "Wherever it is now."

LETTING GO

Let go of expectations and you will be able to let go of judgment. Letting go is an art in itself. It frees you to be what you want to be and let others be who they are. Let go of expectations and you will eliminate disappointment and even anger. Letting go seems to be the answer to eroding judgmentalism.

By letting go, people will be attracted to you. It is as if you become a child again. This is why toddlers and small children are so fascinating. They have no agendas. They have no expectations. They have no judgments. When you are in their presence, you would not be victim to judgment whatsoever. This is a quality worth regaining as adults, a quality that may need to be resurfaced through our jaded, toughened exterior.

IN SUMMARY

Ten ways to erode judgmentalism are:

1. Eroding a lifetime of judgmentalism takes tenacity and time.
2. A simple shift in your cognitive filter can change your results.
3. Erode all three areas ... self-judgment, judging others and judging situations.
4. Get out of your own way.
5. In all problems you are the lock, and you hold the key at the same time.
6. Imagine or learn what it's like to walk a mile in someone else's

shoes. You will see them differently.

7. Differentiate a person from their actions.

8. Situations are neither good nor bad.

9. Revel in the feeling of anticipation.

10. Just let go.

By letting go, opportunities will surface. People and situations will come to your aid. Attraction of the right things happens naturally. You will then be in the perfect place to explore the next Invinceable Principle: Do Everything at Least Once.

PRINCIPLE **5** ... DO EVERYTHING AT LEAST ONCE

"Whatever doesn't kill you makes you stronger."
–Friedrich Nietzsche

Through the doors of opportunity. On June 20, 1978, Jill Kudryk died from a heart attack. I was a junior in high school at this time and Jill was in twelfth grade, a senior in high school with plans to attend a university in the fall. Jill was a friend who always had a kind word. She was loved by many. Then, one day, her weak heart gave out and she was gone.

The funeral was an extremely sad event. It was a heart-wrenching time. I sat in silence as eulogies were spoken. I realized something that day that changed my life forever. I realized that, as teenagers, we thought we would live forever. Instead, life was uncertain. I could go at any time. At that very moment I made a decision to try everything at least once. If an opportunity became available, I would try it. If some new challenge entered my life, I would at least explore it. The only restrictions I put on this approach were that it had to be legal, moral, ethical and not have the potential to hurt anyone else.

Later that year, I kept thinking how I wanted to do two things. One, I wanted to play in our highly acclaimed jazz band. (I played clarinet, and I needed to learn how to play the saxophone.) Two, I wanted to be the valedictorian for our high school in my graduating year. I explored the opportunity. A year later I was a soloist in the jazz band and was elected valedictorian.

The next year I thought I might want to be a doctor. So, I took the recommended pre-med courses. I hated it, but I learned about recreation administration where I could take a mix of business and social science courses.

During college I helped run a family video business where we shot weddings and special events on the less expensive VHS format. After one job

I was invited to join the Canadian wrestling team as the videographer at the Commonwealth Games, in Brisbane. I had always wanted to see the world. I worked hard that summer, sold my car and everything I owned and traveled to Australia. At twenty, with a backpack, I traveled around the world for a full year. I visited Australia, Papua New Guinea, Singapore, Malaysia, Thailand, India and much of Europe. At twenty-one I returned home after having explored all sorts of opportunities, foods, cultures and experiences. I had a broader curiosity about the world.

During my last two years of college, I was introduced to luge. I ended up competing in the Alberta Winter Games and made the provincial squad to train in Lake Placid. This took me to a job in Calgary.

While there, I attended the Canadian, International and Bulgarian Olympic Academies. I founded and chaired the Alberta Youth Olympic Symposium and sat on numerous Olympic related boards.

I traveled to Europe every summer and after the Olympics took three months off (sold everything again) and visited Hong Kong, China, South Korea and other parts of Thailand.

During the past two decades, I:

- whitewater canoed,

- overcame a total malfunction while parachuting,

- dived with sharks off the Great Barrier Reef,

- hang glided in the majestic Rockies,

- skied to my fifth national record of 135 miles-per-hour in the Olympics,

- bungee jumped off the world's largest permanent platform (229 feet) and

- became a glider pilot.

I write this list of experiences to prove that curiosity to explore uncovers opportunities beyond your imagination. It opens doors that would be previously unavailable. It challenges you to be larger than fear, and find what you are truly capable of. This curiosity builds confidence to take on things you might have previously avoided.

What would your life list look like? Do you have any regrets? What will be different starting today?

Changing "try" to "do"

Every word in this book is carefully selected. None more than the word "do" versus "try." When I first chose to try everything at least once I eventually realized I was "doing" every opportunity at least once. Try is actually a very weak word.

In the movie *The Empire Strikes Back* the character named Yoda says to Luke Skywalker, "You must unlearn what you have learned."

Luke says, "Okay, I'll try."

"Try not," Yoda exclaimed, "Do… or do not. There is no 'try.' "

Indeed, "try" is a non-event. "Do" is action.

Take a moment and put your book down on your lap. Now, try to pick it up. Note, I did not say to pick it up. Trying is everything between where your hand was to just before touching the book. The state of "try" is light-years away from the state of "do."

Learning this can take you to a whole new world. In fact, I recommend that you completely eliminate the word try from your vocabulary for the rest of your life. I challenge you to think of one time when the word try is better than the word do.

"I'll try to call you tomorrow" versus "I will call you tomorrow or I won't call you tomorrow."

"I'll try to do better next time," versus "I *will* do better next time."

"I'll try to do my best," versus "I will do my best."

The message you tell yourself and others with the word try is weak and non-committal. It implies that you might not be counted on. It even indicates the level of integrity you bring to your life. Telling others what you will do clarifies your intent. People like that. You like that. People trust people who take a stand.

"I'll try," versus "I'll do it." This is the most important alternative of all. It shifts from disbelief to belief.

Back to the next scene in the same movie…

Later, Yoda uses the "Force" to bring a downed spaceship out of a swamp.

Know the difference between "try" and "do."

This was something Skywalker was unable to do.

Skywalker is amazed at what he just witnesses and says, "I don't believe it."

"That," says Yoda quietly, "is why you fail."

How big is your world?

Fish hobbyists in Japan often nurture *koi* or carp. Interestingly, *koi*, when put in a fish bowl, will only grow up to three inches. When this same fish is placed in a large tank, it will grow to about nine inches long. In a pond *koi* can reach lengths of eighteen inches. Amazingly, when placed in a lake, *koi* can grow to three feet long.

The metaphor is obvious. You are limited by how you see the world. As you know, how you perceive things is processed through your cognitive filter. Your beliefs (your truths) can, and I venture to say *must*, be expanded. I found this anonymous quote on the Internet: "Life is an ocean—get your feet wet."

You have the same opportunities as anyone else to grow in your own lifetime. Your field of experiences depends on your field of opportunities. Faced with an opportunity for self-discovery, what limits you is internal, not external. Nothing outside yourself truly holds you back. Thinking makes it so.

Life is the path that you chose.
Doors that have opened and closed.
When will we forgive and forget?
When will we live with conviction of the heart?
–Kenny Loggins from Conviction of the Heart.

Opportunities are at your fingertips. They float by like leaves on a stream. As you have learned, your life is a series of opportunities. You must explore what is offered to you. Only then can you be in harmony with the essence of what life is, an adventure.

Some streams move quickly, while some meander. But, opportunities will always pass by. There is a twist. You are moving down the stream too. Sometimes you're in the fast current and sometimes in an eddy. You know it is easier to catch a leaf when you are moving the same pace as it is. The flow of life is different for everyone.

Imagine a universal intelligence, God's way if you will. Imagine that you shadow the flow. Where it goes, you go. Opportunities will be easier to recognize and seize if you choose. And, having choice is the best option of all.

IT IS A SIMPLE FORMULA...

- Is it legal, moral and ethical?
- Have I done this before?
- What is the sacrifice (including time and money) to do this?
- Do I have fear about doing this?
- How can I minimize the risk?
- How much bigger would my world be if I did this?
- When do I start?

OPPORTUNITIES DISGUISED AS PROBLEMS

All problems are potential opportunities—the small problems and the big problems alike.

In 1993, my brother Steve and I took six weeks off work and traveled the south and north islands of New Zealand. New Zealanders have a much more relaxed approach to life than North Americans have.

During a drive to the upper tip of the south island we realized that we would have to hurry to catch the last ferry. Along the way we were getting low on gas, so we planned on stopping in the next small town to fuel up and continue on. We arrived in town at five after six. The one and only petrol station was closed. We went to the hotel to find out where another station would be. "There are none. Ian's is the only petrol station in town."

"But he's closed," we said.

"It's after six," the nice lady told us.

"But we have to make the ferry," we exclaimed.

"Why?" she said with concern.

"To get to the other side," we said in unison.

There was the longest pause while she just looked at us. First Steve, then me—back to Steve and back to me. "Oh," she said finally without any comprehension of what getting to the other side had to do with anything.

"What do we do?" we asked.

"Stay on this side, I guess," she said in a way that indicated the hotel still had some vacancies.

Steve and I went back outside. The town was so small, there was nothing to do. We mulled it over for a while and then went back into the hotel. "Okay, we'll stay here," we stated, as if we had any other options. We took our bags out of the car and each took a shower. We knew we were stuck in this small town, but we were going to make the most of it. At least we could have a good meal. When we came back downstairs to eat. It was 8:35 P.M. and the restaurant was closed.

"It's closed," we stated standing in the middle of the lobby again.

"It's after 8:30," she said. Knowing our next question, she continued on. "None of the restaurants stay open after 8:30, but the pub across the way serves sandwiches."

"That's it," we thought, "this is just plain bad luck."

When we walked into the pub, it was a scene out of an old western. It was as if the music stopped, everyone turned around and just stared. We continued in and went to the bar. "Two sandwiches, please."

In minutes we started to meet people who were quite friendly and curious about where we came from. One thing lead to another. One beer lead to another. At about two in the morning we were laughing and carrying on with a number of locals.

"What time does this place close?" we asked at one point.

"Whenever everyone leaves..."

> # You never know what is around the next corner ... until you turn that corner.

This experience was one of the highlights of our trip. A small problem became an opportunity to slow down and get to know the people of New Zealand. It was testimony to the fact that you never know what is around the next corner until you turn that corner.

Larger problems are opportunities, too. Imagine if you had a teenage son or daughter who didn't come home one night. Your reactions go through the stages of anger and worry. When your child finally comes home, the opportunity exists for you to use the experience as a way to get through to the teen. Instead of blowing up, which is exactly what they are expecting, send them to their room. Let them think about it. Notify your intention to talk to them later that morning at 10 A.M. Prepare your thoughts and present them calmly. Instead of attacking, ask your teenager what it is that you did to have them act in such a way. What was it that they need you to understand? How can you combine forces with your teen to find out how to avoid being angry, worried and confused next time?

You then shift the problem from punitive reactions to an opportunity to gain understanding and an agreement on boundaries for the next time.

Turn your problems into opportunities.

A GOOD IDEA WON'T GO AWAY

Wouldn't it be fun to hook your brain up to a monitor that typed out all your thoughts? Sound scary? Why? What would you learn about yourself?

The subconscious mind is always thinking and always sending messages to your conscious mind. The repeated messages are worth taking note of. Your inner intelligence knows what it is you should be doing. To "protect you" your conscious mind and your cognitive filter block or dismember some perfectly good ideas.

Know that there is a profound mind/body connection. The subconscious mind can send notice to you through what is called "the emotional buzz." If the thought of something gives you some level of a body buzz, it is your

---

The emotional buzz is a message to the body: "Hey! Pay attention to this one."

---

subconscious mind sending you the message: "Hey, pay attention to this one." You may call it intuition. Or you might notice tingles up and down your spine. Or you might feel the hair on the back of your neck stand up. There is power in your mind/body connection.

EXPLORING OUTSIDE THE BOX

Nobody likes to remain uncomfortable. The recommendation of authors and speakers to "work outside the box" implies you should go outside your comfort zone. This would be agony. But growth does not happen inside the box. Essentially, the goal would be to find the yin and yang of living inside the box while visiting outside it on a regular basis. Then you can have safe and new at the same time.

Where does it say that you have to do it all now? Take the first step and explore a little.

When I was fifteen, our family traveled east across Canada to do some exploring. In Toronto, we visited the OmniMax theatre and experienced on the massive screen what it would be like to fly in a glider. I never forgot that time. And, true to form, a good idea won't go away. Twenty years later the opportunity to fly a sailplane presented itself.

Learning to fly a glider was fascinating. The design of the two-seat Grob 103 placed the instructor immediately behind the student. My instructor, Carol, was great. On our first flight together she explained how to turn left and right along with speeding up or slowing down the plane. She taught me about the pattern required to land the plane safely and efficiently. During the flight she educated me on the student-instructor system of communicating. When she would say, "your glider," I would respond with "my glider" and take over where I would learn by doing (praxis). When she would say "my glider," I would respond with "your glider," and she would take over the controls (probably because I was putting our lives in danger).

On our second flight, prior to takeoff she pointed out that it was essential to

* "We don't serve peanuts, just plenty of adrenaline."

keep the glider directly behind the tow plane. I knew what she meant. The previous night I had read how the sailplane has a better glide ratio than the tow plane, which means it will start flying before the tow plane can. As a result, it is important not to get too high. If this happens, the rope will lift the tail of the tow plane, crash the plane's nose into the runway and then crash the glider.

As we got into the plane for our second flight, she had me go through the checklist. Controls working, canopy closed, trim set, seatbelt fastened and so on. "Ready?" she asked.

"I guess so," I replied.

"Your glider," she said calmly.

"Now?"

"I know how to fly this plane. You're the student. You fly it," she said. (It occurred to me she'd done this hundreds of times before.) I wagged the rudder, which indicated to the tow pilot that we were good to go.

As we raced down the runway my heart raced along with it. "Here I go. Outside the box again," I thought to myself.

Prepare, practice, explore—as you learn.

Suddenly the glider popped off the runway and we were flying. Before I knew it, we were looking down on the tow plane. My heart stopped beating. I thought we would kill the tow pilot, then ourselves. I immediately pushed the stick forward and we instantly hit the runway with a thud, then bounced back up in the air.

"What are you doing?" asked Carol in a calm voice.

"Your glider," I said.

"No, you're doing fine," she said as I proceeded to yank the tail of the tow plane left, right, up and down. When we released both my legs started to shake. Flying got easier without the tow plane in front of us.

This first experience felt more dramatic than it actually was. Carol was there to "hold my hand" while I explored outside the box. With each flight, we expanded my knowledge a little more. With each experience I explored new territory outside my comfort zone.

After thirty flights in three months, I was ready to solo. But Carol never gave me advance warning. We went up for our first flight of the day. Reaching an altitude of twenty-five hundred feet following a good tow, we released and flew around the area. I flew the whole time as I had done quite a number of times in the past. I did an excellent pattern and landed the plane capably. As we sat in the plane waiting for the second tow, Carol got out of the glider.

I looked at her wondering what she was doing.

"Okay, this time I want you to do the same thing. Release at twenty-five hundred feet, fly around and then land it the same way," she said matter-of-factly.

"Okay…" I said as it dawned on me what was going on.

"How do you feel?" she said.

"Good."

"Okay, have fun," she said, as she closed the canopy. This time with her on the outside of it.

"So this is how they do it," I thought to myself, trying to drown out the voice that kept saying, "Why, why, do you keep doing this to me? I like it here in the box where it's safe. What did I do to deserve this? What?"

The take-off, flight and landing went flawlessly. I had prepared, practiced and explored as I learned. My first solo flight was a real blast.

When I touched down, Carol took the photo on page 101. She then asked if I wanted to go for another flight. I said, "Sure."

This time I was more relaxed. I was a little more comfortable with the prospect of flying solo.

I went through the checklist routine and then Carol hooked up the tow rope. This take-off went fine until I reached the thirty-foot mark. We still hadn't cleared the runway when I heard a loud click, seconds later, at about seventy-five feet I heard a snap, and before my eyes the tow rope fell away from the glider.

I was faced with a quick decision. The rule of thumb is you cannot turn to land back on the runway unless you have cleared two hundred feet. At the end of the runway was a field of corn that had fully matured. Landing in that would be extremely hazardous. I had precious little runway underneath me, but I went for it. I pointed the nose down and deployed the airbrakes at the same time. As soon as the tire touched down I pulled back on the brakes hard and stopped the glider just a few feet from the cornfield. It happened so fast that I didn't really have time to think. It seemed like the right thing to do, so I did it.

Carol came blasting down the runway in the cart. The first thing she said was, "Do you have any idea what you just did?" (I didn't.) "That was perfect. You handled a rope break perfectly!"

She was clearly more excited than I was. To me, it just seemed like the right thing to do. The more I thought about what happened, the more I appreciated the approach I took to learning to fly.

I thought back to a time ten years prior when I learned how to fly a hang-glider. At the time, I accelerated my learning curve too sharply. I was never comfortable flying a hang glider because I didn't do enough low flights to expand my comfort zone. After ten days, very quick for a student, I took my first high flight off the top of a mountain. I scared the hell out of myself. My knowledge at that point hadn't caught up with my willingness to live outside the box.

This time, learning to fly a sailplane, I consciously did the opposite. Along with Carol, I methodically learned every step of the way. I stretched a little each time.

Stay in the box (your comfort zone) and explore outside a little at a time. When an actual emergency or pressure situation arises, you will be well prepared to deal with it safely and efficiently. If and when the poop hits the fan, it will seem like no big deal.

THE MATHEMATICS OF OPPORTUNITY

This is simple (maybe not easy to do, but simple nonetheless). One opportunity will present two more. Those two hold the potential for four more. Those four have eight more opportunities—an exponential unfolding of potential.

Here is a story about how my wife explored the mathematics of opportunity to take her in directions she never expected. Had she not followed this path, however, we never would have met.

In 1992, Michelle Lemmons, had ambitions of making her own film. The year prior, she left a suffocating relationship behind along with all her belongings and material goods. She picked up and set out on her own in Los Angeles with only a suitcase and a decision to start over.

She was broke and needed a job. So, she answered an ad in the trades from two speakers looking for a marketing person. She didn't have a car, so she took the bus to the corner and walked the remaining block and a half to the interview. She got the job and was amazed that the speaking business even existed. Later that year her father fell ill with congenital heart disease. He was going to die.

Michelle wanted to be with her father so she picked up again and moved to Texas. This time with the decision to start her own speakers bureau. She called it International Speakers Bureau and for the first few weeks, she picked pecans to sell in order to pay her phone bill. She never regretted the move to be with her father as he inevitably passed away.

Five years later, Michelle Lemmons has built her bureau to be one of the top ten bureaus in the United States. As of 1999, she employs nineteen people and has touched millions of lives through her service.

The future is waiting for you to use the mathematics of opportunity to your advantage.

CREATIVITY OF ACTION ... STRETCH

"Creativity is the natural extension of our enthusiasm."
–Earl Nightingale

Creativity is more than painting, music, poetry; it is the ability to solve problems, develop unique strategies and contribute to relationships. The late Sam Walton, founder and driving force behind Wal-Mart, had a simple strategy: get out, look around, carry a notepad.

Stretch—yourself. Bring youthful enthusiasm to newness. Know that young things are soft and old things are brittle.

Stretch. Mind the words of John Norley: "All things are difficult before they are easy." Seek out the little stretches. Wear your watch on the other wrist. Move your alarm clock to somewhere else in the room. Shave with the other hand. Drive to work a different way. Change your routine.

Seek out medium stretches.... Talk to five strangers at the next party you go to. Write a letter to your parents and tell them how much you love them. Spend time visiting old people at a nearby nursing home.

Seek out large stretches. Think of the wildest thing you would love to do. Tell a friend that you are committed to doing it. Buy a plane ticket to a country you've never been and don't make any plans. Just show up, and take it from there. Train for the New York Marathon.

Stretch.

Consistently stretch yourself in all areas of your life. Stretch financially, spiritually, physically, emotionally, mentally. Stretch in your family, work, and other primary relationships. Stretching involves creativity of action.

> ## — S t r e t c h —

Seek out small, medium and large stretches.

The accomplished actor, Alan Alda once said:

> Be brave enough to live creatively. The creative is the place where no one else has ever been. You have to leave the city of your comfort and go into the wilderness of your intuition. You can't get there by bus, only by hard work, risking, and by not quite knowing what you're doing. What you'll discover will be wonderful: yourself.

Edwin H. Land put it more bluntly, "Creativity is the sudden cessation of stupidity."

EXPRESS YOUR COMPETITIVE NATURE

Competitiveness is natural. Everyone is competitive. Some more than others, but even the most giving person on the planet has some level of competitiveness. Plus, it's fun! Challenging yourself to new heights teaches you about yourself. Finding out what you are capable of expands your world.

Recently I joined up with "Mighty Mo" Monaghan, an Olympic qualifier in mountain biking, and her husband, Randy Wallace, in the HiTec Adventure Race series. Adventure racing involves mountain biking, cross country running, kayaking and numerous test events. This might sound like a reasonable thing for a former Olympic athlete, but I had never pushed myself aerobically before in this way. Anaerobically I was fit, but aerobic racing was new territory for me. Although we placed fourteenth out of two hundred racers, it just about killed me. At numerous points, Mighty Mo pushed me up hills during the bike section.

Two months later, Randy was hurt so "Fast Fred" Seipp joined the team. Fast Fred was an exceptional runner and cyclist. In this race he took turns with Mighty Mo pushing me up hills on the bike sections. Again, I was out of my league and I pushed myself to my own physical limits.

Why do this? This question was asked of me five years prior when I trained for a 26.2-mile marathon. "Because it's there" is a lame response. For myself and those of you who explore outside the box, it is to find out what we are capable of. To express our competitive nature and explore our limits.

Jack Welch, CEO of General Electric, says, "If we let our people flourish and grow, if we use the best ideas that they come up with, then we have the chance to win (in global competition). The idea of liberation and empowerment for our workforce is not enlightenment—it's a competitive necessity."

DEVELOP THE RIGHT BRAIN

Remember that creativity resides in the right brain. Developing your creative talents is extremely important to complement your left-brain knowledge.

Albert Einstein said, "To raise new questions, new possibilities, to regard old problems from a new angle, requires creative imagination." Einstein clearly understood that the scientific mind (left brain) needed the creative mind (right brain). Therefore, he constantly sought out new experiences to help boost creativity in his pursuits.

Gary Hoover has been an entrepreneur from a very young age. He also loves to read. Books have always been his passion. Gary opened his own bookstore called BookStop. Thinking outside the box, Hoover took a fresh approach. He analyzed the design of supermarkets where the aisles were wide, the stores were very well lit and the essential products (the milk, bread and meat) were spread out along the back walls.

Hoover took these same ideas and built a multi-million dollar chain of book-stores. After building the business, Hoover sold it and moved on to other challenges. He started Travel Fest with the same concept and is the founder of Hoovers.com, an information source of corporations.

Hoover's advice to people is to explore areas you normally wouldn't think of. He recommends that you learn about things you know nothing about. Read knitting magazines, talk to shoe salesmen, learn how to operate a backhoe. By exploring the ordinary, you will discover the extraordinary.

CREATIVE ENVIRONMENTS

The more companies I work with, the more I see what works and what doesn't. The days of command and control leadership have gone the way of the dinosaurs. Companies such as 3M value creativity. Although dealing with creative personalities can be occasionally disruptive in the workplace, the benefits are great.

Creative types may be impatient with the status quo. They may resist authoritarian control or choose autonomy over mainstream methodology. And, they require high doses of stimulation. In order to compete, corporations must find ways to let creativity flourish, the way 3M has done with great success. Creative geniuses might be in your midst right now. Do they have an environment to express their abilities?

R. Buckminster Fuller was tossed out of Harvard in his first year. Known to many as "Bucky," he had talents with architecture, inventing, engineering, poetry and even astronomy. He invented and implemented over 170 patents. He believed that "people should think things out fresh and not just accept conventional terms and the conventional way of doing things."

Sam Walton, founder of Wal-Mart, leveraged creative opportunities when he had his directors fly out to their regions on a weekly basis. Each week, at headquarters, the regional directors were to present at least one idea worth more than the cost of their trip. Creativity was in their job description. It was required.

Creative thinking at work is improved when there is permission to explore. Jim Reep was the cofounder and chairman of First Consulting Group (FCG) a $100 million information-technology service for the healthcare industry. He said flat-out that he would rather have his people "beg forgiveness over asking for permission." He wanted his people to work creatively. Reep started his company in May of 1980, and his leadership style grew FCG to fifteen hundred employees with offices in Ireland, the U.K., Honduras, Canada and the U.S. It is an American success story that grew out of creativity and innovation.

FIND WAYS TO DEVELOP THE PROPER MOTIVATION

In the *Harvard Business Review* September / October 1998 issue, Teresa M. Amabile, senior associate dean of research at the Harvard Business School, in Boston, wrote how managers are killing creativity in the workplace through traditional management practices. Her research led to two kinds of motivation that impact creativity: extrinsic and intrinsic motivation.

Extrinsic motivation either gives pleasure (more money, benefits, perks) or pain (punishment for falling short of expectations or quota). The second,

---

Success stories grow out of creativity and innovation.

---

intrinsic motivation, comes from within the individual. For example, if an individual loves to organize projects, they might be given the task of planning the annual meeting for the board of directors. Or, if a person is interested in helping others, they might be put in the position of designing and delivering a troubleshooting forum for the human resources department.

The challenge is for leadership to identify what will intrinsically drive the individual to pursue their objectives and provide the opportunities to achieve these objectives. Amabile calls this concept the "Intrinsic Motivation Principle of Creativity, where people will be most creative when they feel motivated primarily by the interest, satisfaction, and challenge of the work itself—and not by external pressures."

This method of motivating others places leadership in the position to direct and facilitate but not to control. Guiding employees to the desired objective is more important than instructing the actual means to get there. Her premise is: "Creativity thrives when managers let people decide how to climb a mountain; they needn't, however, let employees choose which one."

BE INTERESTING

If you met you would you find yourself interesting? A common denominator with most interesting people is a sense of humor, zeal, or both. Charles Shultz is quoted as saying, "No one would have been invited to dinner as often as Jesus was unless he was interesting and had a sense of humor." Laugh at yourself. Think of a time you did something really embarrassing or stupid. Are you smiling yet?

Interesting people might be intelligent, but they are always people who have experienced a great deal, too. They have zest for life, passion and curiosity. They are seekers and explorers. They see the irony in life. In order to be interesting, they do interesting things.

When Walt Disney ran out of money trying to open Disneyland, the landscaping was not yet finished. Without missing a beat he had the groundskeepers run around and place identification tags throughout the park with the Latin names of all the weeds. Now *that's* interesting.

LARGER THAN FEAR

The topic of fear could take up the rest of this book. In a nutshell, fear is the single greatest inhibitor to success. You will never take the first step if you cannot get past the fear. What we fear most is change. Where does change come from?

Change starts with dissatisfaction. If you are satisfied, why change? Dissatisfaction leads to awareness. Awareness of what you want and awareness of what you don't want. You may have awareness that there might be a better way.

Awareness leads to desire.

Desire leads to action.

Then... oh no... action means change.

Change leads to discomfort (which means you fear something). Fear of the unknown is normal, but not insurmountable.

Just remember, if you weren't ready for change, you wouldn't have the desire to change. So now it is time to identify with the fear. Laurie Skreslet, the first Canadian to summit Mount Everest, states, "Fear gets smaller the closer you get to it."

Mountain climbers provide a great metaphor for life. Their whole approach involves preparation for both foreseen and unforeseen possibilities. Only then will they start their ascent with all the provisions they will need. They climb. They find ways around obstacles. They turn back if the danger is too great, and they descend with safe discipline.

Our fears in life find us with the opportunity to climb. Our fears are vast but must be overcome. Fears are natural and so is conquering them. If you have fears of embarrassment, fears of standing outside of the norm, fear of loss—deal with it. Walk straight toward it. There is no greater satisfaction than being larger than your fears.

After the first experience it gets easier. Fear diminishes. This is all part of the process of growing. Make peace with the process. Find value in the negative experiences, learn from them and move on.

MINIMIZE RISK

You will feel better about pushing through fear when you minimize risk. People often think of me as a daredevil who is willing to risk it all for a thrill. Yes, I've done some wild things, but the danger is not what drives me. In fact, the top speed skiers in the world would not be what I call daredevils. They each had a methodical and systematic approach to minimizing risk and maximizing competitive advantage. There was nothing exceptionally daring about racing. Risk existed and it needed to be contained. Only then could we compete at a higher level.

Mihalyi Csikszentmihalyi, author of the book, *Flow,* and a peak performance specialist, wrote:

> What is most striking, when one actually speaks to specialists in risk is how their enjoyment derives not from the danger itself, but from their ability to minimize it. So rather than a pathological thrill that comes from courting disaster, the positive emotion they enjoy is the perfectly healthy feeling of being able to control potentially dangerous forces.

Therefore, it is not the feeling of control, but the opportunity to exercise control in adverse situations that is the attractive force. Hence, it is not possible to get this feeling unless you explore outside your comfort zone.

> *He who is silent is forgotten, he who does not advance falls back;*
> *he who stops is overwhelmed, outdistanced, crushed;*
> *he who ceases to grow becomes smaller; he who leaves off, gives up;*
> *the condition of standing still is the beginning of the end.*
> *—Amiel (Swiss philosopher)*

Now, go!

IN SUMMARY

The ten things to remember about doing everything at least once.

1. Walk through as many doors of opportunity that you can in your lifetime.
2. Eliminate the word "try" from your vocabulary.
3. A good idea won't go away. What is your great idea you're avoiding?

4. Explore, explore, explore.

5. Stretch, stretch, stretch.

6. Express your competitive nature.

7. Establish creative environments.

8. Interesting people do interesting things.

9. Be larger than fear.

10. Minimize risk. Now … go!

> *I shall pass through this world but once. Any good that I can do,*
> *or any kindness that I can show any human being,*
> *let me do it now and not defer it.*
> *For I shall not pass this way again.*
> *—Stephen Gallet*

In order to do everything at least once, you must combine the best of willpower and faith. Let's explore these two powerful words.

PRINCIPLE **6** ... DIG DEEP WITH WILLPOWER AND FAITH

"Faith is the courage to face reality with hope."
–Dr. Robert H. Schuller

The balancing act. Here we go again—two seemingly opposite forces and it's our job to find out how they balance each other. It is another typical yin and yang relationship. Willpower and faith combine to become the sixth Invinceable Principle.

With willpower you can create and enable. You create solutions to problems. You enable your qualities of tenacity and perseverance to flourish. With willpower you are the master of your destiny. You know you have it. You can define it. You can draw from it. But there is a downside to willpower.

Willpower is limited. It is short term and it has a ceiling. When it runs out, you check out. Your power of will has depth, but it has a bottom. Most never know how far their willpower can extend. Most don't want to know, given the high price to find out.

On the flip side is faith. Faith is belief in the unknown. Faith is wisdom to allow. Faith is the power to believe in what you cannot see. Faith has depth with no bottom. Faith has no limits. Faith has no definable boundaries. Faith is indefinable and unexplainable. You either have it or you don't. If you have it, you can strengthen it by adding more of it to itself.

Both willpower and faith exist on a continuum. The willpower line diminishes over time. Faith, since it is indefinable, could be anywhere on the continuum. In the best case scenario, as willpower diminishes, faith flourishes.

Combine willpower and faith and you can have the gifts from God, here on earth.

WILLPOWER VS. FAITH

WITH ACTIVITIES:

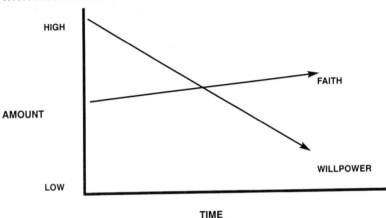

WITH LIFE:

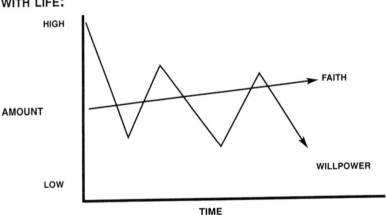

WILLPOWER

Two key words in Webster's definition of willpower are "energetic determination." Willpower is that elusive strength that you call on in times of doubt and weakness. You call on it on days when you know you need to work out today. You use willpower to turn off the television when its mindless programming is turning your brain to mush. Willpower keeps you from eating that last piece of pizza when you are already full.

We even make feeble attempts to apply willpower to our New Year's resolutions. Many people make resolutions and then do not keep them. But there is hope, and willpower is a great starting point.

An American Medical Association survey reported that 61 percent of Americans don't make any resolutions at all. Of the people who make health-related resolutions, 51 percent made the same resolution the previous year and quit. But for the people who did attempt some minor modifications "...every little bit helps," according to the AMA. Dr. Richard Corlin from Santa Monica says you increase your chance of success if you don't make up your resolution fifteen minutes before midnight.

"PLAN OF ACTION" X "WILLPOWER" = BETTER ODDS

Willpower alone is not enough. Giving yourself a plan of action improves the odds. With a sufficient amount of willpower to persevere, you will increase the odds of turning a plan into reality. In *Changing for Good* psychologists John Norcross and Jame Prochaska state that "people who rely on willpower alone fail at double the rate."

Norcross and Prochaska recommend a six-step plan to success:

1. Pre-contemplation. Do your research and know your options.

2. Contemplation. Do the Ben Franklin technique of listing the pros and cons of achieving your goal.

3. Preparation. Here is classic goal setting. Set a date, know the benefits, list the pain associated with not following through and tell others. Emile Coue wrote, "Our actions spring not from our will, but from our imagination." This is why pre-contemplation, contemplation and preparation are critical.

4. Take action. Apply willpower to take it one day at a time.

5. Maintenance. Catch yourself falling into old patterns. Do something, anything, to interrupt the pattern. You can break patterns by using a variety of techniques. Anything will work as long as it is outside of the norm. Stop what you're doing and whistle. Flap your arms. My personal favorite pattern breaker is to cluck like a chicken to the tune of *In the Mood*. (If it's not fun, it's not worth doing.)

6. Termination. Once the resolution becomes a habit or a natural behavior, take on a new challenge.

DELAYING GRATIFICATION

Finding ways to use the potential of your willpower is a life-long journey. Since willpower is like a rechargeable battery, it needs a goal or reward to be refueled. In *First Things First* Roger Merrill and Stephen Covey state that, "It's easy to say 'no' to the less important, when you have a deeper 'yes' burning within." People with goals will be able to support their willpower with tangible reasons to defer or delay gratification.

Moreover, the ability to delay gratification has proved to be a quality in high-performing people. In a study done in the 1960s, psychologist Walter Mischel of Stanford University researched the correlation between willpower (as demonstrated through delayed gratification in children) and social adjustment.

His subjects in the study were a collection of the four-year-old children of the staff and student body at Stanford. In the experiment, each child was offered a marshmallow for taking part. It was explained that Mischel would leave the room for a while. If the marshmallow was still on the table when he returned, the child would get a second marshmallow as a reward. But then the child was told that if the marshmallow was eaten, then he or she would not get a second marshmallow when Mischel returned. Making sure the youngster understood the instructions, Mischel then placed the first marshmallow right in front of the child and left the room.

In two-thirds of the cases, as the door closed behind Mischel, the children reacted the same way. They watched the door close and then immediately covered their eyes or looked down. The children rested their head on the table, hummed a song, swung their feet ... anything to avoid looking at the marshmallow. Mischel was gone for up to twenty minutes, an eternity for a four-year-old. When he returned, the two-thirds that were able to delay gratification, were rewarded with the second marshmallow and given permission to eat them anytime they wished.

As for the one-third who didn't delay gratification, the marshmallow was eaten within seconds of the door closing.

Fourteen years later, these same children were studied again. The delayed gratification group exhibited a high level of social adeptness, above average grades, discipline and ability to get along with others. The instant gratification group didn't fare as well overall. These teens were less likely to complete projects, got into trouble more often, had lower grades and lacked discipline in a number of areas.

Now, if you're like me, you might wonder whether you would have eaten the marshmallow at the age of four. The good news is that learning to delay gratification is possible. Given a methodical approach to goal setting and delaying gratification, you can boost your willpower over time.

Ron Drabman, a psychology professor at the University of Mississippi Medical Center, studied the relationship between children and self-control. His findings support Mischel's conclusions. Children brought up in homes where they did not learn the relationship between short-term sacrifices and long-term benefits are particularly susceptible to struggle later on in life.

We live in a society of instant gratification, making these challenging times. McDonalds, microwaves, the Internet and every service known to humankind seeks to give results ASAP. Our children don't know what it's like to wait for something. Instant food, cars, sex, news, advice, you name it. Our challenge is to educate our youth (and re-educate ourselves) about patience and persistence.

WHAT TO DO WITH CHILDREN

1. **Be flexible.** Too many don'ts are not healthy.

2. **Build in structure.** Give them tangible marks that are achievable with an increasing stretch each time. Set boundaries and monitor their progress.

> # We must educate our youth (and re-educate ourselves) about patience and persistence.

Keep them in the loop so that they know how their actions have measured up to the targets.

3. Lead by example. Teach them through your actions. But be realistic; how high a standard do you hold yourself and them to? Don't be too hard on yourself and don't be too hard on them.

4. Consistently build their self-esteem. "I'm proud of you." Four words that go a long way.

WHEN THERE'S NOTHING LEFT

I have never been much of a runner. I am 5' 9" and 185 pounds. Most of this weight is muscle and bone with reasonably low body fat. The bottom line is God didn't make me "fleet of foot." But, I like a challenge, and one day friends, Sean Cochlan, Bryce Medd, Grant Carlson, and I decided to run an upcoming marathon. The "Do Everything Once" principle kicked in and I trained for four months leading up to the July marathon. We met for a six-day-a-week training schedule. The first time we went out, we started with a two-mile course. We made it one mile before we had to walk. Slowly, but surely, we increased our runs to forty-five minutes with a longer run on the weekend.

In our training we never made it past a run for three hours. Eventually, Grant hurt his knee and Sean decided to train on his own schedule. That left Bryce and me. We anticipated that it would take us four hours to complete the marathon. We were not there to race against each other; we were there to race against ourselves. The day of the race we were ready. My brother Steve, an avid runner, flew in from Las Vegas. Sean and Steve took off at a quick pace. Bryce and I paced ourselves. After the first couple of hours, Bryce and I stayed together, but eventually he pulled away.

Alan Hobson rode alongside me most of the time, as I plodded along. It looked like I was on pace to finish the race in four hours. Then it hit me. Runners call it the "wall." I call it hell.

At about the twenty-mile mark I started to slow down drastically. At times it was all I could do to just walk. Eventually, I could barely stand. My head was swimming and I started to crumble. Then someone from the race medical team happened by and asked if I wanted to quit. Willpower kicked in from somewhere inside.

"No, I'm fine." I marched forward.

Alan helped me by suggesting I focus on a lamppost fifty feet ahead. "Just run to the next lamppost and then walk," he said. Though it was a form of self-torture, this technique worked. It was the single most agonizing hour and a half in my entire life. As I crossed the finish line, both my legs cramped up and I was helped off to the side.

Despite the effort and self-inflicted pain, I realized something about willpower: When it seems there is nothing left, you can still find the strength to push a little further. Break it down to smaller successes and your willpower will be renewed.

FAITH

Believing in something for which there is no proof is a tall order. Yet faith is the cornerstone for achieving anything worthwhile. Willpower's effectiveness is short term and finite. Faith, on the other hand, is infinite and unbounded. Faith is believing in what you cannot see but know in your heart. William Salter wrote that courage and faith go hand in hand. He stated: "As the essence of courage is to stake one's life on a possibility, so the essence of faith is to believe that the possibility exists."

If you factor in the cognitive filter where attitudes, opinions and beliefs are a person's truth, faith plays a key role. If you have faith that God exists, then that is your truth. Imagine trying to convince someone that God exists the same way you convince someone that there is a blue truck in front of you. If you see a blue truck, that is your truth. If they see the blue truck, then that truth is based on what they see, as well. A truth that God exists would depend on their faith, their sight, not yours. So truth and faith are personal and the domain of each individual.

This chapter explores faith, but in a way that leaves the definition up to you. At times, I will explore my definitions but it would be folly to attempt to take a stand of what exactly faith is or should be.

WHAT IS FAITH?

To paraphrase St. Paul, "Faith is the confident assurance that something we want is going to happen. It is the certainty that what we hope for is waiting for us, even though we cannot see it up ahead."

Ian Percy, in his book *Going Deep*, writes "Faith is confidently anticipating a world different from the one we have now." He goes on to say, "Acting on our faith means we must disrupt our current state in order to re-create the desired one."

Sherwood Eddy said, "Faith is not trying to believe something regardless of the evidence. Faith is daring to do something regardless of the consequences." In the land of faith, optimists rule.

OPTIMISM AND FAITH

Matt Biondi won eight Olympic gold medals during his swimming career. He, along with other swimmers, was part of a study by Martin Seligman, a psychologist from the University of Pennsylvania. In the experiment Biondi was told his times were worse than the actual recorded times in a swimming event.

Biondi responded in subsequent attempts, despite the disappointing news, with better times. In addition, his original times were already very good.

At the outset of the experiment, Biondi ranked high in optimistic categories. Some of the more pessimistic swimmers turned in poorer times after receiving disappointing news from the first timed event. Ultimately, regardless of the evidence, optimists have faith where pessimists do not appear to take advantage of any faith capabilities. Without faith and optimism, results go down.

Seligman also worked with MetLife and their sales force. He discovered that people who tested as having a positive outlook sold 37 percent more insurance than the pessimists. In another experiment, Seligman participated in the hiring and screening of new employees. He talked managers at MetLife into hiring a select group of people who scored high on the optimist screening, but failed the MetLife hiring standards. This special group outsold an identified group of pessimistic new hires by 21 percent the first year and 57 percent in the second.

THE "TRINITY OF FULFILLMENT"

Next to optimism and faith, hope is the third key ingredient. Faith, optimism and hope interrelate. You can't be optimistic without hope and vice versa. You will not have optimism and hope without faith. When dealing with the challenges of life, hope makes the difference.

Here's an example taken from Greek mythology:

> Princess Pandora was admired greatly for her beauty. The gods, jealous of her attractiveness, gave her a mysterious box with the instructions to never open it. As with many mythological stories the mortal Pandora was tempted by curiosity. Pandora lifted the lid and the terrible human afflictions like disease, insanity and depression came racing out. A compassionate god witnessed Pandora's mistake and gave her the strength to close the box just in time to retain one quality of hope. The moral of the legend described hope as the one saving grace known to deal with life's struggles.

C.R. Snyder, a psychologist at the University of Kansas, did a study of high school students, ranking them with "high hope" and "low hope." He found that "students with high hope set for themselves higher goals and know how to work hard to attain them. When you compare students of equivalent intellectual aptitude on their academic achievements, what set them apart was hope." If you find yourself struggling, boost your faith, hope and optimism. Empower yourself with the trinity of fulfillment.

RELIGIOUS FAITH

Since faith is not a definable entity, you cannot reason your way to faith. Intellectually, faith has no foundation in science and no structure in philosophy. Karl Marx, Friedreich Nietzsche and Sigmund Freud did not believe in the existence of God. They thought that faith in God was a psychological defense mechanism. They generally felt that God was a human design for self-preservation in a world of struggle.

Faith is not a matter of intellect. It is a trusting that is beyond reason. Tony Campolo, author of *Carpe Diem* and an avid Christian, says, "My reason only makes my faith seem foolish."

Go to any hospital and watch how various people deal with the suffering or loss of their loved ones. People who have religious faith generally have a quiet understanding of God's way. The others clearly flounder more. A faith-based understanding guides people where people void of faith leave their hope and optimism in tatters.

On December 18, 1995, *Time* magazine ran a cover story of the Bible with the title "Are the Bible's Stories True?" Mark Craig, minister of Highland Park United Methodist Church, used the cover story as the basis for one of his sermons. "That is not the point," he preached with regard to the title. "You don't have to read the article to know that *Time* missed the point altogether. The question I ask myself is: Does that work for me?"

His message surrounded the concept of faith. Faith that the messages in the Bible gave understanding to people. Scientists could rarely prove some of the claims made in scriptures. Yet faith in "the Word" has seen millions of people through dark times. That, according to Rev. Craig, is the point.

My wife, Michelle, and I attended that particular sermon given by Mark Craig. It ultimately led Michelle to arrange a meeting with him to discuss something that had been on her mind for a long time.

Michelle was raised by a Jewish father and Christian mother. Her grandfather also played a key role. He was a Southern Baptist minister in west Texas. In her twenties, Michelle looked outside Christianity and studied the Torah under a Rabbi for a year. She also studied the Bible. She was seeking answers to deep questions, "What is right? What is the best way?" Recently she found herself across the desk from Rev. Mark Craig.

She described her internal battle stemming from a background of both Christianity and Judaism. Her questions included whether Christ had risen again. She explained how every time she sat in church there was this underlying confusion.

"Are you a good person?" Reverend Craig asked. "Do you do good things for people?"

"Yes," said Michelle.

"I think you think way too much, Michelle. Why don't you just relax and

---

Faith in the moment gives us the chance to be fulfilled.

---

have faith?"

A weight was lifted from her shoulders when she shifted from rationalization to faith. There was no need for answers that faith couldn't handle. Today Michelle feels that she doesn't have to get as wrapped up in the answers. The clarity she finds now is from her faith.

In life, the mistake we make is when we look outside ourselves for a standard of faith. J.G. Stipe wrote, "Faith is like a toothbrush. Every man should have one and use it regularly, but he shouldn't try to use someone else's."

Like willpower, faith comes from within. Your faith can be your foothold. Over time, it becomes your only foothold when willpower ultimately fades. When people try to achieve fulfillment without faith, they either follow their physical instincts or follow some societal norm. Money, sex, positions of power become the primary motivations. But life is ultimately empty this way. Only faith provides us with the chance to be fulfilled. Nothing else.

SUICIDE

A person void of the trinity of fulfillment—faith, optimism and hope—is in deep trouble. This state is a black hole that can suck a person toward the depths of despair. For some, suicide becomes the only option.

A few years ago, a friend (I'll call him "Jim") and I had a conversation about suicide. Jim's point was that each person has the right to take their own life because it was "their life." Since Jim was an atheist my argument that life was a gift from God had no meaning to him. He wanted facts. Jim was a physician. He relied on physical truths. His scientific background helped him define his world. But Jim had no faith. His simple argument was that God did not exist and that either way, it was his life. Life to Jim wasn't a gift; it was the way of nature.

I agreed: Life was nature and followed a natural order. At a scientific level the purpose of life demonstrated itself in self-perpetuation. But, I argued, suicide interfered with the natural order of things. Jim countered with the argument that if humans were not to interfere with the natural order of things, why did we build irrigation ditches? Why did we build shelters and harvest the soil? Why did we invent medicine?

That is where faith comes in—faith that we humans were special in this world. Our uniqueness celebrates our sense of wonder and curiosity. A sense of hope exists when we use our abilities to make a difference in the lives of others. A sense of optimism encourages us that the world will be a better place as a result of the life we live. Faith—that is our responsibility.

We debated back and forth, but Jim was not to be convinced. He would not believe in something that could not be defined. At the time I thought that this was an innocent debate about God and life.

We spent a good deal of time together over that year and one day he came by to pick up some boxes. He said he was moving to a new apartment. I asked if he wanted to stay for dinner and he declined. He seemed quite preoccupied and distracted. Jim got that way sometimes.

I helped carry the boxes to his car and as he got in the car, he paused. He looked at me and seemed to want to say something, but then just waved, closed the door and drove off.

The next day, I received a phone call and learned that Jim had taken his own life. My friend, the friend of many people, the son, the brother for others, was gone.

No one will ever understand how desperate Jim was. He had attempted suicide once before but had only confided this to two other people. They thought he had seen his way through his hopelessness. But Jim had lost all hope. He had no optimism in a brighter future. He had no faith.

WORRYING: THE CANCER OF OUR EMOTIONS

It is simple physics. No two objects can occupy the same space at the same time. If your thoughts are occupied with worrying, you will not have the thoughts of optimism. If you have fearful thoughts, you don't have faithful thoughts.

From a spiritual standpoint, worrying is a breakdown of faith. Even willpower cannot be applied when worry occupies the mind. Remember, "You will gravitate toward your current dominant thought." Therefore, worrying leads to more worrying.

"Worrying is negative goal-setting. It focuses your mind on what you

Money doesn't control you. You control it.

don't want—so that's exactly what you get," according to Lou Tice in *Smart Talk for Achieving Your Potential.*

With faith, the focus shifts to imagination. Imagination leads to opportunity. Faith therefore, opens up the space, the energy, for better things in life. Worry has the opposite effect.

According to Dr. Charles Mayo, "Worry affects circulation, the glands, the whole nervous system, and profoundly affects the heart. I have never known a man who died from overwork, but many who died from doubt."

It is part of life to worry. It is a natural self-defense mechanism, but you have the power to choose to continue to worry or replace your thoughts with where you want to go next.

FINANCIAL WORRIES

If an extraterrestrial landed on earth, it would think that our favorite hobby is worrying about money. We all do it. Some of us have learned how to deal with it. Others don't have a clue.

I always know when I am preoccupied with money issues. I get a tight jaw, and it starts to ache. You will manifest your worries through your body. Some people get headaches behind their eyes, others feel it in their stomach. So how do you deal with it?

1. Remember that money is a thing. It does not control you. You control it.

2. Use faith to remind yourself that everything will be okay. Look back on your life when you were in a similar situation. Somehow, some way things worked out. Either the money turned up or the events shifted so that you made out just fine. Your basic needs were met. You had food, shelter and clothing. You managed. You will be able to manage again.

3. Take your focus off the lack of money. Refocus on what you have. Put a hundred-dollar bill in your wallet. Don't spend it. If you catch yourself focusing on lack, touch the hundred dollars and reset your focus.

4. You cannot get what you cannot give. If you have five dollars to your name, give it away. You shift from perspective of lacking to a faith-based perspective.

5. Acknowledge that you have fear around the issue of money and then keep moving. Never, *ever*, let catatonia set in. Keep your eye on where you want to be and take a step. Then another.

6. Do not mention your money concerns to anyone. Talking about it only makes it more real. So, instead, talk about the action you will do to replace the space that worry once occupied.

7. Go back to the first step and do it all over again until your money issues are no longer a concern.

THE PRESENT

Living in the present moment is odd advice if you take it literally. You can't and shouldn't completely disregard the past. The future is yours to create. It must not be ignored. Therefore, use the present as home base. Do this and you will be in the best position to develop who you are.

Who you are is expressed in how you think and the emotions that you have. It is in the present that you can explore your inner self without worry or concern. Past pain is left in the past. If you go deep with your thoughts and emotions, you run the risk of this introspection having an impact on your future. But, by keeping the present as home base, you learn to avoid anxiety about something that may or may not happen. If you refuse to go deep with your thoughts and emotions, then you will exist on a superficial level.

At a deeper level lies vulnerability, love and the raw truth. Sound scary? It ought to be. But faith is your trump card. Like the saying goes, "The truth shall set you free." How you live is the truth you tell yourself. This raw truth is not without risk of change and this is where we do not go very often. In fact, some people never go there. They will tackle Wall Street, swim with sharks, go to battle and take on challenges, but never take the not-as-risky-as-you-think journey within.

In fact, emotions are the ultimate expression of the present. You can feel sad over a loss, but that is exactly how you feel now. The sadness will pass, just as the present will. Anchoring your emotions to your thoughts will anchor you to living in the present.

There are two core emotions. Pain and pleasure. Pain in the present is where we feel hurt. Pain from our past feeds anger. Pain related to the future is worry. As you know, anger can keep us in the loop of resentment, guilt and depression. Worrying is an energy drain. Therefore hurt is the source of all negative emotions.

It has been said, "An angry person is a hurting person." This also applies to someone who is worrying, full of resentment, guilt or depression. Since hurt is the source, it is critical to address this emotion before it turns into any other. Experience the hurt, relate to it, know where it comes from, know why it hurts. Address the causation of the hurt. Learn what you can from the hurt and then decide that you no longer want to feel it. A new present moment means the potential for a new emotion.

THANK YOUR SUBCONSCIOUS MIND

The complexity of the mind is beyond our comprehension. With a simple faith in that complexity, you can move out of painful emotions quicker. As a result, I've come up with a technique that works wonders on shifting out of worry and into solutions. In effect, it works this way: Thank your subconscious for giving you this emotion or negative thought. Your mind came up with this for a reason in the first place. Acknowledging that it is there is the first best step in dealing with it and moving on.

When I used to visualize my skiing, my imagery might surprisingly lead to a crash. It was the weirdest thing. I would be having a great run, then boom, out of nowhere, I would catch an edge in my imagination and crash. Immediately, I would stop the image, thank my subconscious mind and refocus. The internal dialogue would go something exactly like this: "Thank you (subconscious mind), but that is not part of my vision." I would then reverse back up to the top of the mountain and start all over again.

The same technique works for thoughts that lead in the wrong direction. For example, you may find yourself thinking negatively. As soon as you notice that your thought has nothing to do with what you really want to occur, say to yourself, "Thank you, but that is not part of my vision." Then, focus on what end result or outcome it is you want in that situation or in your life. This profound strategy is a great way to break patterns of negativity and worry.

Should you not be clear on what your vision is, then obviously it would be helpful to clarify that first.

REALISTIC VERSUS VISIONARY

A friend of mine, Thomas, consistently argued with his wife, Renee, over their need for a new garage. They were newlyweds and, as with most new marriages, the couple stated they each saw the world differently. Their arguments consistently centered on Thomas's "visionary" approach and Renee's "realistic" perspective. Each thought the other was wrong.

Two years after they were married, they bought a house in a revitalized neighborhood. Since their place was eighty years old, it had character and consistently needed little repairs here and there. What it didn't have was a garage. They had space in the back and a garage would raise the value of their property.

One day, Thomas announced his vision of building a garage. Renee shot back that they didn't have the money. Thomas reacted by criticizing Renee for not having any vision. Renee criticized Thomas for always being unrealistic. So it went, back and forth, each thinking the other was wrong. Thomas's optimism was founded in his faith things would work out. Thomas called Renee pessimistic. Renee spoke of being realistic and called Thomas overly optimistic. Who was right?

Eventually, the two were divorced. Within six months, Thomas, on one income, built a garage and even managed to buy some investment property with a partner. It was as if chains were broken and he could now discover new opportunities. Two years later, he sold his first property for a $40,000 profit (30 percent) and held onto his other property. Renee went on to marry another fellow, and the last I heard, they lived "realistically" ever after.

Nothing ventured, nothing gained. Sure, the possibility of getting in a financial bind can occur by over extending yourself. But the age-old wisdom of setting a goal, minimizing risk through a well-thought-out plan and then consistently moving forward is tried and true. You will not be able to guarantee your future. Worrying rarely, if ever, takes you into that future with results that will be fulfilling. If you identify your personality profile with Thomas, then continue to keep your head in the clouds while having your feet on the ground. If you see yourself in Renee, decide now that the pattern of worrying is holding you back.

> # Worry is physically and emotionally unhealthy.

Stop defining worry as being "realistic." This is perceiving worry as a virtue. Theodore Isaac Rubin, M.D. in the book, *Compassion and Self-Hate*, says, "The victim rationalizes anticipation of disaster as prudence." But, Rubin actually proves that worry is one of the many devices for self-hate. "They invariably destroy pleasure and happiness as well as efficiency and effectiveness in current here-and-now activities. They have depleting, fatiguing, constricting effects, and are ultimately destructive to self-esteem and to one's actual person."

Decide now that worrying and anxiety are unhealthy physically and emotionally. You affect yourself and everyone around you by continuing on a downward cycle of negativity. Turn this pattern around and lead yourself to more of what you want in life. Life mastery depends on it.

RELEASING THE EMOTIONAL CHARGE

Your past experiences will fuel your ability to be optimistic or pessimistic. The most difficult memories to shift away from worry are those infused with an emotional charge. Traumatic experiences and even phobias with unknown origins carry particularly deep patterns and are not easily erased.

Finding ways to dispel your own hurt will move you forward in life. Personify proactivity. Discover ways to move beyond trial and error. Learn ways to maximize willpower and faith in yourself. You will then be in a position to have faith in others.

FAITH IN OTHERS

DEGREES OF TRUST

Like respect, trust is either present or it is not. But, when there is trust, there are varying degrees of trust. You can trust someone with your life or you can trust someone as long as they are within view. In effect, trusting others is a leap of faith.

You can trust what someone will do. Or you can have faith that what they do is right, no matter the outcome. If you have that kind of faith, you have the mental space to accept that all things happen for a reason. The end result becomes less important—the moment with another becomes the ultimate objective. Consider how faith in others can pay dividends beyond your knowledge and understanding.

PAYING DIVIDENDS

You never know what impact you have on others. With simple faith in another, you can change lives. Take the example of Scott Adams, creator of *Dilbert*, which is read by more than 150 million people every day. He is also the author of the bestseller, *The Dilbert Principle*. In the July 1998, issue of *Fast Company*, Adams describes his experiences when he was struggling to become a syndicated columnist.

Adams sent his work around to countless editors. Each one rejected his portfolio and one even called back to suggest he take an art class. Finally, Sarah Gillespie, an editor at United Media and a well-known expert in the industry called with a contract offer. "At first I didn't believe her," said Adams. "I asked if I'd have to change my style, get a partner—or learn how to draw. But she believed that I was already good enough to be a nationally syndicated cartoonist. Her confidence in me completely changed my frame of reference. It altered how I thought about my own abilities. This may sound bizarre, but from the minute I got off the phone with her, I could draw better. You could see a marked improvement in the quality of the cartoons I drew after that conversation."

Faith in others is a gift that you choose to give. Delivered with an investment of your time and expertise your faith in others pays dividends for you and others.

Consider the experience of Al Berg, cofounder of Marchon Eyewear. In 1995, Al Berg was leading his sales team through another successful year of growth and increased market share in the eyewear industry. At the time, the growth of the company involved bringing in additional lines. Each addition was felt by the existing sales representatives, since it inherently reduced the amount of "board-space" a rep could fill, thereby decreasing his or her commissions.

The company contracted an outside consultant to run through some team-building exercises. The exercise involved a martial arts technique of breaking boards with the assistance of team members. Two teammates would hold the board. Others would surround and coach the person about to break the board. At the peak of the cheering, the person at the center of attention would lunge at the board and attempt to break it. When the board broke, everyone would go wild. The person succeeded and everyone felt part of the success.

For some, though, the board did not break. Ultimately, in the group of one hundred people, about ten were unable to break the board and were given a second chance. This time with the entire one hundred people surrounding them, eight people broke the boards and the energy level in the room doubled.

This left two people who hadn't managed to break the board. Each person in the room had a chance to offer support. These two received verbal votes of confidence; they were hugged and told they had what it took. The electricity in the air was amazing. Then came the moment when the first person prepared to break the board. She visualized her hand going through the board. She saw in her imagination, how each half of the board was held apart by two of her teammates. Then the moment of truth came. She lunged and "*Snap!*" the board broke. One hundred people erupted in deafening cheers.

Then the second person took her turn. She received the same support and prepared herself. When she broke the board the noise was like a stadium of ten thousand people. The roof could have blown off with the excitement from her teammates. At that moment, Al Berg had an important insight. He realized the importance of what had just happened. It was important to help others.

Al asked the group in the debrief session about what they learned. He asked for a show of hands. How many people got the greatest satisfaction from breaking the board? About 30 percent of the audience held up their hands. Then he asked how many people got the greatest satisfaction from helping others break their boards. One hundred percent of the people in the room held up their hands. The 30 percent clearly changed their minds. "The biggest success in life," said Al, "is helping others succeed."

Each and every salesperson in the room understood the importance of their new partners. They understood the satisfaction of helping others. They understood that, by helping others succeed, *you* succeed too.

THE GIFT OF CONFIDENCE (WRAPPED IN HONESTY)

When I first started public speaking, I dedicated myself to improve my abilities. After committing to the business of professional speaking, I started to call speakers bureaus that might be interested in representing me. The first bureau representative I ever met was Laurie Peck in Edmonton. I was completely oblivious to the nature of the bureau business. Like any other bureau, Laurie's job involved contacting corporations and associations needing speakers. This must be balanced with a comprehensive understanding of which speakers are available.

A typical response you get when you contact a bureau is "Send me your information and I'll get back to you." When I contacted Laurie, I indicated that I was new to the business and that I wanted to work with her. She instantly responded, "When are you speaking in Edmonton?" Within two weeks I had Laurie in my audience for a full 60-minute presentation. Moreover, she spent an additional two hours giving me tips on how to improve my message and ways to work the crowd.

Looking back, this was an amazing gift she gave. I still apply some of the strategies we discussed. Her gift of confidence, the faith she showed in my abilities, clearly paid dividends for me. I know that she feels a good deal of satisfaction when she hears of my success, too.

Sometimes the gift of confidence is wrapped in some "honest" feedback. If you are a speaker and you want to get "the straight goods," then ask a bureau representative what they think. They are not in the business to sugar coat their responses. They simply cannot afford to send a speaker to a client who will not shine and be a perfect fit for their client's event. If the bureau reps sense this, they will tell you.

Soon after I met Laurie, I met Linda Davidson, the president of CanSpeak Speakers Bureau out of Vancouver, Canada. I know Linda as incredibly supportive and professional. She knows the speaking business as well as anyone. If you ask her for feedback, you'll get it. When I did I was unprepared for the answer.

At the time I thought I had arrived. I was getting good responses from my audiences and I could see my Olympic story was making a difference in the lives of others. Linda saw the potential in my message and agreed to a meeting at her office. When we met, I asked her when we could start working together.

She responded that I was not ready yet. I needed to improve my message and get back to her when I had improved. I did not understand the way Linda packaged her support. I took her feedback negatively and later shot back a letter saying how I was good already but that I would improve. I wrote that the next time she saw my speech, it would "blow her socks off."

Linda and I look back on those awkward beginnings and chuckle. Her honesty actually inspired me. Linda actually thought I hated her, but her perspective inspired me. She states today that she always knew I would grow in the speaking business. I was too deaf from defensiveness to hear it though.

Between Laurie, Linda and the many other bureau representatives who have shown their support over the years, I have learned a great deal about faith in others. Their time was a gift of their faith. Their gifts, I hope, bring them successes too. Your gifts of confidence, wrapped in truth, have value beyond measure. Give your gifts wisely and freely. Then stand back and enjoy.

THE LACK OF FAITH IN OTHERS

Everything has a flip side. The absence of faith in others is evident in the realm of victim-like behavior—a counter-productive way to live. It leads to more negativity and less rationality. The barometer for this behavior is the explosion of lawsuits filed in our society.

In 1994, the estimated cost of lawsuits to businesses and consumers in the U.S. was $152 billion. Moreover, the average case took close to three years to resolve where between 50 to 70 percent of every jury-awarded amount went to lawyers and legal costs.

Within the last decade, there has been a backlash. Anti-lawsuit abuse organizations are motivated by stories like the following:

> A convicted serial killer in the Orange County prison sued a writer for
> $60 million based on what was written about him. Despite the fact that

he was on death row for the murders of sixteen people, the convict claimed his innocence and described the book as misleading, false and said it had "defamed his good name." Moreover, he claimed the book would erroneously cause him to be "shunned by society and unable to find decent employment" once he was released from prison. The publisher spent $30 thousand in legal fees. When the case went to court it was thrown out in forty-six seconds. (Source: Citizens Against Lawsuit Abuse)

On one Fourth of July, a man was invited by his parents for festivities at their home. In an intoxicated state the man tried to ignite one of his firework items. He stood back, yet nothing happened. He went back to inspect the reason and it went off in his face. He sued his parents, the owner of the store that sold him the firework and his employer. (Source: Alabama Voters Against Lawsuit Abuse)

A San Diego man went to an Elton John-Billy Joel concert where he witnessed a woman using a urinal. He sued $5.4 million for the "emotional trauma" he claimed to have suffered and stated that his right to privacy was violated. (Source: American Tort Reform Association)

A minister and his wife sued a guide-dog school for $160 thousand after a blind man stepped on the woman's toes. The school is reported to be the only one of its kind in the Southeastern United States. It raises, trains and provides seeing-eye dogs at no cost to the visually impaired. The reverend and his wife each sought $80 thousand. Thirteen months after her toe was stepped on she reported the blind man broke the toe. Under the supervision of an instructor, the blind man was learning to use his new seeing-eye dog, Freddy, at a shopping mall. Witnesses on the scene recalled the minister's wife not moving out of the way of the dog on purpose and hearing her say she "wanted to see if the dog would walk around me." Source: *Houston Cronicle*, October 27, 1995.

BE ACCOUNTABLE

We all slip into the victim-mode now and then. The difference between choosing to take responsibility for the solution or pointing the finger at the problem is the difference between moving forward or staying stuck in victim mode. Take accountability for everything in your life. Even if things that happen are out of your control, the attitude of responsibility for your next choice is your next best step. Take responsibility for your actions. Choose to be empowered, not helpless.

Speaker and author Mark Sanborn, calls this "the age of foolishness and stupidity" where paranoia from liability and lawsuits has gone too far. Mark has a collection of signs he has seen over the years. In a restroom he saw a sign that said, "Please do not drink the water from the toilet bowl." Another sign he saw at a hotel said, "Please do not use the soap dish for support." Mark's comment to this was: "What kind of pin-head would do pull-ups in the shower off a soap dish?"

Mark's perspective clarifies that we are increasingly losing our faith in others. We each have to take responsibility for our own lives and trust others to do the same. By doing so we turn the tides.

I have five employees. They all work in an environment that demands accountability. Since I travel a great deal, I naturally depend on them to hold themselves to high standards of personal responsibility. The interesting by-product is that they, then, take a pride in not letting me down. Time and again, they each mention that, with my faith in them to make the right decisions, they hold themselves to even higher standards. The net effect is that we all win.

The concept of "do it right, do it yourself" is a myth. It bears fruit that is sour and unwanted. People need to be believed in and they need to believe in themselves. Your contributions to the lives of others depend on your ability to believe in others while taking responsibility yourself.

In Summary

1. Learn to maximize the best of your willpower and faith.
2. The willpower to persevere will increase the odds of turning a plan into a reality.
3. Learn to nurture your ability to delay gratification.
4. When there's nothing left, dig deep and use willpower in tiny chunks to get you through.
5. Believe in what you cannot see with your eyes, but know in your heart.
6. Pursue your future with the "trinity of fulfillment"—faith, hope and optimism.
7. Worrying is the cancer of emotions.

8. During a negative thought, interrupt your subconscious mind then move on to what your true intention is.

9. Having faith in another will pay dividends to you and the person who receives it.

10. Give the gift of confidence wrapped in honesty.

With the best of willpower and the profound nature of faith you will take your results to the next level. This book is not written for the neophyte to explain the concept of achievement. Instead, it is assumed that you have achieved a certain degree of success in your life, and you are looking for more. You are now in the position to frame the art of achievement.

PRINCIPLE 7 ...FRAME THE ART OF ACHIEVEMENT

"Life is way too short." –Ernie Poscente*

Beyond the basics. This book will not aim low. In other words, I assume that you inherently know what it takes to achieve anything worthwhile. You already know that achievement is a simple (maybe not easy) formula that combines perseverance, flexibility and curiosity. In the past you learned that your approach was critical—perseverance with tenacity and clarity of purpose. You remained flexible to conditions and turned any problems into opportunities, all the while maintaining a consistent curiousity. You observed and took advantage of opportunities along the way.

I also used this kind of approach when I reached every single goal in my life. Each accomplishment built on the next. The formula for achievement that I used to get me to the Olympics is virtually identical to the one I use now in my speaking and writing business. This chapter is not about how to achieve. It will focus on framing the art of achievement instead of what it takes to achieve something. Framing the art of achievement means clarifying what will give you the best experience as you approach, deal with and look back on achievement. Think of a four-sided frame that surrounds achievement.

1. **How achievement is approached** (Have No Regrets)

2. **How achievement is perceived in retrospect** (Your Best is Good Enough)

3. **How achievement is embraced** (The Courage to Endure)

4. **How achievement is finalized** (Letting Go)

---

* Spoken by my father three months before he died, at age 59, from a year-long battle with brain cancer.

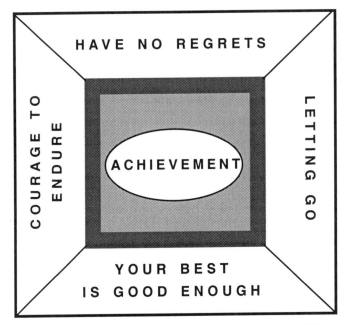

FRAMING THE FINE ART OF ACHIEVEMENT

HAVE NO REGRETS

"I hated every minute of training, but I said, 'Don't quit.'
Suffer now and live the rest of your life as a champion."
—*Muhammad Ali*

In 1988 I seriously began pursuing my dream of competing in the Olympics. At the time, I knew that there were two ways to do things. By trial and error (the hard way) or by learning from others' experience (easier than the hard way). In my hometown of Calgary, lived "Jungle" Jim Hunter. He had competed in the Olympic Winter Games, in 1972, in Sapporo, Japan. He had brought home medals for Canada and became known as "The Original Crazy Canuck."

I phoned up Jungle Jim out of the blue, introduced myself and announced my intention of going to the Olympic Games. I'll never forget his reaction.

"Let me get this straight," he said. "You want to go to the Olympics but you have never ski-raced before. Is that correct?"

"Yes," I said. "This idea of mine just won't go away. So, I quit my job and committed everything I am and have to seeing if this can happen. I've learned you won't know unless you try. So ... do you have any ideas on the best way for me to get to the Olympics?"

There was a long pause. Finally Jungle Jim broke the silence with three words I'll never forget. He said, "Have no regrets." He continued by saying, "When it's race day and you look back you know you have no regrets. You know that every single day of training you did your absolute best. Know that at race day you could not have possibly done anything more to reach your goal. You will then look down the mountain, without one single regret." He paused again and then added with clear intent on driving this point home. "Then your best is all you can ask for. And Vince ... your best can be the best in the world."

Jim was absolutely correct. In each and every race run (including the finals in the Olympics), I looked back and had no regrets. It was an extremely liberating feeling to know that my best was all I could ask for. Plus, the best part of this advice happened during training. The day-to-day routine leading up to race day I've approached with the no-regrets philosophy.

Each and every step along the way it was as if I had the voice of Jungle Jim echoing those three words, "Have no regrets." I would be doing push ups and decide that I would finish at one hundred. Then, "have no regrets" would start to echo in my brain at around ninety, despite the fact that my arms would be shaking. Then at one hundred, I would add five more, or ten more, whatever my arms could handle.

In other situations, I would wake up in the morning and start to think, "I'll read that mental training book later." Or, "I'll decide to skip writing in my training diary today." Or, "I'll call potential sponsors at another time..."— whatever... Then *Have no regrets!* would ring in my ears and I would give it that little extra effort.

> # It's not how much you do.
> # It's how often you do it.

It's not how much you do, it's how often you do it. It simply doesn't matter if you make some monumental effort at any given time. You have it in you to give that extra little bit. You know that you could add that finishing touch. You know you can take that extra step.

Recently, the Buffalo Bills quarterback, Todd Collins, injured his shoulder, and the backup-quarterback, Billy Joe Hobert, was called up in the middle of a game to take over. On his first three passes Hobert threw two interceptions. He admitted after the game that he hadn't prepared for the match. He frankly admitted that he usually does, but this time he "just glanced at the playbook." Contrast this to Buffalo's new backup quarterback, Doug Flutie, and the 1998–99 season.

Here was a short guy whose situation demanded that he measure up to the task. Despite winning the Heisman Trophy in 1984, his NFL career was never given a solid chance given his five-foot nine-inch frame, small for a quarterback. In the Canadian Football League he became a record-setting player, Grey Cup winner and carried marquee status. At thirty-five, Flutie signed a $2 million contract in the role as back-up quarterback for the Bills. Later that season the first-string quarterback, Rob Johnson, separated some cartilage in his ribs and for Flutie a new window of opportunity opened up. Flutie came to the rescue during the first quarter against the Indianapolis Colts. The Buffalo Bills went on to a 31-24 win and the thirty-five-year-old Flutie shone in the process. In the 1998 season, Doug Flutie created a following with his exciting play and took his team to the 1999 playoffs. You can guarantee Doug Flutie was ready for that first game by living the philosophy of "have no regrets."

Without proper preparation, the hazard of poor results looms large. Experiencing regrets for not meeting your potential is called "the sting of regrets." We have all experienced the sting of regrets. You know what it feels like. The bigger the sting, the more you would never want to have that feeling again. Use Jungle Jim's three words of advice. Have them echo in your brain when you approach life. You will then have no regrets.

"REGRETS? WE DON'T NEED NO STINKING REGRETS!"

Knowing how awful regrets feel, it is surprising how many people still march ahead and put themselves in positions they will regret. Look at individuals the media have been able to hang before the juries ever got to them: Bill Clinton, Prince Charles, Frank Gifford, Marv Albert, Tammy and Jim Bakker. Yet, these people still had the opportunity to go the straight and narrow before they put themselves in a vulnerable position with the media. They were willing to risk the sting of regrets.

In some cases, people do not seem to understand consequences. Much like any other parents, the role that my wife and I play in raising our children is to teach them the consequences of their actions. As a part of the empathy covered in Principle 1, children are born with empathy but learn over time the consequences of their actions to others and, of course, to themselves.

I am convinced in this society of instant gratification, we are losing our grasp on consequences. Covering your body with tattoos, branding scars, driving your car irresponsibly or unprotected, promiscuous sex. It just doesn't bode well for our future. Plus, eventually the consequences catch up. You will pay the price—a completely unnecessary price. You could be doing something a lot more productive.

I have an acquaintance who is the classic "slow-to-mature" type. He is forty years old. While a youth, he became involved in the wrong crowd and experimented with drugs of all sorts. Over time he was able to get his life back together, but he lacked a certain degree of maturity. It would not be out of character for him to blurt out a hurtful or a grossly inappropriate comment in his attempt to be funny. He would regularly drink too much and often drove while intoxicated.

One evening he was pulled over for drunk driving and spent the night in jail. When discussing his situation, his only response was, "That's what I got for taking that way home that night." He simply avoided the reality that he needed to understand consequences a little better. His instant gratification mentality and ignorance of consequences will one day catch up to him, and he will suffer the sting of regret.

Jungle Jim's "have no regrets" is much like the rocking chair theory. When you are sitting in your rocking chair in your twilight years, what will you be thinking to yourself? Will you have any regrets or will you think that you did it all? In the words of Frank Hand, "You'll only regret the things that you don't do."

Again, it is not how much you do, it's how often you do it. Doing a little counts more than anything. You will have regrets if you knew you could do a little more. Andrew Carnegie, in a graduation address, said "There are several classes of young people. There are those who do not do all their duty, there are those who profess to do their duty, and there is a third class far better than the other two, that do their duty and a little more... Do your duty and a little more and the future will take care of itself."

You will never have regrets when you do your duty and a little more. In fact, the impact is not just on you. It becomes a huge impact on the lives of those you touch. You then shift from satisfactory to *significant*.

FROM SATISFACTORY TO SIGNIFICANT

By virtue of my business of professional speaking, I fly a great deal. Living in Dallas, the head office and hub location for American Airlines, I get to see the best and the worst that happens in that company. The front-line people are the ticket agents and flight attendants. The more I travel, the more I realize the importance of a high-performing mentality in the individuals of this and any other corporation. Whether it is a fast food franchise, delivery service, department store or airline, the individual employees have the responsibility to lead by example or tear down with their actions.

Recently, I came across one of the best examples of that high-performing mentality. When I met Linda Farrington, she had been a flight attendant for American Airlines for thirteen years. As I boarded business class for my two-hour flight to Dallas, she proceeded to memorize each of the names of the twenty people in that section. Within five minutes she referred to everyone by their first name.

As a part of working in business class or first class, the flight attendants hand out moist, hot towellettes to the passengers. Linda did this, but placed two tiny wine glasses full of dry ice and water on the tray. She delivered the towellettes in style with dry-ice fog spilling over the edges of the trays. All the while, she had a comfortable rapport with the passengers.

The highlight of the flight (highlight and flight are two words you would never think belong in the same sentence) came later. Linda kept saying, "You'll have to check out the lavatory," with a smile. Pretty soon, it became obvious there was something up in the "lav." Upon entering I couldn't believe what was there. Linda Farrington had set up an entertainment motif and sound system in the corner. With a Walkman! and two small speakers, she had the sounds of Vivaldi's *Four Seasons* playing. Covering the cassette player was a colorful fan-shaped motif with flowers and decorations. Now, we're talking the corner of the tiny shelf in the lav. This wasn't an elaborate thing. But it was clearly significant.

Each and every person who came out of the lav was smiling. You could visibly notice people in the section become more sociable. People were talking to others across aisles and over seats. At the end of the flight, I witnessed each person thank Linda for her exceptional job.

It turns out that Linda Farrington does this on all of her flights and has been doing so for seven years. She said she had nineteen different motifs depending on the time of year and the occasion. On July 4th she sets up a star-spangled motif with the music of John Phillip Souza. At Christmas she has a festive motif with "politically correct" holiday tunes. On Valentine's Day the love songs are played with cupids and hearts surrounding the speakers. You name the day, Linda has a motif for it.

Linda Farrington clearly understands the value of doing her job with excellence. The extra effort she put in was minimal yet the impression she made on the customers was exceptional. In fact, this experience with her clarified the need for employees in corporate North America today to do their jobs… with caring.

"PRESS THE BUTTON IF YOU WANT ME TO CARE…"

Like anything, we have to take the good with the bad. The dark side of customer service was apparent on a flight I took in the United States in January of 1998. My wife, six-month-old son and I were flying back from New Zealand. Our trip from Auckland was a twelve-hour flight on Air New Zealand. Max, our son, started to run a fever about four hours into the flight. His fever had gotten so bad that he started to vomit and we had to put cold, wet towels on him to keep the fever down. The flight attendants were fantastic. They helped out and, since we were new parents and clearly green at this parenting thing, they were very good with us, too. When we got off the plane, we were met by an emergency team, but by that

Understand the value of doing
your job with excellence.

time Max was feeling better and we decided to spend a couple of days in Los Angeles while he recuperated.

Before we traveled, we got clearance from a doctor. Max was weak but recovering. Back in L.A. we boarded our flight. As we got on, we let the flight attendants know that we had a sick baby. We assumed that they would want to know in case they had experience with this sort of thing. During the entire three-hour flight, the flight attendants did their jobs. They explained the emergency procedures, how to buckle a belt and where the exits were. They did not smile. They passed up and down the aisle with carts of drinks and food. They did their jobs.

By the end of the flight, both Michelle and I were surprised that no one made a point of coming over and asking how Max was. In a way, we had the feeling that we didn't matter. Both Michelle and I own our own businesses and employ many people. The more we talked about it the more we realized our experience as customers and passengers was underwhelming. We decided that we would talk to the flight attendant and give some unsolicited feedback. Our approach was completely non-confrontational. We smiled and explained that we managed our own companies and knew the importance of honest feedback from customers. We continued that as customers, it would have been nice to have someone come by and check on how Max was doing.

The reaction we got was not what we expected. The flight attendant recoiled, got flustered, became defensive, mumbled a few words and walked away. She came back within two minutes with more composure this time and explained in a condescending tone, "The little orange button above you is called a call button. If you wanted us to come by, you should have pressed the button." Instantly, Michelle and I thought we hadn't properly explained why we brought up our comments and worded them differently.

She then repeated her previous response: "If you wanted us to come by, you should have pressed the button." At this point, Michelle and I couldn't help but burst out laughing. She honestly didn't understand what we were trying to do was help her with future customers. At a loss, we asked for the head steward.

He came by. We explained to him the intent of our comments. The steward said, "Folks, if you wanted something from us, you should have pressed the orange button. Plus, we do our job and we are very busy." He walked off, leaving us wondering why the heck we even brought it up.

The best part came about five minutes later. Witnessing the flight attendants collecting at the front while talking in hushed tones and frequently glancing back at us, we saw the original flight attendant come back toward us. "Folks, you have to understand, if you want something…" she said before we chimed in, "press the button."

"Yes, well, there's something else," she said. We looked puzzled while tingling with anticipation. "I have to know if you are going to write a complaint letter. Because if you write a letter, I have to write a letter, too," she said with a smug look.

"No, we have no intention of writing a letter," we said. She walked off and Michelle and I just looked at each other, not sure if our flight was going to Dallas or Pluto.

My wife has an exceptional ability to assess a situation. She never ceases to amaze me with her capability of saying the right thing at the right time. On the way off the plane, Michelle touched the flight attendant on the arm and said six simple, but profound words. "You know, it's just about caring."

It was clear that the flight attendants on this flight took the position that they were doing their jobs. They had probably experienced more than one irate passenger in the past. So, what my wife and I experienced was probably a culmination of negative prior events combined with myopia of what their jobs could be. The situation created a great deal of defensiveness and ill feeling in the flight attendants. Michelle and I became just another couple of whining passengers who needed to be handled. If these people had demonstrated the mentality that Linda Farrington displays on a daily basis, the outcome may have been dramatically different. Plus, the flight attendants would have enjoyed their roles much more.

Most people want their work and lives to be significant. They want to create value. They want to do things that matter. They want to know that they make a difference. Think of how much happier this flight attendant would have been had she made the shift to making a difference by adding value and a dose of caring.

A law in physics states that every action will have an equal and opposite reaction. When we choose to bring happiness and value to others, we receive happiness and value in return. What you sow is what you reap. What you give is what you get.

Look at your own life. Where are you doing your duty but not that little extra? Where could you add more caring? How can you take your life from satisfactory to significant?

YOUR BEST IS GOOD ENOUGH

Look around and you will find a general consensus that the "good enough" mentality is unacceptable on the road to success. While I agree that slackers and the slovenly have low levels of "good enough," there is an important distinction. The problem with "good enough" occurs with perfectionists. This is the source of the disease of perfectionism. Actions, results, feelings, relationships, events, memories and goals are never "good enough" for a perfectionist.

If you are a perfectionist, a candidate for perfectionism or even a recovering perfectionist, you may see the merit in a healthier philosophy where your best is good enough. But first you must be clear on your definition of "your best." Remember the case study of Elaine and Gerry and their unhealthy marriage. What is your best? Elaine continued to have an affair. Gerry asked her to stop. She repeatedly said to Gerry that she was doing her best. Maybe she was. It seemed odd, though, that she was capable of committing to being at the top of her class in high school. She was an accomplished athlete, had outstanding grades in college, and then she became a doctor. Learning this piqued my curiosity about the definition of best. Obviously the word means something different to everyone.

WHAT IS YOUR BEST?

Let's agree that your best is accomplished when you do everything you can think of with the resources you have available to you. Given this definition, when someone else doesn't meet your expectations, is it possible this truly was their best?

I consider myself a recovering perfectionist. I used to think that perfectionism was okay. With this approach, I knew that my sights would be aimed high. Of course, I knew that perfectionism was an impossible task, but I truly believed that I would accomplish more by attempting perfection versus "just excellence." What I didn't realize, and more important internalize, is I would *never* be satisfied. In other words, I would *always* be in the state of dissatisfaction. *Ouch!*

"The Relentless Pursuit of Perfection" is a slogan for a car—a great slogan, but I get a sting every time I hear it. It is a sad statement if applied literally. A life full of a relentless pursuit would be a life full of disappointment.

Stop thinking of best as an end result. In fact, best is dynamic and evolutionary. Your best today is your best... today! But not necessarily tomorrow. The standard may be higher and you have new levels of what best really is. Do you remember what Mother Goose said?—"Good, better, best; never rest till *good* be *better* and better *best*." Your best can be improved, but for sanity today, your best is good enough. In your journey to understand and define your best, remind yourself of these three points when evaluating your best:

1. When you have done everything you can think of given your resources.

2. Perfectionism does not work in any form.

3. It is a dynamic process.

THE PURSUIT OF EXCELLENCE

Three months before I was to compete in the Olympic Games, I took a course that literally changed my life forever. It was the single greatest investment that I have ever made in my life. It was called "The Pursuit of Excellence." Just prior to that I met Mara Vizzutti. In our conversation, she mentioned a course that I might be interested in, it was called "The Pursuit of Excellence." Without trying to understand the course, I said arrogantly, "Mara, I am going to compete in the Olympics. What could I possibly learn about excellence?"

As a representative for the company Context Associated, Mara had heard it all. This didn't faze her in the least. She said, "I know you might find value in this; I'll send you some information." Something about the course caught my eye. Despite the fact that I was in a failing marriage, I keyed in on the part about making more money and getting more satisfaction out of work. It turned out to be a great learning experience for me and what I brought to my marriage. It even helped me focus better at the Olympics rather than be consumed by my marital difficulties.

After finishing "The Pursuit of Excellence," I was very excited about its benefits. I had learned that one of the coolest experiences in life is learning about one's self. We wander through life thinking we know everything about ourselves, but we really don't. It isn't until a different approach is pursued that the self-discovery is allowed to flourish. One day, I called my cousin about it.

"I took this great course and they have an introductory session on Wednesday. The course is called 'The Pursuit of Excellence.' Would you like to check it out?"

She recoiled and said sharply, "I have no interest in being perfect." It became clear that not everyone shared my enthusiasm. Looking back, I used to think that only weak people took personal development courses. I am now a firm believer that some of the healthiest people on the planet are consistently and proactively working on themselves. I often think about what she might have learned had she taken the course.

There were various levels in the course. The second level, "The Wall," covers more in-depth personal discovery where the participant walks away knowing their purpose in life. The third level was called "The Advancement of Excellence" and was more or less a practicum from the material learned in the first two courses. The fourth course, "Mastery," was the most amazing experience for me. For most people it is a combination of going deep within to simplify life and fine tune what is not working. It was there that I realized how thick-skinned I was regarding perfectionism.

Through a series of modules I learned something about myself that had remained well hidden. I looked back over my life and tried to think of a time when I ever gave myself a break. Suddenly a memory came flooding back to when I was five years old. I was in the kitchen and I was showing my mother a finger painting that I had just completed. Like any mother, my mom started to gush about how beautiful it was. How the colors were great. How perfect it was. I distinctly remember thinking "It's not perfect." I looked back at the painting and looked at the mistake that I made where my finger went off the side of the paper. I did not keep the paint within the boundaries of the paper.

Then another memory flashed, and another. I thought about the first time I won the Canadian Championships in 1990. After the race I was extremely upset that I did not win by a larger margin. Instead of enjoying the moment, I was dissatisfied, unhappy, unfulfilled.

November 19, 1992: Standing by the ocean with the memories flooding back, I started to fall apart and sob. I could not think of one single time that I had given myself a break. I looked back at how I had consistently managed to break my own heart. It felt as if I were my own worst enemy and it was very, very sad to learn. This was a regret that was not addressed in over thirty years. It was the sting of regrets that I was now paying the price for.

But, from that day on, life has been a thousand times easier. It was as if the biggest chain that I had around my neck was put there by me. It is gone and life seems different now: more of a joy to discover. Now I know that my best is good enough. And, I have achieved new heights personally and professionally well beyond what I was capable of in the past.

Your journey may sound similar to this or you may find a much different path to self-discovery. The path is on a journey that has no real destination. In a Robert J. Hastings poem, *The Station*, the concept of finally getting somewhere doesn't actually exist in life. Instead, we live in anticipation of one day arriving; when we get there, "that will be it." We forget that we must relish the moment and savor it completely. He concludes the poem with, "Life must be lived as we go along. The station will come soon enough."

WHO FEELS GUILTY?

Athletes, parents, salespeople, teachers, construction workers, professionals, musicians, writers, entrepreneurs, the physically challenged, politicians, Buddhist monks on the top of a mountain, etc.—everyone is

---

Your best is good enough.

---

guilty of being too hard on themselves at one time or another. The varying levels of self-berating distinguish how far one must climb to get out of the hole of perfectionism.

Athletes look at the goal. They reach it and then the goal is old news within a short period of time. If they don't reach the goal, the agony can be immense. So, they try harder. What if they still don't make it? What then?

Think of parents looking to raise good and happy kids. The most frustrated people on the planet are parents who think they could have done more, spent more time with their children, lived a better example. It is far too easy to be hard on oneself as a parent. Remember this as a parent: *Your best is good enough!*

Salespeople are constantly haunted with feelings that they could be doing more. Should I have made that extra call? Did I drop the ball with that customer? Did I miss the opportunity to close the deal in our last negotiation? Should I have worked less and played more? Should I have played less and worked more?

Do you see yourself in any of these profiles? Okay, it's time to stop the madness. You have done enough to be hard on yourself. Even if you are pretty good at self-compassion, there is always room to grow. Reading this book can be a turning point for you. Right now, bring to mind your greatest frustration. What is it? Is it something at home, a person at work, a situation, a relationship, a personal problem? Think of something that is eating away at you.

Now say to yourself— "What is ... *is!*"

Staying in the mode of self-hate or resisting what has happened will only serve to auger you down. Accepting that "what is ... *is*" will be the turning point for you to rise up instead of spiral down. Should you accept, you can move forward toward your clarity of purpose (see Principle 12) and take action. Here you will continue to rise up. Or, you can continue to resist what you experienced and end up resenting it in some way. You then may find ways to get revenge, feel guilty, and then loop back to resentment again.

There is an often-quoted saying by Somerset Maugham, "If you refuse to accept anything but the best in life, you very often get it." Here is this saying with an Invinceable Principle twist, "Refuse to accept anything but your best, accept your very best as good enough and you will experience true fulfillment."

ARE YOU A PERFECTIONIST?

Have you read all this about perfectionism, acknowledged the liability of perfectionism yet find yourself still embracing it as serving you in some way? Answer these questions (if yes to any of these... perfectionism has its hooks in you):

• Do you feel that some of your achievements are never quite good enough?

• Have you (or are you) putting off a project before getting it just right?

• Do you acknowledge the liability of perfectionism but still justify it as working to your advantage?

• Do you push yourself to give more than 100 percent to avoid mediocrity or failure?

Not only will you rob yourself of satisfaction, you will limit your performance. Look for the warning signs that have an impact at work, in relationships, and at play:

1. Fear of failure. Hardcore perfectionists would sooner lose a limb than fail. Failing is a part of growing. Therefore, put yourself in a position where if you fail, then you can act. Repeat frequently. Like my dad said, "Life is way too short."

2. Fear of rejection. Nobody likes rejection. Get over it. Rejection is a part of life and is a necessary step to find the yes. Ask any successful salesperson how they get through rejection and they'll tell you it means getting one step closer to another yes.

3. Fear of making a mistake. Mistakes can be embarrassing, frustrating, awkward, costly and even deadly. Big mistakes in life-and-death situations, like those for a surgeon, or the less obvious death-defying procedure of driving a car, are completely avoidable. That is where preparation, due diligence and careful attention to detail are important. In lesser situations, mistakes are how you discover a better way. In most situations, making a mistake is okay. Learn and move on. Making the same mistake twice is inexcusable, if you truly learned from past mistakes.

Buddha was quoted as saying, "It is our very search for perfection outside ourselves that causes our suffering." Let go of any expectation and perfectionism disintegrates on the spot.

THE VICIOUS CYCLE

If you do not accept your best as good enough, you may be trapping yourself in a vicious cycle. The cycle goes something like this:

1. **You set a goal.**

2. **You're a perfectionist, so your goal will never be achieved.** You have set yourself up for failure.

3. **But, you persist, frustrating yourself and limiting growth, while, spending energy on an attitude that begins to suck you dry.**

4. **You beat yourself up for failing and disintegrate your already tarnished self-esteem.**

5. **You give up and experience some degree of depression.**

6. **You get sick of being down and snap out of it by setting another goal.**

You can get out of the vicious cycle by setting more attainable goals, defining what your best will be (given the circumstances) and holding yourself accountable to accept your best as good enough. Next, set a higher goal, or goals, with an even higher "stretch." Use the next part of framing achievement by having the courage to endure.

COURAGE TO ENDURE

"He conquers who endures."
—Perseus

Sure ... anything is possible. But the sacrifice is commensurate with the magnitude of the goal. In order to conquer, you must endure and you must be willing to pay the price. Often, the price is an unknown draw on you physically, emotionally, financially and sometimes spiritually. In the words of Stephen Covey, "Real excellence does not come cheaply. A certain price

THE VICIOUS CYCLE OF PERFECTIONISTS

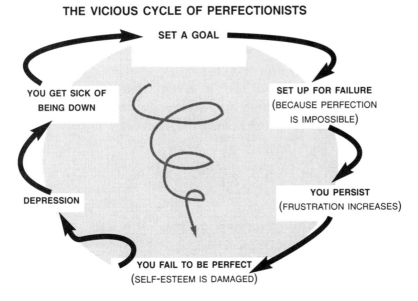

SET A GOAL

YOU GET SICK OF BEING DOWN

SET UP FOR FAILURE (BECAUSE PERFECTION IS IMPOSSIBLE)

DEPRESSION

YOU PERSIST (FRUSTRATION INCREASES)

YOU FAIL TO BE PERFECT (SELF-ESTEEM IS DAMAGED)

must be paid in terms of practice, patience, and persistence—natural ability notwithstanding."

Given the worthiness of the sacrifice, the feeling of satisfaction can be beyond your expectations. The impact on those around you can be equally exceptional.

Last year I flew to San Diego to speak to the Maaco annual franchise meeting. On the way I met about six young Marine recruits on their way to boot camp. These young men looked awkward and unsure. Despite their puffed-up pride in entering the Marines, they instilled very little confidence in me. It even crossed my mind that the Marines must have changed their entry guidelines. I couldn't help but think that this was not a promising future for the Marines.

Three months later I was back in San Diego and happened to run into four of the original six. In fact, I didn't even recognize them. They came across a food court to say hello. What I witnessed was nothing short of a complete transformation. They were confident, seemed empowered and stood taller than I remembered. We talked about their experiences.

They spoke of a great deal of pressure from the drill instructor. They were trained to be unfailingly loyal to their unit, to *never, ever* let down their platoon. They said it was the hardest thing they had ever done but also the most satisfying. They clearly made friendships for life and grew in the process.

The Marine Corps pushes recruits to their physical and emotional limits. All the while, they learn about their potential and their growth capabilities. These young men were simply exposed to a new world that demanded more from them than home or school had. They literally changed from boys into men.

I think back to my childhood and realize that my parents knew this principle. Not that they remotely resembled drill instructors in the Marines, but they did make a point of exposing all three of their children to as much opportunity as was within our resources. We tried music, hockey, swimming, debate clubs, different types of jobs and even the Sea Cadets (that was interesting considering we lived in the prairies of Alberta).

The sacrifices in these situations were small, but perfect, for children. The experience of trying new things was a stretch but prepared us well for life's future challenges. At the other extreme, sacrifice on a grander scale is a different issue. No longer is a sacrifice a stretch for growth, but a stretch for survival.

In his book *Man's Search for Meaning*, Victor Frankl writes about his horrific experiences in the concentration camps of Nazi Germany. His background as a psychologist and scientist resulted in a first-hand perspective on sacrifice. His observations concluded that the way to endure the horror was by attributing meaning to the suffering and pain. The people who did not do this did not live long in the camps. Across the English Channel was a different form of sacrificial challenge.

THE ULTIMATE SACRIFICE

The ultimate sacrifice is human life. On D-Day, June 6, 1944, the biggest military fleet in history left from Portsmouth, England. There were fifty-nine convoys spread across a hundred miles, led by six battleships, twenty-two cruisers and ninety-three destroyers. They made up part of an Allied force of 2.5 million strong with five thousand ships and four thousand additional small craft in the armada. The approach to D-Day was a massive effort and now regarded as the single greatest turning point of World War II.

On the same day of the fleet leaving from Portsmouth, twenty-three thousand Allied paratroopers prepared to land behind the German's beach defense. As the planes took off, Eisenhower and his staff saluted them. One of the masterminds behind the push, Eisenhower knew the magnitude of the sacrifice that his troops were making. When he turned away, he had tears in his eyes.

This commander knew that casualties as high as 75 percent might be sacrificed for this offensive. He remembered a comment from Churchill who said, "When I think of the beaches of Normandy choked with the flower of our Allied youth, and when in my mind's eye I see the tides running red with their blood, I have my doubts. I have my doubts."

By nightfall, 156,000 Allied soldiers were on the beach in Normandy; yet the total number of killed, wounded and missing in action was estimated at less than five thousand. These five thousand souls and the efforts of the surviving troops gave the most profound sacrifice. These soldiers and their leaders had the courage to endure.

With all these examples of willingness to pay the price, the method to reach the goal was based on a dedication to do what it took until the job was done. They stayed in the process.

STAY IN THE PROCESS

I hesitated putting the section of staying in the process in this book, since it is well known that you simply need to be determined not to quit. But, as obvious as it may seem, remind yourself of the examples of great people before who did not quit.

Alexander Graham Bell is one inventor who understood this fully. "What this power is I cannot say; all I know is that it exists and it becomes available only when a man is in that state of mind in which he knows exactly what he wants and is fully determined not to quit until he finds it."

Thomas Edison estimated to a friend that he had failed to produce a stor-

> # When you're in the middle of a mess ...
> # this is a good sign.

age battery even after ten thousand experiments. When his friend sensed Edison was despondent, Edison perked up and said, "Why, I have not failed. I've just found ten thousand ways that won't work." Edison is credited for 1,093 patents in his lifetime.

These people almost seem super-human with their accomplishments that changed the world. Most of us are just regular folks doing the best we can. Given my position in helping others with personal growth and peak performance, I come across people daily who are frustrated and struggling. More than anything, the process can be frustrating. Time and again I witness people deciding to take their lives to the next level, only to find they are in the middle of a mess. Believe it or not, this is a good sign. The best way to describe this is by an analogy of cleaning a closet.

CLEANING THE CLOSET

Imagine you have a closet that you walk by every day. There may be things that you would rather deal with later, so you toss them in the closet. The longer you ignore what's in the closet, the more stuff that ends up in there. Finally, you get to a point where you either can't take the fact you have ignored the closet or the closet is full and needs to be cleaned out.

The only way to clean the closet is by emptying it out. As you take stuff out, memories come flooding back. You come across matters left undone; you start to pay the price that you previously ignored. Finally your closet is empty, but you find you are sitting in the middle of a mess at its worst point. You might not even know where to start and at times it is overwhelming how much stuff there is. Take heart.

Finding yourself at the peak of a mess means you are halfway. You then systematically decide what it is you want to keep, what you want to deal with and what you want to toss. Progressively, you follow a process similar to closet cleaning that clarifies your priorities. As the mess is reduced, the cleaning becomes easier. In time, you are in the position to decide whether you will fill the closet with stuff again or stay in the process of a well-managed and controllable closet.

THE THREE MENTALITIES TO ENDURE

The "start … finish" mentality: When quitting is *not* an option, it is called the start … finish mentality. It wasn't until a few years ago that I thought everyone thought the same way I did. One glowing example of this happened when I joined a group of friends on a rigorous trek along the famous West Coast Trail in British Columbia.

The West Coast Trail covers a forty-seven-mile-long (seventy-seven-kilometer) route between Renfrew and Bamfield on the unprotected west coast of Vancouver Island. Its origin was as a "life-saving trail" for nineteenth century shipwrecks. It is now a protected area that is federally maintained by Pacific Rim National Park Services.

The terrain is far from easy to traverse. It is a test of fortitude and determination. Along the way the forest trails are surrounded by western red cedar, hemlock and Sitka spruce. The sandstone beaches are exposed at low tide, combined with striking, and sometimes dangerous tidal surge channels. Taking a break from the huffing and puffing along the way, there are scenes of osprey snatching salmon from the ocean, whales, curious seals and unbelievable sunsets. To make the four- to seven-day hike even more challenging, there are the intermittent torrential downpours that soak the dirt trails and the trekkers. With frequent rainfalls, there is plenty of water in the cascading creeks and a vibrant green in the thick rain forest.

On our trip there were six people, each loaded with forty- to fifty-pound packs. Since the West Coast Trail is not serviced with amenities, you must bring everything that you feel you will need along the way. The night before our departure, we split up the provisions and ensured each person took a fair share of the load. On the first night, we camped outside of the park boundaries, preparing for our early-morning departure. That night it was raining lightly, but steadily.

All the next day it rained and was somewhat dark from the clouds. With each step the ground got softer and the pack got heavier from the rain that found its way past the waterproof covering. With each passing hour the mood became darker and darker. After we hiked for eight hours and covered just nine miles, the rain stopped and we stopped by a picturesque waterfall. We actually saw the sun as it set with the colorful purple and orange hues bouncing off the scattering clouds. Our spirits started to pick up. All was well until we woke up the next morning.

Nature's alarm clock was the incessant sound of rain hitting the nylon covers of the tents. It was a classic West Coast downpour and everything was either wet or damp. The packs seemed to weigh seventy-five pounds each, and every other step was a slip in one direction or the other. The mood of the group turned sour very quickly. In fact, people started to snap at each other and it was becoming very uncomfortable, notwithstanding being wet and chilled to the bone.

The rain never let up. In fact the clouds got darker and it seemed like night at 2 P.M. After a few more miles we came across the Nit Nat Lake crossing. There, a native Indian family makes a small fortune shuttling people from one side of the lake to the other. During the crossing, unknown to the rest of the group, one person in the group decided that she could not go on any further. She told her husband and his choice was obvious. Despite the fact that he had coordinated the whole trip, he had to stay with his wife.

Normally, on the West Coast Trail, the only way out is by an emergency helicopter that patrols the trail once or twice a day. You could signal the coast guard with flares or a fire, but quitting was typically not an option. There are no phones on the West Coast Trail and when you make the decision to start ... you finish.

In a clearing, not far from the lake, we assembled for a team meeting. The couple announced their intentions to quit and take the boat up to Nit Nat Village. Within seconds, the three other members of the group decided that they would quit, too. These were people in their twenties and thirties. They were fit and healthy. Yet, given the opportunity to quit, they did. I just stood there with my mouth open.

"We can't quit, we just started," I protested. But with the rain coming down and the sun obliterated by dark clouds, my cajoling was pointless. I was faced with a decision. I had no hiking experience. Traveling alone meant that if I got into trouble, I would have to pray it was on the trail where others might come by and help; and I would have to carry a greater load, since I would have to carry all the camping gear plus food. But the more I thought about it, the more I couldn't accept quitting. "We aren't dying; we are just uncomfortable," I thought to myself.

"Fine," I said, "anyone who wants to change their mind can come with me. I'm going. It will be dark soon and I need to get to the next camping area before then." As I was re-packing and adding gear that others had in their packs, each person separately came over to convince me to reconsider. "It's probably not safe to go it alone," they would say. It became obvious that they thought I was being unreasonable. To me, I had no choice. Start … finish. It's that simple.

At last I was ready to continue and said my goodbyes. One of the females in the group started to cry and kept saying, "Be careful."

"Don't worry about me," I said with as much confidence as I could muster. Then I walked out of the clearing into a break in the trees and brush where I turned right. No sooner did I turn the corner than I slipped and fell over. When you slip with a sixty-pound pack on it's like a W.W.F. midget throwing you down to the ground. I looked around. No one saw me. Since the pack was even heavier than before, I remained temporarily stranded like a turtle flipped on its back. I righted myself and walked on. I kept a brisk pace to reach the next camping area before dark.

It was a long and miserable hike in the rain. I wondered a couple of times if I had made a mistake, but it seemed like the right thing to do. Nothing ventured; nothing gained seemed like an all-too-appropriate cliché at this point.

By the time I reached the camping area it was dusk. Better still, it stopped raining. The camp was simply a beach where there were three other groups. I set up near a couple of hippie/biker types who were very friendly. They made a bonfire that was huge. It was at least eight feet at the base and threw a flame ten to fifteen feet in the air. The fire was purely for practical purposes, to dry clothes. We strung up ropes and dried everything, especially the sleeping bags. It worked great!

Before long I got tired and checked my sleeping bag. I felt it up and down and it seemed perfectly dry. I got in my tent, stripped down to my boxer shorts and T-shirt and then slid into the bag. The next feeling was that of disgust and foreboding. I had forgotten to turn my sleeping bag inside out when I was drying it. My thorough check did not involve an inside check. But, I was so exhausted that I just figured it was a fitting end to a very wet couple of days.

"Do you like adventure?"

The next morning the sun came out. As luck would have it, it remained that way for the balance of the trip. When the skies are clear, the beauty of the West Coast Trail is truly exceptional. Moreover, the balance of the hike took a welcome twist.

Five or six hours after my camp departure, I came across a family that I recognized from the night before. They had an earlier start, but I caught up to them. They were the Byl family, Frank, Lorraine and their two sons, Jeremy and Daniel.

Frank and I walked side-by-side for a half mile or so exchanging small talk. Frank was a big guy. He was about six-foot-three and very broad. Yet, he had a boyish quality about him. We instantly connected. Later on, after a few minutes of silence, Frank looked at me in a curious way.

"Do you like adventure?" he said.

I didn't have a clue where this question was heading. I paused, trying to think of what he meant. Finally I said, "Yup ... I like adventure. Why?"

"Were going to take the Adrenaline Surge route."

I couldn't believe he just said that. At the trailhead the park wardens forbid the hikers from this route. Each year, inexperienced hikers try to navigate Adrenaline Surge, where the channel meets up with a waterfall and cliff. Since the channel is cut deep into the sandstone beach, one slip and a hiker falls in, they are unable to climb out of the slippery sides— they drown. Two people that year had already died and the route was closed. Plus, Adrenaline Surge was only navigable at low tide. Moreover, Frank's boys were nine and eleven years old, hardly the ages to cover dangerous territory.

"Are you kidding?" I asked immediately, feeling more than skeptical.

"No, I'm serious. I have hiked the West Coast Trail a dozen times. I teach physical education and I take high school students along here all the time. I know exactly how to get across Adrenaline Surge. It just would be nice to have another strong guy along to be on the other side of the safety rope. Plus, I know a special route most people never get to see."

He was convincing. I joined up. We proceeded to see and do things I never imagined. We went to an area of a natural waterslide. It was molded, rolling rock that was covered in green algae. We slid down this series of slides from one pool down to the next. It was a blast.

The next day we reached Adrenaline Surge and I then fully understood what all the fuss was about. You actually had to walk through the waterfall while trying to keep a foothold on a little four-inch ledge of rock. There were no handholds and you had to keep your pack on. One slip and you would simply fall directly into the surge channel, which was a sheer and slippery seven feet on either side.

We hooked each boy onto a safety rope with a strap and a caribiner. If they slipped, we would hold them up and get them to regain their footing. We did the same for Lorraine. I was the last to come across.

"What if I fall in?" I asked Frank, trying to make my voice heard over the sound of the waterfall and the crashing waves in the surge channel.

"You'll get very wet," he yelled from the other side. He then smiled and held up the rope.

I nodded, took a breath, then carefully made my way across the four-inch ledge. Piece of cake (if you know what you're doing).

From Adrenaline Surge we continued along miles and miles of sandstone beach. The views were stunning. The blues of the ocean contrast to the greens of nature, the earth tones all around us and the wildlife in the sky, ocean and land. It was nothing short of breathtaking every step of the way.

I later learned that the only other route was inland. From all the rain, the trail was muddy. Each step was a struggle. Plus, the view never seemed to change, since the hike was lined with trees on either side. Many of the hikers I met up with later complained that it was the hardest slogging of the whole trail. Me? I said nothing about my adventure. Why rub it in?

At the end, all I could think about was how grateful I was for the experience I had just had. I felt bad for my former hiking group. They had missed an experience of a lifetime simply because they had quit. They did not embrace the start ... finish mentality and they lost out on an extraordinary opportunity.

ANOTHER EXAMPLE OF "START ... FINISH"

In 1991, Alan Hobson and Jamie Clarke joined a Canadian expedition to climb Mount Everest. Despite their roles as communications specialists, (they would send satellite transmissions from base camp), they were also part of the climbing team attempting to summit the world's highest peak. The team fell short, held back by an early monsoon and fierce winds.

Although Alan Hobson, a native of Ottawa, Ontario and Jamie Clarke, born in Calgary, had known each other only for a few years, they each had a life-long dream to climb Mount Everest.

Immediately after the team's first attempt, Alan and Jamie decided to organize their own team of climbers and faxed China for a permit to attempt a summit bid in 1994. This time they hand picked a collection of Canadians and gained sponsorship from Emergo, Canada. With Alan and Jamie lower on the mountain, their lone hope of summiting lay on the back of John McIsaac. Just 162 meters, a couple of city blocks, from the peak, McIsaac was forced to turn back due to severe problems breathing. In a few short hours it became apparent that John McIsaac was in serious trouble.

He kept sitting down in the snow where the seduction of just closing his eyes and sleeping was death's way of taking over at those altitudes. On the radio, the team patched in his two daughters from at home in Canada. They urged their father to keep walking, "Please Daddy, come home."

Somehow, McIsaac managed to stumble into Camp 6 at twenty-six thousand feet. The team doctor quickly diagnosed pulmonary edema. His lungs were filling with liquid and his only hope of survival would be to descend immediately. Unfortunately, he fell unconscious and a few hours later he had to be carried down the mountain from the 23,500-foot level.

A collection of Canadians and climbers from other countries contributed to the 33-hour-long rescue and John McIsaac was reunited with his wife in base camp soon after.

The team felt satisfied that their summit had been accomplished, but Alan and Jamie had started something, they needed to finish. In 1997, they made a third attempt on Mount Everest. Or, as the Sherpas call it, *Chomolungma*, Mother Goddess of the World.

Any climber who has attempted to reach the top of Mount Everest will tell you that the mountain decides if you summit. It is a combination of good planning, proper weather, solid leadership, a strong team and healthy climbers. Even the 1996 disaster that claimed the lives of nine people on the side of Mount Everest did not deter their plans.

This time, Alan Hobson and Jamie Clarke selected a team of climbers from both Canada and the U.S. They received sponsorship from Lotus and Colliers International. This time, Alan and Jamie hoped they would have what it took to be the ones to make a summit attempt.

On May 20, 1997, at 7:10 A.M. Jamie Clarke and their Sherpa partners, Lhapkpa Tsering and Byalbu Sherpa, stood on top of the world. Alan Hobson was to follow. At 9:00 A.M. he also summited with his Sherpa partners, Kami Tsering and Tashi Tsering. All descended safely and remarked on the intense satisfaction of accomplishing a lifelong dream. Persistent people like Alan Hobson and Jamie Clarke, as much as anyone on this planet, clearly understand the power of a start ... finish mentality.

START ... FINISH MEANS *START* ... *FINISH!*

In the early 1990s, two speakers and members of the National Speakers Association joined forces with an idea that they thought was pretty good. Their names are Jack Canfield and Mark Victor Hansen, and their idea was a book of short, non-fiction, inspirational or touching stories from various authors.

Once the book was near completion, they struggled with a title. One evening, Mark and Jack were on the phone and agreed to meditate on a title before they went to sleep. In the middle of the night, Jack Canfield called up Mark Victor Hansen and said excitedly, "I've got it ... *Chicken Soup for the Soul.*"

Mark instantly loved the title and they soon took their idea to a publisher. They could have easily self-published the book but had bigger plans for *Chicken Soup for the Soul*. The publishers they first approached summarily turned them down and sent them on their way.

In total, Jack and Mark approached thirty-three publishers until finally a small publishing house called Health Communications Incorporated (HCI) said yes. This was the best decision HCI ever made. In fact, HCI recently took out an ad in the *New York Times* thanking the thirty-three publishers for turning Jack and Mark away. Because in that time, the *Chicken Soup for the Soul* idea turned into a series of best sellers, consistently on the *New York Times* best-sellers list with over 30 million copies sold. (In the publishing business, if a book exceeds one million, it is an incredible hit.) There are now books like *Chicken Soup for the Teenage Soul* (I and II), *Chicken Soup for the Mother's Soul,* and *Chicken Soup for the Pet Lover's Soul.* Jack Canfield and Mark Victor Hansen have plans for seventy-four "Chicken Soup" books in the near future.

The fact is, once their book was first published, people loved it, but HCI had less marketing clout than the big seven publishing houses. Therefore, Jack and Mark got creative and they used non-traditional points of sale. Hair salons and chiropractic office waiting rooms had copies to read and a stack for sale at the desk. Some bookstores were confused and put the book in the cooking section. This worked to their advantage since shoppers would scan the shelves and be intrigued by the title. Jack and Mark even had a network of their friends and colleagues peddling the book to their friends. At each town they visited, they arranged book signings and media interviews. They, of course, sold it at the back of the room at their speaking engagements.

Pretty soon, they hit what Jack Canfield called "flashpoint." The combination of word of mouth and persistent marketing paid off. The book shot up the bestseller list to number one and their start ... finish mentality paid off. They simply believed in their idea and never gave up on it. They knew what their objective was and they saw it through. They now continue to set new goals and continue their successful start ... finish pattern of achievement.

Think back to goals you attempted and did not reach. No start. No finish. We all have something that we did not see through. You will never know what benefit you could have seen had you applied the start ... finish mentality. You may have missed out on the beauty of nature beyond your wildest imagination, like the hiking group I was with missed on the West

---

Pay your dues.

Persist ... you will hit flashpoint.

Coast Trail. Or, you may have missed out on reaching extraordinary heights like Alan Hobson and Jamie Clarke. Or you may have passed on fame and fortune similar to what Jack Canfield and Mark Victor Hansen now enjoy.

Given the ability to minimize the risk, weigh the odds and accept the short-term sacrifice, the start … finish mentality is an essential tool for life mastery.

The New Altitudes mentality: The second kind of mentality, or approach, applies in a different scenario. In this case, the goal is not defined. It's more like a project that calls your name. Like a good idea that won't go away, it pesters your thoughts until you see it through. Some call it discovering your destiny or meeting your fate or even a trust in karma. The truth is, destiny, fate or karma are nothing more than consequences of your own actions. It is the pride in that consequence that will take you to new plateaus, a higher plane, to "New Altitudes."

Some say that there is no such thing as a born salesperson. Well, they never met my brother, Steven. One time we planned to have a Kool-Aid stand out in front of our house, selling drinks for a dime. Steve was six years old and I was seven and we went to the kitchen to mix our product and get the ice. Within seconds Steve was gone somewhere leaving me to finish the preparation. He reappeared in time to help carry out a small card table to the end of the driveway. He promptly vanished again, leaving me to make the signs and carry the inventory to the table.

Finally we were ready to go, and Steven stood out on the sidewalk to wave the customers in. Three cars drove by and Steven turned to me and said, "Well this isn't working," and disappeared for a third time. Despite my age, I knew I was getting gypped. Here I was doing all the work, and I would still have to share the profits—notwithstanding if there would be any profits.

Five minutes later Steven came back with an eight-year-old female neighbor. He had talked her into wearing a bikini and holding our sign. "This will get them looking," Steven said to me confidently.

He then said to the girl, "Okay, stand and look sexy." He showed her how to stand in a provocative pose.

It worked. People would stop and chuckle while Steve would up-sell the Kool-Aid, "Two for twenty cents. Only while supplies last." would be his pitch while I just sat there amazed. After an hour or so I paid our helpful assistant.

As she walked off, she turned to me and said, "Your brother is sooooo cute." (If I had a nickel for every time I heard that....)

Steven is now a master sales trainer for Wickman Enterprises. He draws from years of door-to-door sales and real estate experience along with his "oh-sooooooo-cute" charm. Steven Poscente is an amazing salesperson!

Back when I got the idea to race in the sport of speed skiing, I thought that I might follow Steven's lead. He had just been in real estate for a year and had already been a top producer in his office. He was a finalist in the Calgary Real Estate Board's Rookie-of-the-Year and qualified for the prestigious Million-Dollar Club.

I watched Steven making money and doing deals at will. Since I needed a job to support my racing, "How hard could it be?" I thought to myself. So, in November, 1988, I quit my sports administration job with Alberta Luge and took the real estate course. I printed up some Century 21 business cards and proceeded to go broke. For six months I sold nothing, listed nothing and showed nothing. I worked hundreds of hours, but I came face to face with the fact that I knew *nothing* about sales.

Eventually I started to sell a house here and there while keeping up a full-time commitment to racing and training. The four years leading up to the Olympics of 1992 was a very difficult time for me, and the time following the Olympics was even more difficult.

At the games all the athletes were mobbed with autograph seekers. It was fun. The reporters and the attention made me feel pretty special. On the flight home I started to realize I was broke and needed to hit the ground running. I didn't win the gold and there were no mega-endorsement deals waiting for my return.

Five days after the Olympics, I returned to win the Canadian Championships at Big White, British Columbia. The sense of urgency to start making money was front and center. I had bills piling up.

In the past I had a good deal of success door-knocking for business. Trying to find people who were looking to sell their home or buy in the near future

Become a student of your own vocation.

was the name of the game.

Ten days after the Olympics I had my suit on. It was a cold March day and I walked up to my first door. "Hi, my name's Vince, and I'm with Century 21 Real Estate—" I was interrupted by a door being slammed in my face.

FROM HERO TO ZERO IN TEN DAYS FLAT

It didn't seem right, and the more I persisted, the more difficult it became. But then something inside me clicked. I realized that I knew very little about sales. It became my quest. I wanted to learn more. Instead of quitting and finding a better-suited job, I realized that a solid foundation of sales meant learning about the sales process. I became a student of my own vocation.

I decided to work smarter rather than harder. I focused on the location of the greatest buyers, not the newspaper, not open houses, but other Realtors. I researched the best door-knocking track that was out there. It worked fantastic. I got two leads a day from a more polished presentation.

I researched the odds of selling a house and found that less than five percent of sales came from newspaper ads and open houses. These were simply used to pick up buyers. I focused my time and energy on marketing to the four thousand Realtors in the city. If each active Realtor had about three or four buyers each, then I would raise the odds of selling my listings faster.

In addition, I was adamant about balance. I did not work weekends. Since I did not do open houses, nor run newspaper ads, this wasn't necessary. I partnered with an officemate to cover for me should an offer come in on the weekend, which it never did, and I had some semblance of a life (unheard of with most Realtors).

Imagine the look on a client's face when I would say I did not work weekends, I did not advertise in the newspaper and I did not do public open houses. They would quickly see the logic when I reviewed the statistics and unfolded my strategy and budget for marketing to the Realtors.

In the two years following the Olympics, I was consistently in the top ten salespeople in an office of one hundred Realtors. I learned a great deal about sales, which I knew would serve me in the future. Real estate sales was not my dream vocation. It was an opportunity to reach "new altitudes" for learning more of what life had to offer. After these couple of journeyman years, I was offered the position as vice president of the Wealth Builder Program for North America's largest real estate investment service.

Constantly seeing things through is the key to reaching new altitudes. Do not leave things undone, if there is an opportunity to gain a better perspective, skill or position (which is the case 99 percent of the time). If you see an opportunity, take the leap and see what the future holds for you. You never know the riches you will collect from your new altitude.

DOING WHAT IT TAKES

In 1983, Karen Behnke was a nurse making a comfortable living in the Bay area of California. Except, burning inside Karen was her self-professed mission "to save the world." She started a company that would serve the healthcare industry. Nine years later she sold the business for $4 million, followed with a marriage to one of the top interventional cardiologists in the U.S. and a beautiful baby boy named Jake.

Karen's easygoing demeanor belies her drive and determination to succeed. She reminisced that starting the business was one of the hardest things she ever did. She began with no business background, no money, no contacts and no business plan.

"I was a nurse and I knew that 80 percent of all diseases could be prevented. I wanted to literally save the world and that is what drove me at the beginning," she said in a recent interview. In the beginning she used seventeen credit cards to juggle a $2,500 line of credit. Using the single most "expensive" money she could find, she followed her ambition. Karen Behnke knew that with her business she would "either be poverty-stricken or a millionaire." After putting her house and everything on the line, she moved forward.

Karen learned along the way. Her natural talent for marketing served her well and her drive evolved. No longer did she idealistically just want to save the world. She also balanced that with wanting to run a profitable venture for herself and her shareholders. In time, 350,000 people enrolled and over 2 million lives were touched with her worksite wellness programs. She even met her promise to shareholders to consistently beat the S&P Industrial Average.

Her decision to sell was not based solely on money. A large part of her decision was to leverage the concept to more people. This meant joining forces with Pacificare, an $11 billion company. Karen estimates that 2 million people are involved in worksite wellness program initiatives, and this number continues to grow.

Karen Behnke's decision to do what it takes truly did take strides toward saving the world. Plus, she reached new altitudes of success and opportunity. In addition to her great family, she sits on the board for 24-Hour Fitness, overseeing 280 clubs, and she is retained by a venture capital firm in San Francisco. She and Howard are building their dream home in a secluded area in the trees over-looking the Bay area. Karen Behnke knows that the persistence she used with the new altitude mentality paid off in spades.

NEW ALTITUDES OF EXCELLENCE

Sugar Ray Leonard had it all: an Olympic gold medal, a prolific professional boxing career, a world title and financial security for the rest of his life. Yet deep down he still felt he had left something undone.

After a lengthy retirement, Leonard decided to challenge Marvin Haglar for the middleweight championship of the world. Skeptics abounded. In his last professional fight, Leonard had almost lost his vision in his right eye; he hadn't boxed for five years and Haglar was undefeated for over ten years. But for Leonard, his boxing career needed a *coup de grace*. His New Altitude had to do with his intrinsic definition of a higher order of excellence. His desire to satisfy his curiosity was that which only he understood. Something was left undone and he was going to do something about it.

This time, more than ever before, the chasm between him and victory was wider than he ever remembered. This drove him to prepare harder than he ever had in the past. He trained as if obsessed. In most ways, he was. He knew he would have no regrets.

The fight went the distance, Haglar was clearly the more powerful boxer, but Leonard won on his overall boxing skill. Leonard won the $11 million purse and the bragging rights as middleweight champion of the world. Sugar Ray Leonard reached his own new altitude and continues to do so in his everyday life.

The "do or die" mentality: The third mentality is applicable only in life-threatening situations. The interesting thing that I found in research was a common denominator—defining the importance of family. Each story of survival revealed an inner drive to reunite with their families. The family is one of the most meaningful and intense relationships in our lives. It is not surprising that the family is one of the strongest motivators in the do-or-die mentality. Here are four stories where each person was taken to the very extent of their limitations.

NANDO PARRADO

In 1972, a rugby team boarded a flight from Uruguay to Chile for a tournament. The Fairchild aircraft was chartered and the team had a collection of relatives and acquaintances joining them. Despite being temporarily grounded just a few hours into the trip, the pilot and the forty-five passengers and crew on board continued on their way to a destination of disaster.

Due to heavy crosswinds and thick cloud cover, the pilot mistook his bearings and assumed he had cleared the last mountain range in Chile. As the plane descended, they immediately found themselves in the midst of the Andes and far too low to avoid crashing the plane. Their futile attempts to climb full throttle first clipped both wings, then broke the fuselage in half, killing all the passengers in the back one-third of the plane. This left the front of the fuselage in the shape of a giant torpedo to launch over the other side of a steep ridge where the projectile, with sixteen people on board hanging on for dear life, slid down the hill at over 150 miles per hour. The fuselage came to a sudden stop toward the bottom, rendering a number of people dead, others unconscious and some without a scratch.

One of the survivors was Nando Parrado. For seventy-four days the group survived the horrific cold, lack of food and water and a deadly avalanche. Their story of survival was sensationalized with the discovery that they survived off the flesh of the dead people. In the words of Nando, they "had no idea why God had tested them with such a terrible decision to stay alive in such a way." Quite simply, they had no choice.

For days on end, Nando Parrado was fixated on climbing out. Listening to a small radio found in the crash, the group discovered that the rescue attempts were called off after eight days. In a personal conversation with

Nando, he kept repeating to me that his "personal affections, the thought of reuniting with his father" were what kept him going. Nando had lost his mother and his sister in the crash. He was determined to reunite with his remaining family.

After a nearly impossible climb across the massive mountain ranges, Nando Parrado and Roberto Canessa found help. Nando Parrado credits the opportunity to reunite with his father and family as his primary motivation.

BECK WEATHERS

The do-or-die ordeal that Beck Weathers faced at just over twenty-six thousand feet on Mount Everest is amazing in its own right. Beck, nearly blind due to an earlier eye surgery, was left waiting at 27,600 feet while his other climbing colleagues made their summit attempts. In the next forty-eight hours, nine people would die in the worst climbing disaster on Mount Everest. Statistically, one out of every four climbers who attempt to summit do not make it down alive. Considering the challenges Beck Weathers would face, his odds of surviving were practically zero.

With his condition and a promise to team leader Rob Hall, Beck stayed put until another team leader happened across him. By this time a surprise storm was unleashing its full and deadly force. He and the other exhausted climbers were led down to an area where the camp was supposed to be, but it had been blown off the mountain!

Beck's group had no choice but to continue descending in hopes of reaching Camp 4. In the fury of the storm—the darkness, blowing snow and an ineffective flashlight beam of three feet—their condition worsened.

Weathers spent the night freezing to death, lying on his back with his right hand exposed and his face open to the elements. By morning his face was coated with ice and his breath and heartbeat were barely perceptible.

Beck awoke with the thought of not wanting to leave his family without a father—not wanting to leave his wife without a husband. Somehow, he managed to get himself mobile while noticing one of his companions, Yasuko, had frozen to death right beside him.

Blind in his right eye and only able to focus three to four feet with his left, Weathers managed to walk, directly into the wind, toward Camp 4. Ninety

> # He was driven by the desire to go home and be with his family.

minutes later he arrived at the camp to the amazement of the remaining climbers. The storm continued to rage on. It would not let up. Beck was given what attention they could offer, but he was obviously too far gone for saving. His hand and face were completely frozen solid and he was hanging on to life by a thread. At this altitude and no way to get him down, Beck Weathers would soon die.

Yet, he was driven by the desire to go home and be with his family. He would not die. The next morning the climbers prepared to descend. They checked on Beck last because they thought he was dead. To their shock, he was not dead at all. They slowly made their way down the mountain to Camp 3.

Still hanging on to life, Beck was transported out by the courageous Lieutenant Colonel Madar Khatri Chhetri of the Nepalese Army. It was thought an impossible task to get a helicopter to that altitude, yet Beck's fortune smiled on him again.

In retrospect, Beck Weathers tells anyone who will listen that your family is the most important thing you have and he would not be alive today had he not kept that his focus.

JAMES FIERRO

In the span of less than two years, in his late thirties, James Fierro experienced more stress than most people experience in a lifetime. It's his belief that this stress brought on a rare form of skin cancer called *mycosis fungoydis* which could have taken his life had he not turned things around. Again, the realization of not wanting to leave his children, parents and all that was important to him drove him to climb out of his do-or-die situation.

James Fierro lives and breathes business. The art of doing the deal is as natural to him as flying is to a bird. Living in Vancouver, British Columbia, James built up a microchip company that in a three-year period was negotiating contracts for hundreds of millions of dollars with government and corporate giants like Chrysler, GM and Caterpillar.

During one particular three-week business trip to Asia, a small but hostile group of stockholders moved to take control of the company. By the time Fierro returned home, it was too late to turn the tides. And worse, his hands were tied because he had invested most everything he owned in the company. He also had $100,000 of company debt on credit cards, and he had mortgaged his house to channel all his available capital into the company. Worse still, he had his mother, brother and family members heavily invested too. They were counting on him. Since most of the deals were made by Fierro, the company hung in the balance while the new group scrambled to get control.

Despite his disgust with the people who "stabbed him in the back," he was figuratively handcuffed and unable to take legal action for fear of the damage to the company and all those who had invested in it. He had to assist where he could trying to keep the now volatile deals and financing alive. He repeatedly fielded questions from shaky contract negotiations and attended meetings with investment bankers. He tried to instill confidence to keep the contracts and financing from crumbling.

Meanwhile, he was scrambling to pay what had become a substantial monthly personal overhead and keep from going under. His wife didn't like the way things were going, and she soon left James, despite their attempts at counseling. Shortly afterward, she hired the services of a lawyer whose ad in the Yellow Pages depicted a pit bull with a studded collar and the caption, "When we bite in, we don't let go."

In less than four months, James Fierro went from a stock position approaching $27 million to nothing. He was flat broke and scrambled to secure short-term consulting projects, while leaning on his original event marketing company for a small draw in order to survive.

Because he had two kids involved, he refused to get a lawyer and "roll around in the mud with a messy legal battle." He openly admits it might have been a mistake because the judge ordered James to pay his wife $10,000 per month.

He was astonished and couldn't believe the order since he had no money to pay even his most basic current bills of rent and payroll. He immediately secured some consulting on the side to meet his escalating obligations. Amidst all this, he noticed a bruise on his chest that wouldn't go away.

Then the bruises started to appear under his armpits. After a couple of months of worry and a biopsy, he was instructed to go to a specialist across town. As he pulled up he saw the sign—The B.C. Cancer Clinic.

"No way. I can't believe this," he thought to himself in shock. Minutes later he sat in a waiting room thinking of his mounting debt, his $10,000 payments, keeping his former microchip company together and general survival. He was in a fog of disbelief and numbness.

When the team of doctors came into the examination room, one woman stepped forward and said in a cold, calculated way, "You have a rare form of cancer called *mycosis fungoydis*, which attacks the largest organ in your body, the skin. It can move to various parts of the body and other organs, if it hasn't yet. There is no known cure and our recommended therapy is intense radiation-beam treatment. The treatment resembles being put on a barbecue spit and rotated, while being bombarded by intense radiation beams to completely burn the outer layer of skin off your body. You will be incapacitated for six months while multiple layers of your skin dry up, die and fall off. All of this is accompanied by a full course of chemotherapy treatment."

"I could feel my heart pounding—sweat began pouring from my forehead and I couldn't breathe," said James. "I got into my car and I had an overwhelming feeling that I couldn't identify with ... I was in a daze. I couldn't even speak."

Soon, with a collection of close friends and Y.E.O. forum members, James uncovered the source of his despair. More than the prospect of the cancer or dying, he couldn't stand the thought of leaving his kids and mom behind. He couldn't imagine his kids growing up without knowing him. "This was the turning point of being able to deal with it," confessed James.

He immediately researched his options, conventional and otherwise. Through Y.E.O. Inventory of Skills he was contacted by leading doctors from Sloan Kettering and the Mayo Clinic. He took his driving style in business to his drive to survive. He met with a fellow who had cured himself of cancer. James created his own regime of diet, vitamin and mineral nutrition, activity, meditation, visualization, parasite cleansing vegetarian meals and drinking plenty of wheat grass. No radiation and no chemotherapy. He believed at his core that, if this disease was manifested by the stress in his life, he could create his new health.

Three months later all the spots were gone and forty-five days after that there was no sign of any cancer. Incidentally, the doctor was not the least bit interested in the solution that worked for James. "I couldn't believe it," said James. "I was excited to share what I had discovered and he didn't take a single note."

During this period, James built and launched a highly successful e-commerce company. Three years later, he still has no sign of cancer and his life is better than ever. He now heads up Venture Resource and three new exciting start-ups. Business is better than ever, and he's having a ball with his children. He's grateful that his children will get to know their father— the way he intended it all along.

The Van Den Berg family

One of the most famous survivors of the Nazi concentration camps, Viktor E. Frankl, commented that "when we talk about attempts to give a man in camp mental courage, we said that he had to be shown something to look forward to in the future. He had to be reminded that life still waited for him, that a human being waited for his return." The story of the Van Den Berg family is an incredible example of what Frankl was talking about.

During World War II word traveled fast in the streets of Amsterdam that the Nazis were sending all Jews to concentration camps deep within European confines. Mani and Hugo Van Den Berg of Amsterdam, first hid their sons Zigmund, six, on a farm and Arnold, three, in a religious household in the country. Then, they too were in hiding, protected by the Bundt family. Despite the fact that the Bundts knew the punishment for hiding known Jews was torture and death, Mani and Hugo stayed hidden in a ten-foot by ten-foot room with no light.

One evening, Mani and Hugo could not take it anymore and they sneaked out at night to try to see the children. They were soon pointed out by other neighbors and arrested on the spot. Not mentioning anything about their children, they were transported immediately in a cattle car to Auschwitz. Thus began the most horrific and terrifying days of their lives.

The men and women were separated upon entry. Women were regularly raped, molested and abused by soldiers. They, like all prisoners, were forced to work in inhumane conditions and some were executed at random to maintain a high level of fear.

According to Mani, "The single most important element of my drive to stay alive was to see my children again." Regularly, the prisoners were lined up and a Nazi captain would throw a hat and tell one prisoner to go for it. He would then shoot that person in the back. He would repeat this a few times a day, every day.

By the time the Russians were advancing, the Nazis increased what they called "production" and were slaughtering ten thousand people each day. Soon, things began to unravel. Pandemonium ensued and Mani made a run for it.

A Nazi soldier had her facing a gun barrel, and she said to him, "I've gone through all this just to see my children again. I am a mother and you are a father. Please let me see my children again."

The soldier replied, "You are all dead and we are all lost." Then he waved her off and she was free.

Hugo's experiences were just as horrific. Hugo constantly thought about his wife and his children. He knew he needed to stay strong for them if and when he got out. But luck played a role too.

One time Hugo was among twelve people digging a ditch. As they heard the distinctive whistling scream of an approaching bomb, eleven men went right and Hugo went left. The bomb killed the eleven other men, but Hugo survived. Another time, Hugo took a piece of bread. He was caught and the usual order was instant death. Instead, he was "taught a lesson" by being beaten to a pulp. Yet, he survived once again.

Finally, at the end, he joined ten thousand prisoners on a "relocation march." By the end of the march only eighty made it the grueling distance. The Nazi captain said casually, "You are all free to go." Hugo immediately went sideways to lie down in a haystack while the others continued down the road to the nearest town. As the seventy-nine kept walking they were gunned down from behind. The Nazis took a body count and realized there was one person missing. Miraculously, Hugo remained hidden.

Over the next few weeks, Hugo was found and transported back to Amsterdam by the Red Cross. He ended up in a rehabilitation hospital. He asked the authorities to locate his wife, yet she was presumed dead. When he arrived at the hospital he weighed eighty pounds which was a grotesque ninety pounds shy of his normal body weight. He was nothing but organs, bones and skin.

A few weeks later he was out for a walk and passed by a friend of his struggling to get a cart over one of the steep Amsterdam canal bridges. Hugo stepped in and assisted his friend.

The friend, who hadn't seen Hugo for years, said, "Hugo, you are alive. Mani never mentioned that you were still alive."

Time stopped. Hugo, in a shocked state, breathed the question, "My wife is still alive?"

"Hugo, your wife is alive and staying at the Red Cross in Harlem, sixteen kilometers away."

Hugo immediately walked the full distance in his frail state and found his wife. Their reunion was full of the greatest depths of emotion possible. They then looked for their boys who were also barely alive. The Van Den Berg family had overcome incredible odds. From a genocide of 6 million Jews, their family remained intact. But, much of their extended family was completely wiped out. Both sets of parents, five brothers, five sisters and all the respective children were killed.

In 1949, they prepared to emigrate to the United States. In two tires of a bicycle hidden in a barn, Hugo hid gold, what remained of his family's life savings. He gave a large portion to the Bundt family and used the rest to help them move to East Los Angeles where a relative was located.

By the time they moved to Los Angeles they had two more boys, twins, Egon and Donnie. Today, three of the four sons are self-made millionaires from simple saving and investments in compound interest bearing vehicles. Their mother, Mani is still alive today and she knows the family remained intact due to their strong bond.

Whether life is on the line or business success is the challenge, Lee

---

Failure gives perspective.
Perspective gives clarity of direction.

Iacocca said it best: "I've had a wonderful and successful career. But next to my family, it really hasn't mattered at all."

COURAGE TO LET GO

For most, the courage to endure is an easy concept to grasp. It takes courage to persist. It takes courage not to give up. It takes courage not to quit. But, for many, the courage to quit doesn't make sense.

There are times when giving up is the only logical option. You may have tried everything in your power yet you still are unable to succeed. In motivational books, it's far from popular to recommend that quitting is an option, yet, under the appropriate circumstances, quitting is the smartest, healthiest thing to do.

FAILURE VERSUS QUITTING

In the minds of most strong-willed people, quitting is paramount to failing. To quit means to fail and the perception remains black and white. You either persist until you succeed or you quit and are a failure.

Failure gives perspective. You may fail and then discover a better way. But failure may also be a clue that what you're doing just isn't going anywhere. How you read the clues, the perceptions that you become savvy to, give you the power to better guide your destiny.

In the words of Rich Adler, "Failure isn't what it's cracked up to be." To fail means your approach didn't work this time. To fail repeatedly means your approach needs a serious change in strategy. To repeatedly fail, given a different strategy each time, might just be your clue to quit. Yet, what about Edison and his ten thousand experiments toward the storage battery?

This is when letting go of certain fixed ideas may be appropriate. Instead of all-out quitting, letting go of elements of your approach may be a better fit. In the end the question you must ask yourself in persisting is...

AT WHAT PRICE?

The overall balance you engage in any pursuit involves the ancient concept of yin and yang. Friendships that you imagine will last forever evolve and sometimes evaporate. Your challenge is to accept the loss with the gain. The lesson with the pain. The process with the end result.

If you have done everything possible in a relationship, with a business or on a project, there comes a time when you need to face the prospect of letting go. Letting go is never easy.

When I was twenty-three, I graduated from college and found a job in Calgary, three hours south of my hometown in Edmonton. When the moving date came, I was very excited. I saved a great deal of money living at home during my studies but I was ready to move on.

When I discussed my plans to move, my parents offered to help me with the move and get me settled in my first apartment. During the move my mom stayed close and she left in tears. Even my dad got a little emotional. Me, the insensitive dope that I was, didn't understand what the big fuss was all about. It was not until recently that I realized their emotions rose from letting go.

They didn't quit being parents, but they had reached a point of letting go. Our two children (as I write this book) are nineteen months and six months. Before long they will have their first day of school and the chapter of pure innocence will be lost. For most parents this is the first of many times where they are faced with that impending event of letting go. I can only imagine how difficult it may be.

The yin and yang of the whole equation is that letting go opens the door for new opportunity. Distancing myself from my parents opened a whole new avenue for us to communicate. I got to know my parents from a different angle and they witnessed new growth in their son.

Letting go of an employee is hard for any employer. Firing is such a negative event. Yet time and again, an employee let go from one job is relieved and goes on to flourish in another scenario.

Letting go of a boyfriend or girlfriend could be the best thing. To date, you may have been kidding yourself that one day it will work ... the birds will sing, the rainbows will light up the horizon, the sun will light your way… *and a cow will jump over the moon.* Sometimes, letting go is not the same as quitting. Instead, it is the next best available option.

The question remains, when is the right time to let go? Answer this question with another question, at what price?

At what price would our relationship have suffered had my parents resisted my move to Calgary? At what price would hanging onto that problem employee do to the company, the other employees and your sanity? At what price is staying in this dysfunctional relationship doing to your future? Would it take six months to work things out? Six years? Sixty? At what price are you willing to make it work?

JUST LET IT GO

I was talking with a friend and colleague Thelma Box, who facilitates a self-development course called Choices. Thelma is one of those people who wouldn't know how to mince words if she tried. If you ever want the truth in its raw form, just have a conversation with Thelma.

In our conversation I mentioned that my wife and I had an agreement to never go to bed angry. But I had gone to bed angry a couple of times in the last few months, and Thelma's reaction was immediate and to the point.

"So, you'd rather be right than happy!" she said staring at me without blinking.

Here's a clue: if something stings it's probably a truth. Thelma was right. I went to bed mad about something that I had a different point of view on. Like every other human being on the planet, I like to be right. But at what price? My happiness, for one.

Thelma's simple truth made all the difference in my marriage. Now I always ask myself, do I want to be right or happy? It's often an easy choice.

In a conversation with an Ayurvedic teacher from India, I asked him if he ever got angry. He said, "Yes I do. Then I ask myself, 'What is the use of this?' and then I let it go." Basically the same equation. Would you rather be right or happy?

The healthiest approach is to know what is past is past. Even a sense of humor helps out now and then. Bob Uecker is a sportscaster and is highly

Do you want to be right or happy?

regarded as the most mediocre major league baseball player ever. Bob was once asked how he handled the pressure as a player. In classic Uecker fashion he said, "It was easy. I'd strike out and put the pressure on the guy behind me."

HITTING YOUR FIST AGAINST A BRICK WALL

Personally, I didn't fully grasp the concept of quitting versus letting go until I had a conversation with a close friend about my failing first marriage. I had gone through hell and back many times over and I couldn't see an end in sight.

As we sat by the Bow River, I said in a feeble voice, "I don't know what to do."

My friend knew my situation, and he knew the facts from the past three years. Then he said the word I could not accept—"Quit."

"I can't quit. I do not quit at anything," I replied.

"Vince," he said, "It's like you're trying to knock a hole in a brick wall by just using your fist. Pretty soon your knuckles start bleeding. But you keep banging away at the wall. Eventually, your fingers fall off. You keep banging. Now you're down to the stub of your wrist. But you're not a quitter. So you keep banging. Judging by what you have gone through emotionally, you're down to your elbow and you're still trying to succeed. When are you going to figure out that it is okay to let go when the cost has become too great?"

Since that time, I have recognized the qualities of a number of people who spent a good deal of their lives trying to make dysfunctional relationships work. When they are in the throes of a separation or divorce, they can't stomach the thought of quitting.

In most frustrating scenarios in life, it is sometimes best to just give up for the day. I have five staff members at my office and there is an unwritten (but often quoted) rule that if it's not fun, we go home. We know we're not good to anyone if we're feeling miserable. Usually, just the knowledge that one could just go home at any point makes the rest of the day go smoother.

Even in cases where one of us feels out of sync with the flow of the day, it means that it's time for a break. A quick pattern interruption helps, with a walk down to the corner, and then it's back to the task at hand.

IT MAY BE YOUR DESTINY

Letting go is like surrendering to God. How could you possibly know what is in store for you? How do you know you aren't getting in your own way? The challenge is to detach yourself from your results. Make the process ultimately more important than the result. Letting go might very well be the best option you have yet to exercise.

IN SUMMARY

1. Have no regrets.
2. Shift your actions from satisfactory to significant.
3. Your best is good enough.
4. Perfectionism is the lowest form of excellence.
5. Have the courage to endure through the sacrifice.
6. When you're in the middle of a mess, the closet is halfway cleaned.
7. If you start something, finish it. "Start ... Finish."
8. Raise yourself to new perspectives, "New Altitudes."
9. Cherish your family, because they're the only thing you truly have.
10. Ask "At what price?" If it's too high, have the courage and the intelligence to let go.

Excellence in achievement has never been easy. It is a constant flux of dogged determination balanced with a methodical approach. Keeping everything in perspective involves an awareness and an elusive objective—self-honesty.

Figuring out achievement is sometimes a moot point. When other people get involved, achievement can take countless other twists. So, the next Invinceable Principle involves strategies and approaches for dealing with others. Utilizing the four rules for strong relationships will take you to even higher levels of life mastery.

Principle 8 ...Utilize 4 Tools for Strong Relationships

Depending on your day today—pick the most appropriate quote:

"Hell is other people."
–Jean-Paul Sartre*

"Relationships are meaningful because they are opportunities to expand our hearts and become more deeply loving."
–Marianne Williamson**

The four tools: If you do nothing else, use the following four tools and your relationships will strengthen and your life will flow just a little better. The first is "F³P²," which is an acronym for "First Find Facts Then Present Perspective." By first finding out what the other person is saying, or implying, or even rumored to have done, and then presenting your perspective, it will be more accurately delivered.

The second tool is simply to talk about others as if they are present. All too often we verbalize our frustrations about others only to suffer the embarrassment of being catty about another person. Plus, you have signaled to others that you and your opinion about others cannot be trusted to be held in confidence.

The third tool is the twenty-four hour rule. When in doubt, don't. At least, not just yet. Before you send that e-mail, make that retaliatory phone call, biting comment or nasty letter, wait twenty-four hours.

Finally, the fourth and last tool is to accept the burden of responsibility. Hold yourself accountable for all your results, and you will move forward with a more empowered state.

Before we explore the details of these four tools, let's first get an overview of the situations and relationships to which they could apply.

* Considered the father of modern existentialism. **Author of *A Return to Love*

> # The Latin root for the word communication is "to make common."

THE BIG PICTURE

We are not alone in this world. Francis Bacon said, "Whosoever is delighted in solitude is either wild beast or god." Sure, we are all faced at some time or another with the special qualities necessary to live in solitude. But more often than not, we go to work, home, restaurants, shopping and there they are ... people.

If we master communication, we strengthen our relationships. The Latin root of the word communication is "to make common." In other words, through communication, we make common our likeminded perspectives or disagreements. Without communication, a dozen eyewitnesses to the same event cannot agree on a single explanation. Hence, we are somewhat shut in by our own subjectivity.

Your truth is *your* truth. Others have their own truth, too. This book has covered how people think, we have explored the ways to erode judgmentalism, and we have searched for ways to have faith in others. Yet as the opening quotes indicate, people (relationships) can be the bane or the beauty of what life has to offer.

ACCEPTANCE

People are not perfect (especially stubborn perfectionists). Get over it. People will never cease to amaze both positively and negatively. Acceptance is "what is, is."

For a while I sold new homes and was amazed at the expectations of some buyers. Some buyers would simply lose patience if there were cracks in walls or things were not exactly as they visualized. Think about it.

First, wood is an imperfect material. It expands, contracts, dries and bends with changes in heat, humidity and age. Second, people draw blueprints. Third, over the course of five months, a few hundred imperfect human beings were involved in the process of building the house. Plus, as one builder put it, "All the doctors and lawyers were busy, so these are the people we had working on your house." He sarcastically implied that some of the tradespeople might not have thought their whole responsibility through to an intelligent conclusion.

So, every so often I'd have a furious buyer threatening to sue because he found a crack in the wall or a white fridge instead of a black one. Clearly, there was either an unavoidable situation or a failure to properly communicate. The bottom line would always be: Let's find the solution and move on.

In sales I learned that before communicating, it helped me to categorize the individual first in order to get my message across best.

EINSTEIN, PICASSO, MOTHER THERESA, GENERAL PATTON

By finding out how people process information, you will enjoy a better hit ratio with the messages you send. In no particular order, the four personality types are as follows:

1. Einstein. This kind of person loves to analyze and collect data. The more information they get, the better they feel. They will rarely make a decision without collecting all the facts and they love analyzing all the details.

2. Picasso. This person is more of a creative type. They have a talent for looking at things from different angles, if any angle at all. They're more interested in the doing than the method. They live in the now, and time is often irrelevant. They often live by the motto, "Ready, fire, aim." They don't understand the Einstein types, and vice versa. They like to make quick decisions as long as fun has something to do with it.

3. Mother Theresa. This type is your classic caregiver. They love to help others and would rather play a support role than lead. They know people well and can size them up quickly. They are great at building a support network and prefer to make decisions by consensus.

4. General Patton. Being last on the list drives them crazy. They love to be out front and better still, organizing others. They know they are right and are frustrated with others who haven't caught on to it yet. They make great delegators and make decisions based on a quick study. But most important, they want to do the talking and they definitely want to make the decisions or lead the decision-making process.

Despite the fact that these four personality types are generalizations, the usefulness in sizing up a person before you talk to them is obvious. You wouldn't expect to get a quick decision from an Einstein any sooner than you would expect to get a well-thought-out plan by a Picasso.

Any combination of the above personality types is also possible. There may be a dominant General Patton type with a good deal of Picasso. Entrepreneurs would fit this type of profile. There may be a Mother Theresa type crossed with an Einstein profile. Medical professionals and university professors would fit this description.

Just remember what kind of person you are dealing with and then you are better prepared for a positive interaction. There are three areas that are critical to how you interact with others. They are:

1. Family: Families are where you will learn the most about how to best communicate. Why? Because they're not going anywhere and they keep coming around every so often. Families are also a curious collection of personalities and personal agendas. Interaction is always an adventure of either nerves or carefree bliss. You can practice unorthodox communication styles with your brother that you wouldn't dare try on a coworker.

Families are the ultimate training ground for acceptance of others. Whether you are a parent with higher hopes for your twenty-year-old than she has for herself, or you have expectations that your parents should be a certain way. No acceptance ... meltdown.

Think of the words from Paul the Apostle who wrote, "Let each of you esteem and look upon and be concerned for not (merely) his own interests, but also each for the interests of the others." Families hand you those challenges and opportunities in abundance.

2. Marriages and Primary Relationships: Bill Cosby said, "For two people in marriage to live together day after day is unquestionably the one miracle the Vatican has overlooked." Again, acceptance is a key ingredient in a healthy marriage or primary relationship.

According to Charles L. Allen, "One of the important things about marriage is to be accepted. Love is the basis of marriage, but there are many married people who have never felt accepted. Marriage is not a reformatory, and spouses need to reach out to each other without criticism or reserva-

> # With the foundation of acceptance, the relationship is then allowed to focus on communication and self-esteem issues.

tions. To live with a wife or husband who does not accept you is a dark valley to walk through."

With the foundation of acceptance, the relationship is then allowed to focus on communication and self-esteem issues. Research by Dr. Robert C. Kolodney shows that at the Masters and Johnson Institute in St. Louis, 90 percent of the therapy focuses on communication and self-esteem issues and only 10 percent focuses on the physical and sexual problems in the relationship. Interestingly though, a large percentage of counseling is initiated with the primary intention of working on the physical issues, and it is not until later that communication or self-esteem issues surface.

3. Work: Work has become our extended family. With dual-income households, the family unit has evolved into an odd three-way family of divided loyalties. Acceptance of this work family is no different. Of course, there's always the choice to leave, but the large part of our day is a struggle with accepting our bosses, peers and subordinates.

For all of the above, acceptance is a base from which to communicate well and utilize the following first tool for building strong relationships.

Tool #1—F^3P^2 First Find Facts Then Present Perspective

How important is effective communication? According to leadership author Max DePree, "there may be no single thing more important in our effort to achieve meaningful work and fulfilling relationships than to learn to practice the art of communication."

Peter Drucker claims that 60 percent of all management problems result from poor communication. In addition, a poll of marriage counselors surveyed indicated that more than half of all divorces are a direct result from ineffective communication between spouses.

F^3P^2 is simple ... listen, understand then talk. The sad fact is that listening is rarely part of the equation. Relationship guru, Leo Buscaglia states, "Most conversations are just alternating monologues. The question is, is there any real listening going on?" The other day I went out for lunch with a friend. I might have gotten a couple of dozen words in during the hour we met. At the end of the meal, my friend said he thought "it was a great conversation," and that he found me "very inspirational." Interesting. Maybe this is what William Shakespeare meant when he said, "Men of few words are the best men."

The ultimate in rude and immature behavior is people who talk while another person is speaking. Sure, you can get away with it in a large crowd. But how does this make it any more acceptable? I have a colleague who works with such an individual. He regularly talks or makes a loud yawning noise when others speak at their company meetings. Yet, when it's his turn to speak, he expects rapt attention from everyone and draws out his thoughts in a random, disorganized manner. In effect, he manages to alienate most of the people around him with his egomaniacal behavior. One day he was overheard wondering why at age thirty-five he still hadn't found that "special someone." One wonders who would put up with that kind of self-centered arrogance? F^3P^2 is more than a communication technique. It is common sense.

The net effect is that good communication relies on good listening, first and foremost. Do the opposite and you will end up being a lonely and annoying person.

DO *NOT* RELY ON FIRST IMPRESSIONS

It normally takes just seconds to size up a person and gain a first impression. Bad, or good, the first impression is there for a long time. An expert in communication, George Walther, does an extraordinary exercise in one of his presentations.

He gets the audience to pair up and then describe their favorite dessert in less than fifteen seconds. The roles switch and the next person describes qualities about his or her favorite dessert. Then, George instructs the audience to come up with adjectives each person would use to describe his or her partner.

The results were interesting. Each audience member had little difficulty being able to size up his or her partner in under fifteen seconds. The exercise made it abundantly clear how important a first impression is. It also became clear that unconscious messages might be sent to others that you don't want to give or that aren't particularly accurate.

Last year I attended a reception during a showcase for meeting planners in search of speakers. At the reception I was introduced to a speaker named Joan Brock. She held out her hand and I shook it. Joan had somewhat droopy eyes and didn't bother to make eye contact with me. I instantly felt like she was somewhat rude, and I soon turned and walked off, muttering to myself that I had better things to do than to be ignored in such a way.

The next day I sat in the crowd observing the other speakers. Then Joan Brock was introduced and led up to the stage. She was completely blind. If I could have crawled in a hole, I would have. I felt like I had just been crowned the king of all assholes. I felt like a total jerk.

Fortunately, Joan didn't know I had done this until I apologized to her afterward. Still, I learned my lesson again: F^3P^2 applies to first impressions as well.

FIVE STEPS TO F^3P^2

1. Be a sponge. Take in any and all information. You choose later what you want to keep and what to discard.

2. Catch yourself resisting anything that is said to you. Do not hang on one thought while the talker is communicating. Listen from the first word spoken to the last.

3. Do not interrupt.

4. If confused, clarify what you believe their meaning or intent was. Clarify facts as you interpreted them. Then and only then—

5. Present your perspective.

COMMUNICATION TECHNIQUES

One way to understand how to do something is to first understand how not to do it. Notice in both the following cases the communication was one-sided and stilted.

When I was first married and having difficulty, I was approached out of the blue by my father-in-law. He tore into me like a man possessed. He knew his daughter was in emotional pain and to him it was clearly all my fault. The more he talked, ranted, insulted and demeaned, the more I reminded myself that he had only heard one side of the story. I didn't say more than a few, "I understands," followed by, "You feel protective of your daughter."

The tongue-lashing lasted about twenty minutes and then he stiffened up, looked me square in the eye, reached out to shake my hand, said "Well I feel better!" and walked off to his car.

I stood there for ten minutes wondering what happened. Sure, this fellow needed to get something off his chest, and I did use good listening techniques, but he alienated me in the process.

Here is another example of not listening: It happened when I was winding down my real estate responsibilities and speaking professionally on a part-time basis. At the time, there was a local company that put on a course for people wanting to begin public speaking. It was expensive and lasted three days.

One of the representatives kept calling me to get me to take the course. I kept saying that I wasn't interested and already had a good head start in my speaking business. "You can always learn something," he said.

"For that much money, I'd want to learn a whole lot," I said and added that I didn't have the money to spend anyway. More than anything, I was skeptical about whether I would gain enough knowledge warranting the time and cost.

Finally, I gave in to his persistence. The bread and butter for the company was a customer service program that was taught nationwide, and I finally figured there had to be something they could offer. Plus, they promised a complete money-back guarantee. I verbally confirmed this with the rep and then I sent deposit of a hundred dollars.

In the past, I had taken adult learning courses and knew the value of getting involved. Despite my skepticism, I made a commitment to give 100 percent all the time. It would simply not be fair to take the course, arms folded, and expect to learn something through osmosis.

I quickly learned that the course aimed to meet the needs of people across the board. Some there were afraid of public speaking, while others were curious about the speaking business. I was the only one who had done any professional public speaking.

Each module in the course covered a variety of areas in the business and techniques of speaking. With each module I got involved and tried to learn something. With each module my frustration grew for saying yes in the first place. Halfway through I was asked how I was enjoying the course and I said I was disappointed. "Don't give up," I was promised. "There's more to come."

The "graduation" involved each person doing a five-minute presentation. One person went crying out of the room in fear of making a fool of herself.

After the course I thought long and hard about the value that I got from the course. In the end I was extremely disappointed and called the company to let them know. "Heck, they're a customer service company. If anybody would know how to handle a situation like this, they would," I thought naively.

The wailing and gnashing of teeth that followed was unbelievable. My explanation of giving 100 percent in order to give it a fair shot did not sink in. The representative was clearly hurt by my dissatisfaction. Moreover, he was shocked to learn I wouldn't pay the balance. "You took the course, you stayed, you should pay!" he exclaimed.

Later that day I received a phone call from the owner of the company. While putting me on speakerphone (since he had more than two people in his office he proceeded to slice and dice me). He insulted me, questioned my ethics, condescended by going through each module like someone with a superiority complex. His phone call succeeded in embarrassing and pissing me off all at once.

This, so-called customer service expert managed to feign listening skills where he made sure that I knew I was wrong and he was right. The whole thing turned into a huge farce. Still, to this day, I am amazed that the worst customer service experience of my life came from a company that teaches customer service... Just when you think you've seen it all!

To this day I come across these people at various times and the reception I get is straight out of junior high school. I even made a point of saying "Hi" once and the owner looked at me and said, "You've gained weight, haven't you?"

The point of the story is this: What could have been different had they listened and understood more? Communication involves a balance of listening, understanding and then talking. The following is a blueprint you can use to this end.

BLUEPRINT FOR COMMUNICATION

In the process of P^2 you still need to exercise some listening savvy. It is critical to communicate in a way that is without judgment of another. In order to truly communicate, it is necessary to get through the mired confusion of timing, intent and interpretation. The following seven-step plan can act as a blueprint for how and when you get your message across.

1. The Go-Ahead: "May I check something out with you?"

Find out if the timing is good to bring up what is on your mind.

2. The Intent: "My intention of bringing up what happened last night is to have a better relationship with you."

The intent of conversation needs to be set as a beacon for the balance of the communication. If you leave out the intent, you may be subject to deaf ears. The person may assume that your intent is to attack or make wrong.

Since there are approximately fourteen thousand interpretations for the five hundred most-used words in the English language (resulting in an average of twenty-eight meanings-per-word) the importance of the intent cannot be underestimated.

Worse, there are more than 700,000 kinds of nonverbal communications. Therefore, the intent of your conversation must be clarified. Ensure the receiver knows your intention. Listen and ensure that your intent is clearly received and understood.

3. Clarify: "I noticed you slammed the door last night. Do you agree that you did slam the door?"

Clarify what you noticed and gain agreement that this is the way they saw it, too.

4. Categorize: "I heard and saw you slam the door after hearing that we were going out to dinner without you. I couldn't help but think that you were hurt by being excluded from the group."

Instead of judging someone as wrong or right, categorize the action in a way that you experienced it with one of your five senses (i.e., "I heard, saw, touched, smelled, tasted"). Add your interpretation or perception without making the other person wrong for their actions.

5. Agreement of Your Perception: "Is that the way you see (or feel, or understand) it?"

Instantly check in with them and get an agreement of your interpretation or perception.

6. How It Makes You Feel: "I felt misunderstood at that time. I actually didn't know you were home at the time."

Give the receiver perspective on your feelings. People are less inclined to shut you out if they know your feelings are on the line. Don't get confused with the line "I feel you were wrong." That is NOT the way to open the dialogue.

7. Desired Result: "Next time I will make a point of checking the house to see if you are here."

At this point, the discussion may very well open up for a more detailed dialogue. The result is to set the tone for better communication and may even be an end in itself. Let's recap.

RECAP:

1. **"Go-ahead"...** "May I..."

2. **Intent...** "My intent is..."

3. **Clarify...** "What I noticed is..."

4. **Categorize...** "I interpreted this as..."

5. **Agreement...** "Is this correct?"

6. **Feeling...** "It made me feel..."

7. **Results...** "I would like to..."

> # What could have been different had you listened carefully and understood more?

"A good listener is not only popular everywhere,
but after a while he gets to know something."
—Wilson Mizner

NEGOTIATION AND GAINING AGREEMENT

Any kind of agreement involves some form of negotiation. As a result, following a few simple rules will get you further than a haphazard approach to winning someone over. Follow this ten-step process and repeat it until you are satisfied with the result.

1. Dedicate your negotiation to win/win. Give the other person every confidence that this will be your approach.

2. Be crystal clear on what you want to accomplish. Know exactly what you want as a result from this meeting. It never hurts to tell the other people present the end result. For example, when I walked up to the negotiation table during a real estate transaction, the first thing I would say was: "First off, I want you to know, we are going to sell your house, tonight!"

3. Ensure all decision makers are present. If they are not, you are spinning your wheels. Get the decision maker(s) there and then proceed.

4. F³... more than ... P². Listen, probe, understand and clarify. Finding facts means finding their facts. What do they want to accomplish?

5. Find common ground on the topic. Build rapport. Know your commonalties and build from there.

6. List wins for the other person. Take a run at interpreting the various wins that the recipient may get from dealing with you. Show that you care about the position that they will take away.

7. State your case. Now is the soonest you would start selling your point of view and position. The recipient is expecting to find out what you want in the deal.

8. Verbalize your concerns and obtain more information if possible. Deal with those concerns and the solutions as you see them. They may have objections and you must deal with these before you move on to step 9.

9. Ask for a decision. If you get a yes, congratulations! If you receive a no, go back to step 1 and keep looping through steps 1–9 until you get a yes.

10. Follow-up. It never hurts to find out someone's thoughts through follow-up. There may be something both of you missed the first time. Give them a chance to tell you about things that have come up in the meantime. Following-up proves that you are committed to a win/win scenario.

In situations of conflict there are some landmines and overriding rules.

• Never give ultimatums. This will lead to win/lose or lose/lose every time.

• Stay on topic. Conflict can surface other issues that distract from the task of gaining agreement. Through active listening you must notice the distractions and offer to discuss those later.

• Always be accountable. Never come from the place of playing the victim. You lose credibility and diminish your empowerment toward finding a solution. This takes any pressure off the other person to have to change. You then are wasting your time.

FEEDBACK

I don't know too many people whose first reaction would be, "Oh goody... feedback." All too often we are dishing out feedback with the intention of straightening someone out. Who likes to be straightened out?

But, there is a time and a place for feedback, and there is a better way to give it. With F^3P^2 we will be better equipped to deliver and receive it effectively.

How to apply the F^3P^2 formula to receive feedback:

1. Find facts on why they gave you feedback.

2. Find facts on their feelings about what they said.

3. Present your perspective on your feelings about the feedback.

4. Present your perspective on the feedback. You may agree with some parts and disagree with others.

5. Agree on results or agree to disagree. Agree on where to go from here.

BOUNDARIES

Sometimes it is just untenable how a person is or what they do. Your place is not to judge them, yet the very qualities or patterns that this person exhibits get under your skin. Your best solution is to set a boundary for that person to know about when they are around you.

For example, you may work with someone who controls situations with anger and flys into a rage when things do not go their way. Instead of telling them they are wrong for doing that, use a personal boundary for them to make a choice. Follow the seven-step blueprint for communication.

BLUEPRINT FOR BOUNDARY COMMUNICATION

1. Go-ahead... "May I bring up the time you yelled about the quota report the other day?"

2. Intent... "My intent is to have a stronger working relationship with you."

3. Clarify... "What I noticed is you yelled a lot and it seemed it was important to you to ensure you got your way."

4. Categorize... "I interpreted this as one of the ways you have historically communicated your point of view."

5. Agreement... "Is this correct?"

6. Feeling... "It made me feel extremely uncomfortable and it simply doesn't work for me."

7. Results... "I consider this a boundary preventing us from having a strong working relationship. Therefore, when working with me, I'll ask that you keep your voice at a moderate level. Should you fly off the handle like that, I will simply leave the room. I am not saying that you need not do this with anyone else, it's just that I will not work this way."

From here on in, your coworker will know the rules that work for you.

Ensure that you make it clear that they are not wrong for doing what they do. Clarify that it just doesn't work for you and you will absolutely not be a part of it.

This boundary strategy works at home, with your parents, with your kids, with your spouse and anyone else with whom you interact closely. It is not easy and sometimes the message is not fully understood. Exercising your boundary will send a clear message that you meant what you said.

Once you set a boundary, keep it. If things should change, then go through the communication seven steps of the blueprint and reestablish your ground.

Be aware that this blueprint is a powerful tool that can sometimes be used to manipulate for negative purposes. This is *not* virtuous and will only serve to hurt. If your intent is constructive, generally only good can come from it. If your intent is destructive, then you may have won the battle but lost the war.

TOOL #2—TALK ABOUT OTHERS AS IF THEY WERE PRESENT

Think about something negative that you said about someone else recently. Would you say that same thing in front of them? It really is quite easy to say things behind someone's back, but, it will come around to bite you later.

Sure it would be interesting to call off all bets and just let your comments fly, like the ongoing bitterness between British politicians Winston Churchill and Lady Astor, where numerous sarcastic exchanges were recorded. Once Lady Astor, upset with Churchill for a stand he took, said, "Sir Winston, if you were my husband I'd poison your tea." Churchill shot back with, "Lady Astor, if you were my wife, I'd drink it."

Another time Lady Astor, disgusted with Churchill's drinking, found him inebriated at a public gathering. "Mr. Prime Minister, you are drunk," she said loud enough for all to hear. He responded with his quick wit, "Yes I am drunk and you ... are ugly. But tomorrow, I will be sober."

Clearly a strategy of telling others what you think with a sharp tongue has its price. Behind someone's back, or to their face, cutting comments fail to go in the right direction. This will only breed resentment and revenge.

Choosing what to say about another sounds easier than it really is.

ARE YOU BEING THE WAY YOU WANT THEM TO BE?

This is a tough question to get past if your comments are critical or judgmental. Just for practice, pick a person in your life you love to gossip about. List off the qualities you would want them to have or display. Now, go over the list and *honestly* pick which things *you* are currently doing.

If there are things that you find you are not doing, you've got some work on your hands. Either you can change the way you do things or you can knuckle down and accept the way they are.

WHAT UNDERLYING MESSAGES ARE YOU TELLING THE PERSON WITH YOU?

Imagine you are talking negatively about another person. You have succeeded in giving your opinion about another. You have also succeeded in conveying to them you can't be trusted with what you might think about them. Every time I hear someone's character get slammed by another person, I wonder when it will be my turn to get talked about.

When I was the managing director of the Alberta Luge Association, we often had dealings with the national associations in Ottawa. One administrator in particular would regularly complain bitterly about the incompetence or stupidity of somebody. She openly labeled people left, right and center to the point where we wondered if anybody could do something right. Even at the tender age of twenty-three I wondered when it would be my turn at being talked about in such a manner. (It turned out to be sooner than I expected.)

The effect these people have is the exact opposite of networking. They alienate people and cause an environment of distrust. The best thing to do with people like this is just steer clear. Sometimes that is impossible. Just don't get reduced to their level. If you do, catch yourself and "zip it."

A CASE STUDY: BILL, JUNE AND THE MOTHER-IN-LAW

It became clear in the marriage between Bill and June that June's mother got under Bill's skin. He was civil to his mother-in-law but behind her back he would steam about some of the things she said. Even if she said nothing, Bill would be irritated for one reason or another. Some of the same things that bothered Bill also bothered June.

Sometimes at night, June would openly complain about her mother, and this, to Bill, would be like throwing gasoline on the fire. He would chime in and it became a lynching without the mother present.

One day, Bill was frustrated about his mother-in-law for something she did and June had had enough. She encouraged Bill to talk with his mother-in-law. After a couple of weeks and a good deal of encouragement, Bill went to talk with her. What ensued was like a bad train wreck.

Bill let it slip that June had also been irritated by what her mother said. He didn't have much experience communicating in situations like this, and the mother-in-law felt verbally attacked. Plus, the mother-in-law chose not to find the intent behind Bill's efforts. June found out about how hurt her mother was and asked Bill what he said to hurt her mother so much.

Bill was angry with June for sending him in to speak to her mother only to be criticized for how he said it. June was angry with herself for saying disparaging things about her mom. The mother-in-law was angry with both of them for attacking her in person and behind her back. They were angry with her for being so stubborn.

This problem happened fifteen years ago and there is still tension among everyone. According to Bill, "The whole thing is still a mess and nobody gets along." What did change was that June made a commitment always to talk about others as if they were present.

RAPPORT

Talking about others as if they are present has a great deal to do with rapport. Think of rapport as a combination of trust, harmony and cooperation in a relationship. Usually, rapport is thought of in a casual context. But rapport has critical applications in any relationship.

Consistently check your rapport. Is the trust being strengthened, is harmony being cultivated, am I focused on cooperation where everyone wins? Keeping this approach will take you further away from ever wanting to say a disparaging thing about another person again.

Consistently check your rapport.

TOOL #3—THE 24-HOUR RULE

One day I was at the office and I had been upset about something that happened with a client. This client was the president of a large real estate franchise and had purposely set up a win/lose situation. He won and I lost. I immediately sat down to write a scathing letter outlining how this person had been wrong and was out of line. I was so angry that I made a point of adding extra adjectives to make my point.

I sat on the letter for a few minutes having printed and aggressively signing it—practically ripping it as I did so. I stewed for a little while longer and then thought I might call my dad for his advice. This is when he told me of the 24-hour rule.

He, too, wrote letters, but he made it a policy to wait at least twenty-four hours before he sent them. He would always leave the envelope open and reread the letter the next day. If he still felt it was a good idea, he would seal it up and send it off. But most of the time he would just chuckle at the thought of what kind of mud slinging this letter would bring and toss it in the garbage.

I waited twenty-four hours. This was sufficient enough time to cool off and reconsider the intelligence of sending this diatribe. The letter found its way to the garbage can the next day.

WHEN IN DOUBT, DON'T

E-mail is probably the worst avenue for this kind of slip up in judgment. With this instantaneous communication, in writing no less, the results can be less than charming. Compound this with "cc's" sent to your address list and you could be the next Bozo-of-the-Year award winner.

Chat rooms on the Internet are prime locations for regrettable prose. Liability should always be a concern where each word must be carefully considered.

Cocktail parties are a place where a few drinks add meaning to the cliché, "Loose lips sink ships." It can be difficult to know exactly what you should and should not say in today's politically correct environment.

The bottom line is then—when in doubt, *don't.* If you doubt sending an e-mail—don't. If you doubt typing something in a chat room is the smartest thing to do—don't. If you find yourself wondering if what you might say about another person at a cocktail party might come back to haunt you—don't.

STRAIGHTENING PEOPLE OUT

"Consider how hard it is to change yourself and you'll understand
what little chance you have of trying to change others."
–Jacob M. Braude

In more visual terms, my Irish grandmother often said, "Straightening people out is like straightening a dog's hind leg. The minute you let go, it just goes back the way it was in the first place." In effect, the 24-hour rule gives you breathing space just to take the emotion out of a letter or comment. Given a more logical approach, your choices may be different.

Still not convinced? Think of the advice from the great American philosopher, Thumper: "If you can't say anything nice, don't say anything at all."

BURDEN OF RESPONSIBILITY

Are you fulfilled in your life? What areas are lacking? What are you searching for? These are all questions that you ask yourself either consciously or unconsciously, but they are always present. But there is one question that can get you into a whole quagmire of confusion, if you're not careful: What are you counting on others to provide?

If this question resonates with you, you are unconsciously delivering a message to others, "I have needs that you *must* provide." On the flip side, if you do not ask this question, you open the door for better self-acceptance and will be in a position to feel better about others.

Yes, we all have expectations of others, but relying on others to meet our needs leads to disempowerment. The hierarchy of needs was made famous by A.H. Maslow in 1954. In order, from primary to higher-order needs, they are:

1. **Physiological.** Survival needs. For example, food, drink, physical health.

> # Relying on others to meet our needs leads to disempowerment.

2. Safety. Physical and emotional security. For example, shelter, clothing, protection from attack (unemployment insurance, old age pension).

3. Affection needs. Affection and the need to belong. For example, the family unit, loved ones, work groups.

4. Esteem needs. For self-respect and achievement. For example, recognition and appreciation of accomplishments.

5. Self-fulfillment needs. Otherwise known as self-actualization, where people use their potential to achieve their maximum capability.

As the primary needs are met, a higher-order need can then be satisfied. First, confusion occurs when the burden of responsibility is shifted externally. For example, shifting the responsibility for your affection needs to another is reasonable, but first you must bear the burden of the responsibility for making it happen. Put yourself in amidst others. Ask for a hug. Lead by example.

You will empower yourself more if you recognize that you are responsible for each need. What will you do to make it happen? You will then shift into solution mode quicker. By taking the burden onto yourself, you immediately take pressure off others.

It's like pushing on another person. In order to keep standing they have to counterbalance their weight back at you. The more you push, the more they need to push back. But, the second you take the pressure off, you both stand fine on your own.

The second possible confusion occurs after safety needs are met. Affection needs must be met in some ways in order to meet esteem needs. In order to do this, you may consider joining a group or a service club. Do not become an island. Get back with family, join groups at work, spend time with old friends. You will then be able to nurture self-esteem and the esteem of others.

SELF-ESTEEM

Nathaniel Branden, Ph.D., the author of *The Art of Living Consciously,* defines self-esteem as "The disposition to experience oneself as being competent to cope with the basic challenges of life and of being worthy of happiness." Through an approach subscribing to the burden of responsibility, Branden offers six practices that are the "pillars of self-esteem."

1. The practice of living consciously—It is about knowing your conscious and unconscious truths. This relates to your cognitive behavior model where you are aware of the reasons for your results.

2. The practice of self-acceptance—Attempting to live without negative self-judgmentalism. You have feelings and thoughts that must be dealt with as part of a process of seeking fulfillment.

3. The practice of self-responsibility—Be accountable to yourself for all your actions and even results. Empower yourself to move forward.

4. The practice of self-assertiveness—Draw on your own strength. You know what your boundaries are. You know what will and will not work for you.

5. The practice of living purposefully—Live "on purpose." Do this through proactive self-discovery. You know who you are and you know (as best you can) your purpose on earth.

6. The practice of personal integrity—Walk your talk. Your walk must be symbiotic with how you feel and think.

Obviously this is an ambitious list. I believe that is why self-esteem is a rare commodity today. It takes work! It takes time! It takes commitment! Especially, it takes a journey within, which I have learned, most people do not want to take.

Interestingly, if you apply each of these six things to an infant, each quality is inherent. A child will live consciously. There is no judgmentalism. A child will always initially attempt to be self-responsible. "I want that toy, I reach for it." A child knows his or her boundaries and will let you know when those boundaries are crossed. A child naturally lives on purpose. A child lives in integrity. There is no hidden agenda nor playing politics— just simple truth.

As adults, we have unlearned these practices. It will take effort to own them again. But please, *do not take any of this to an extreme.*

On one extreme is the self. The reader may interpret that I am proposing a narcissistic or megalomaniacal approach. We are part of the whole, we are not alone and we must find a way to strengthen self-esteem to contribute to our relationships.

On the other extreme is part of a spiritual movement that implies turning your self-esteem problems completely over to God. Bob Osborne, the minister from my hometown church, calls it "the Jesus blind." There is a myriad of solutions available. We have a window of opportunity, and we will limit ourselves by pulling down the blind. The challenge lies in recognizing God's wisdom in giving us the strength to be proactive. Use your God-given talents for curiosity and potential for growth.

There is a balance, which is—as usual—a process. By reaching for your highest potential, and finding yourself, you will strike the best balance of self-effort and the natural order of things, or God's way.

Whose problem is it?

Answer this question and you will know where the burden of responsibility lies. Dr. Howard Lauria (the renowned heart surgeon mentioned in the last chapter) mentioned something interesting to me. He said he was consistently amazed that when people are told they are smoking too much, eating food too high in fat, or not exercising enough, they seem to be looking for a solution outside themselves. His patients seem almost in a mild state of shock when they are asked to decide what kind of life they want to lead. They sometimes ask for a special medication or new kind of treatment. Bottom line—it's not Howard's problem. Howard knows they will be empowered by making their own choices and acting on them.

I am amazed when the American freedom of rights are twisted around to meet the needs of radical interest groups. It does mean a freedom of rights, but *not* a freedom from responsibility! We each have a personal accountability and also a social accountability. Be the change that you want to see in the world. Whose problem is it? Each one of us must say "me!"

Follow the leadership adage: Give me solutions not problems. What are the problems you observe? How are you being part of the solution? Inaction

> # Freedom of rights? Yes.
> # Freedom from responsibility? No!

means you condone it! Shift from victim to responsible behavior. Global warming, water shortages, over-population, violence in movies/video games/music, the neighbor's dog that defecates on your lawn... Whose problem is it?

IN SUMMARY

1. Accept others for exactly who they are.
2. Before delivering information, use the categories of personality types to your advantage. Is that person an Einstein, Picasso, Mother Theresa or General Patton?
3. F^3P^2—First Find Facts (3 Fs), then Present Perspective (2 Ps)
4. Memorize and use the blueprint for communications.
   - Go-ahead ... "May I..."
   - Intent ... "My intent is..."
   - Clarify ... "What I noticed is..."
   - Categorize ... "I interpreted this as..."
   - Agreement ... "Is this correct?"
   - Feeling ... "It made me feel..."
   - Results ... "I would like to..."
5. Talk about others as if they were present.
6. Are you being the person you want them to be?
7. Practice the 24-hour rule.
8. When in doubt, don't.
9. Own the burden of responsibility.
10. Always ask "Whose problem is it?" Then look in the mirror for the answer.

The source of all effective communication is truth. Telling the truth is as old as time, yet it still manages to confuse the heck out of some people. What to do and how to do it is covered in the next chapter.

PRINCIPLE **9** ...TELL THE TRUTH

"You keep lyin' when you know you oughta be truthin'..."
—Nancy Sinatra*

Just a little lie. I've lied a few times in my life. Funny things, lies; they start small. As kids, we lie to cover our backsides: "What happened to the rest of the cookies?"

"I don't know. I think they were finished yesterday."

If lies work to protect us, to give us the edge we need or to give us the status we're looking for, we often keep on lying, often believing the lies we create. If we're not careful, or if we don't make a conscious decision to stop lying, we can end up lying for the rest of our lives.

"Did anyone see the change that was on the dining room table?"

"What change?"

"When we called Randy's place at midnight, they said you weren't there."

"I fell asleep in the basement and maybe he didn't know I was there."

"Do you love me?"

"Why do you ask?"

"I submit that you were cheating."

"You're wrong."

"Were you aware, Mr. President ... ?"

The majority of people lie, in all kinds of personal, corporate, government and other situations. And the choice, at any time we want to make that choice, is to keep on lying, or to stop—and attempt to make the honest way our way. Forever. Saint Augustine said it this way, "When regard for truth

* From the song, *These Boots Are Made for Walkin'*

has been broken down or even slightly weakened, all things will remain doubtful."

REGARD FOR THE TRUTH

The following is a quote of Confucius which was recorded in *The Analects*. As with most of Confucius' teachings, it was simple and profound. The decision to tell the truth must be in front of you at all times.

> Be sincere and true to your word, serious and careful in your actions; and you will get along even among barbarians. But if you are not sincere and untrustworthy in your speech, frivolous and careless in your actions, how will you get along even among your own neighbors? When standing, see these principles in front of you; in your carriage see them on the yoke. Then you may be sure to get along.

In 1982, I went to the Commonwealth Games in Brisbane, Australia with the Canadian Wrestling Team. I was not a wrestler; I was not a participant in the games. I was contracted as a videographer.

In events of this kind, athletes invariably travel with their support team. There are doctors, trainers, managers, publicists, and people of all kinds, who are necessary adjuncts to their competitions. Their expertise helps the athletes to maximize performance, to permit the athletes to focus better on what they're supposed to do—win medals.

I was envious of the status the athletes held. They received attention from the media and red-carpet treatment wherever they went. One day I sat in a public area with the athletes and a young child approached us for autographs. I was about to say no when the wrestler beside me said, *"Go ahead, what's the harm?"* I signed an autograph and it felt good, in a way.

I began to imagine myself as one of the team. At the beginning, it was a fantasy. It wasn't long before other athletes in the village and members of the public had me figured for one of the team. I did not go out of my way to correct them and in retrospect, quite foolishly, it was the beginning of convincing myself that I was part of the team. It was a fantasy that evolved into a lie.

Two months later, when the games and the post-games activities were over, I was ready to leave Australia. On a sunny Queensland morning, I checked in at the airport to continue my trip.

The immigration officer took my passport and saw the Commonwealth Games stamp.

"In the games mate?" he asked, smiling and excited.

"Er . . . yes," I said, lying, but just a "white-lie" I thought. (I should have brought back to mind the famous saying from Sir Walter Scott's *Marmion*: Oh, what a tangled web we weave ... when first we practice to deceive!)

"What sport were you in?" He was genuinely interested.

"Wrestling," I said. "I was in wrestling." My voice trailed off. I wanted no more questions.

"Did you win?" he leaned forward.

I paused and then said, "No."

"That's okay. How did you do?"

I stopped breathing and finally said, "Fourth, I finished in fourth place."

He put his arm around me.

"There's nothing wrong with fourth, mate," he said, in a very consoling way. "You did your best. You should be proud of yourself. You've made your parents proud. You did it for your country ... and remember, there's always next time."

I could have shrunk into a hole. I was disgusted with myself and the lying route I had chosen to take. I was a traitor to the real team, to Canada, to my family, but most of all I was a traitor to myself. I acknowledged the immigration officer's remarks, but more than that, I think I was acknowledging the lesson he had just taught me. It was as if he somehow knew—that my term as a liar should end right then.

The incident affected me deeply and I made a decision there and then to stop lying, to end the B.S. No more of this. From then on, I would tell the truth to others. I would be true to myself. I decided to heed the words of Albert Schweitzer: "Truth has no special time of its own. Its hour is now, always."

I am now convinced, more than ever, this was an important turning point in my life. My discomfort with lying led to an honest pursuit of a dream. To compete in the Olympics struck a chord deep within me. I knew I would only know that I had what it took if I made the steps to get there. I was not satisfied with the fantasy. I was not going to pretend.

Sometimes, it's not easy to take the honest way. As I write this book, I look back on what I call my journey of integrity and feel deep, profound satisfaction for pursuing my dream. Regardless of my results, the journey of integrity is what is satisfying. Had I felt comfortable lying to that passport official in Australia, do you think I would have had the fortitude to pursue my Olympic dream? My guess is *absolutely not!*

WHITE LIES AND BLACK LIES

M. Scott Peck defines a black lie as "a statement that we know as false." A white lie is "a statement we make that is not in itself false but that leaves out a significant part of the truth." The most frequent lie is withholding the whole truth. To protect someone's feelings from being hurt, we often hide some of the truth to avoid hurt feelings.

"Do you like my science project on amoebae?"

"It's great… just what I've always imagined."

"Does this make my butt look fat?"

"Not at all. You look great."

"Would you like to spend Christmas in Abilene, Texas, this year?"

"I've always dreamed of a Christmas in Abilene."

In a way, white lies are socially acceptable. We raise children under the guise of white lies. It is often perceived as essential to protect their innocence. Not telling children about some of the financial stresses, marital problems, family disputes, etc., keeps children out of that uncomfortable loop. But, children know they are being shut out. In turn, they don't benefit from some of the life skills that would serve them later. At the right age it might serve them better to involve them in the truth.

The yin and yang of this dilemma is to know what is necessary information and information that may be blown out of proportion in their young minds. Getting a job offer in another part of the continent may only be at the initial offer stage. Burdening the kids with this information could throw them

Never be satisfied with fantasy.

into a tailspin of despair over leaving their school, losing their friends, finding a new home and the like.

In addition, withholding your opinion is best done if there is a remote chance that your truth may not necessarily be the truth for another person; or, just as important, they are not ready for this information.

"I think your wife is having an affair with her tennis instructor."

Or, "Your new car was just rated the lowest on the *Consumer Reports* survey."

M. Scott Peck recommends seven rules for a dedication to the truth:

> 1. Never speak a falsehood. Speak the truth and nothing but the truth.
>
> 2. Withholding the truth is potentially a lie. Each time you do this you are exercising a moral decision.
>
> 3. Withholding the truth should never be based on personal needs, power, acceptance, greed or any other ego-based gain.
>
> 4. Withholding the truth should *always* be based on the needs of the person receiving the information.
>
> 5. By following a maxim of a genuine love for another, you will be able to meet the complex responsibility of assessing another person's needs.
>
> 6. Be aware of a person's needs to use the truth for spiritual growth.
>
> 7. Know that our tendency is to underestimate another's capacity to "handle the truth" both practically and spiritually.

People generally want to grow, and the most growth frequently occurs in an atmosphere of truth. Knowing your spouse is unfaithful will lead to growth, probably painful at first, but growth nonetheless. The truth withheld in a relationship is like a cancerous tumor. Truth about your performance at work is better known sooner than later.

The greatest truths are those that you discover about yourself. Since we wander around in the confines of our skin every day, we get lulled into believing that we know everything there is to know about ourselves. In fact, a lion's share of what makes us tick is active only in the subconscious mind. Finding out the truth about yourself can be liberating. In taking

> # Finding out the truth about yourself
> # can be a pretty cool feeling.

courses, reading books and participating in self-help group discussions, new discoveries happen all the time.

PAYING THE PRICE OF LYING

I find it amazing that a vast majority of the sit-coms on television have story-lines based on how one of the main characters lies and spends the rest of the show trying to cover for the lie. The sophomoric message is always the same: "Oops, I lied, but you forgive me and we will all laugh about it in the end."

In real life, when you lie, you pay. Here's a vivid example of that: Three friends qualified for an adventure race in California. Adventure racing has its roots in ten-day races like the Eco Challenge and the Raid Gulloise. It follows the same format of backcountry running, mountain biking, kayaking and special tests like crawling through mud, climbing twenty-foot walls or jumping over obstacles in a coed team and racing in under four hours.

The trio planned on flying to California to attend the race. In order to transport their equipment, they had to disassemble the bikes and put them in boxes. One of the travelers had often, in the past, avoided paying the $35, one-way fee for transporting the bikes by saying that the boxes contained survey equipment or a tuba. (Apparently, the airlines will charge for bikes but not for survey equipment or tubas.) This time however, the experience was different.

"What's in the boxes?" the ticket agent asked.

"Survey equipment," one said.

"What kind of survey equipment?" she persisted.

"Oh ... the kind with frames and mechanisms and the like ... "

"I'll have to open the boxes to make sure there's nothing dangerous in the boxes."

As she opened the first box, one of the travelers said sheepishly, "Actually ... they are bikes."

She looked at the trio, looked in the box and then slowly looked back at the three like she was playing Quick Draw Jesse in *Gunsmoke*. Something seemed to click inside her head, and she was obviously biting her lip.

The pennywise, pound-foolish friends were charged double for transporting the bikes due to what the agent called "The Wright Amendment." Instead of paying $105 extra, they had to pull together $210 on the spot. Plus, the agent made a note in the computer to notify the return ticket agent that the men had lied and to charge double the normal fee.

CAN'T SLEEP AT NIGHT...

A friend of mine, after moving from Canada to the U.S., learned that his insurance rate would double because he had two previous traffic tickets. Somehow, in some demented logic, he didn't think it was fair that traffic tickets from another country should follow a person around. He proceeded with the stab-in-the-dark idea that if he retook the driver's exam and the driving test, his record would start anew. After he went through all this, he called the best-priced insurance provider he could find and lied about not having any tickets.

A couple of days later, the phone rang and it was a Mr. Roberts from the insurance company. He proceeded to scold my friend in an officious tone. "There seems to be a problem with your application. Is there something you're hiding from us?" he said.

Ultimately my friend did end up paying higher insurance premiums...

EVEN THE SMALL STUFF COUNTS

Lying just isn't right. Repeated enough, it disintegrates the trust another person will have in you. Even the small stuff counts, like your score in golf. Golfing with my brother as we grew up is a classic example.

We had the biggest fights over golf scores. Separated by a year in age, Steven and I were fiercely competitive in all things. We used to go to family weddings and would pick out one particular girl. We would proceed to put on all the moves known to bachelors around the world. It would be a no-holds-barred, anything-goes competition to see who could be her favorite by the end of the night.

But, on the golf course there were rules and we knew them. Every once in a while, however, I would catch Steven kicking his ball onto a better lie, or pretending to find his lost ball or just plain making up a lower score for the hole. This drove me crazy. Plus, I would always follow him around while paying attention to my own play to make sure he was being honest. This was nuts—but that's brothers for you.

Today, Steven's golf has improved vastly, but history is etched firmly in my brain. Even when Steven shoots a great game and tells me over the phone—I am skeptical. Despite the ancient history of our youthful contests, I still can't shake my doubts.

This case in point proves that some people have a difficult time shaking off the past. Lying to a person in the past will continue to haunt you. Make the decision now to tell the truth. Even the small stuff counts, especially with your spouse or significant other.

WITH YOUR SPOUSE

Telling the truth with your spouse or mate seems obvious at the outset. Small examples would be "Why were you late?" Large examples would be "What's this lipstick doing on your shirt?" Your "emotional bank account" (according to Stephen Covey) determines the reception you will get.

The emotional bank account is the investment in trust that you have either built up with another person or are overdrawn on. Coming home late while your emotional bank account is well into the black would receive nothing more than a casual, "What took you...?"

Coming home late when your emotional bank account is in the red and only getting deeper means you'll get a distrustful and wary reception no matter what your answer is. It is possible to build your bank account back up, but the deeper you are, the harder it is to regain ground.

Trust is also like a ball of crystal. If it is shattered, it may never come back to its original state. You're better off just doing what's right and staying far away from ever having to lie or tell half-truths.

In my first marriage, I used to think that I would always tell the truth. In retrospect, I couldn't tell her about the things that might have caused conflict and sabotaged the relationship. I desperately did not want to rock the boat and I suffered the consequences of my lack of forthrightness.

Now, in my present marriage, everything is different. Our relationship is based completely on truth. If either of us is angry, the other finds out about it very quickly. Coming from a place of commitment, we have no fear of consequence from the truth. We trust one another implicitly and it works a million times better than the method of fear and distrust.

CHEATING

The Olympics mirror what is good and bad in society. It is a microcosm of real-life struggle and drama. It involves winning, losing and striving for excellence. It involves pure intent and cheating. It has it all and that is part of its appeal.

In 1988, I went to Seoul, South Korea, to attend the Summer Olympics as a spectator. My original plan to help the athlete's commission failed, but things worked out for the best since I got to see a number of the events with no restricting commitments. In fact, I even saw the much-touted final 100-meter race featuring Ben Johnson and Carl Lewis.

When Ben Johnson shattered the world record and won a gold medal for himself and Canada, I was beside myself. It was immensely exciting. But, as the history books bear witness, Ben Johnson's gold medal was stripped from him in a whirlwind of controversy.

Unknown to me, the same morning the news hit the press, I had a meeting at the Shilla Hotel where the bulk of the International Olympic Committee were staying in their five-star accommodations. I had arranged to have breakfast with one of the IOC representatives from Canada who agreed to meet with me to discuss my future intentions of assisting the Olympic movement back home.

When I walked into the hotel, the press were like sharks who were swimming in bloody waters. They lined up at all the phones and had just caught the story of a lifetime. Ben Johnson had cheated by testing positive for anabolic steroids. Lost his gold medal. He disgraced himself and his country. It was ugly.

I hurried through the lobby and realized what all the commotion was about.

> # Coming from a place of commitment, you will have no fear of the consequences of truth.

I even had a Canadian Olympic Association blazer on that I quickly took off and threw over my arm. "No point in attracting attention to myself," I thought.

When I got on the elevator I pressed the button for the fourteenth floor. I remember thinking as the elevator ascended, that there was no thirteenth floor—a common practice in hotels due to an odd superstition. "How unlucky could thirteen be?"

Then I realized that the fourteenth floor was in reality the thirteenth floor. As the elevator slowed to a stop, I mused again, "How unlucky could thirteen be?" Then the doors opened. There standing in front of me was Charlie Francis, the coach who provided Ben Johnson with the knowledge and mechanisms for taking the steroids.

"Geez," I thought. "This ain't too lucky at all."

I look back on that whole event and realize that Ben Johnson cheated. To some in Canada, his biggest crime was that he got caught. It mattered not that the Olympic Games were the one venue where the pure intention of the Olympic ideal would be to celebrate the excellence of effort, not performance-enhancing drugs. The equal playing field, built on honor, fairness and truth was destroyed by one person's willingness to cheat.

The spirit of competition mirrors the spirit of life. Do what is right. Do it with integrity. Tell the truth. Live the truth, or squander your potential in the fantasyland of lies.

THE FANTASYLAND OF LIES

> *"The easiest person to deceive is one's self."*
> *–Edward George Bulwer-Lytton*

Think back to Bill Clinton lying under oath and to the world regarding his relationship with Monica Lewinsky. It's clear he spent much of his life carefully wording his statements and probably out-and-out lying when required. Prior to his first term as president, Bill Clinton was a guest on the *Arsenio Hall* talk show. He played the sax with the band and then talked comfortably with his host. Hall had a good rapport with Clinton and the conversation led to being a musician in a band. Out of the blue, Hall asked Clinton if he had smoked marijuana. It is a classic scene where Clinton said, "Yes," froze, without blinking for a second, and then added… "but I didn't inhale."

Pleeeeease. That's like saying, "Oh, I chewed the donut but I didn't swallow." Or, "I only held the beer in my mouth, but I certainly didn't drink it."

Yikes!

Now let's look at recent history. How did Clinton back himself into the corner with the "inappropriate" Lewinsky relationship? A pattern of lying builds on itself, much like how people become thieves and white-collar criminals. Studies prove that white-collar criminals start out small—stealing pens from the office, and take home bigger things later on. Small subversive activities can naturally lead to larger ones.

Connect the dots: Bill Clinton's comfort with lying started small and it grew. It grew to the point where finally, at some level, he believed he was immune to retribution.

In addition, there is a thrill, however large or small, in getting away with something. Criminals are regularly quoted as saying something like, "It is a thrill to be able to sneak into someone's house. You get a buzz from stealing their stuff and all the while they are sleeping in their beds. Give me something else that feels that cool and I would do it." Adventure or extreme sports, speeding well past the posted limit, vandalism, various forms of breaking the law and for some—lying. Although each pursuit is mutually exclusive, the common denominator is the adrenaline buzz. Adrenaline junkies are like attention seekers who get attention in either positive or negative ways. Getting a buzz from lying is another component of the complex and sticky web of dishonesty.

Do you know anyone who lies and yet seems comfortable with it?

We all know people who live in an obvious fantasyland of lies. I remember one of the organizers in my sport of speed skiing who compounded his lies into incredible tales that convinced others, and I'm quite sure became real in his own creative imagination.

He believed he had skied at 133 miles (214 kilometers) per hour, long before any other Canadian had done so. The fact was, he was a terrible speed skier. He claimed to own a motorcycle that was custom-made especially for him by Honda. His apartment was adorned with medals that were actually extras not used in previous ski races he helped to organize. He claimed to have hung out with Mario and Michael Andretti at the 1991 Vancouver Indy. Mario, he said, had given him his Indy car to take a spin on the course.

I can still hear him saying, "Wouldn't you know that I crashed in the same corner as Mario did in the race. Mario, Michael and I had a good laugh about that!"

I once worked with a guy who convinced everyone, and probably himself, that he was in the U.S. Army's prestigious Delta Force. Despite the fact that the Pentagon still refuses to acknowledge its existence, Delta Force recruits from the U.S. Army's Special Forces, Green Berets and Rangers. He told how he and his unit went behind enemy lines before Desert Storm, and (in disguise) walked among the Iraqis gathering intelligence. We were impressed with his stories, but later discovered that he wasn't even in the military at the time.

Another time, I had the opportunity to spend time with Kurt Muse, an American businessman and Rotary Club member who has an amazing story. Muse spoke of his experiences in Panama where he could not stand the dictatorial rule of General Manuel Noriega. Muse was eventually taken hostage. He was jailed for operating an underground radio station, and he spoke proudly of the Delta Force rescue. When I returned to the office the next day, I recounted the story to my colleague. I told of how, in operation "Just Cause," Delta had landed paratroopers on the rooftop of the jail and fought their way down to the second floor and back out again to a waiting MH-6. The small helicopter sustained damage from gunfire and was forced down. Fortunately there was a passing UH-60 that picked up the infrared and a radio signal that the Delta trooper was protecting the P.C. Muse was rescued and later learned that "P.C." stood for "precious cargo." With an odd smile, this coworker slipped into his fantasy mode again and told of how he was across the street sneaking into Noriega's office and stole a knife-like letter opener off his desk. I recently checked facts and dates and there is no possible way this coworker could have participated in operation "Just Cause," which was initiated in December 1989.

He had countless other stories of being a high-performing professional cyclist, an internationally acclaimed martial artist and chief executive officer of five martial arts schools. Fabulous, completely fabricated stuff! He ended up being fired when it was discovered that he forged signatures on contracts, stole the entire client and supplier database, wrote bad checks to various people and misrepresented himself on behalf of the company.

Clearly, Albert Einstein was right when he said, "Whoever is careless with the truth in small matters cannot be trusted with important matters." If we carelessly tell lies, we will lose sight of the truth. The truth becomes an enigma where once it was crystal clear.

No matter how well we may cover ourselves in the short term, we become trapped by our lies. Our lies will continue to destroy us from within. If and when others catch us, our destruction will come from our environment.

There are no rewards in virtual achievement. "Integrity is the glue that holds our way of life together," advises the spiritual leader Billy Graham. The satisfaction, the real satisfaction in life comes from actually doing it.

IN SUMMARY

1. Tell the truth.
2. Tell the truth.
3. Tell the truth.
4. Tell the truth.
5. Tell the truth.
6. Tell the truth.
7. Tell the truth.
8. Tell the truth.
9. Tell the truth.
10. Tell the truth!

PRINCIPLE **10** ... ACCESS THE ALPHA

"The ultimate beatitude of man consists in the use of his highest
function, which is the operation of his intellect.
Hence, the blessed see the essence of God."
–St. Thomas Aquinas

Pure potential. Peak performance is my thing. It fascinates me to know what makes people tick, what makes them do what they do and, most of all, what makes them climb higher. In the quest for peak performance, the physiological source of pure potential is located in the brain when it functions at the alpha level of brain waves.

BRAIN WAVES

The brain functions by sending electrical signals between nerve cells along with changes in voltage. These variations are displayed in wave form or brain rhythm and frequency. If you hook up a person to an electro-encephalogram, you will note patterns indicating cycles per second (CPS). The higher the frequency, the higher the cycles per second.

There are four common wave forms:

1. Beta: The beta wave form occurs when you are wide awake. Here you process information through active thinking. You are alert. The conscious mind, especially the logical, left brain is in full gear. In this beta rhythm the brain "revs" between thirteen and twenty-five cycles per second.

2. Alpha: This is the state of relaxed alertness for your brain. It is widely regarded as the ideal learning state where your brain is most receptive. At about ten CPS the brain uses both right and left brain. This is a powerful state, full of potential. When the creative is linked to logic and understanding, learning and growth are taken to a new level.

You naturally slip into alpha every day on a frequent basis. Sometimes, through daydreaming, the mind wanders off and slows down to ten CPS. Some unenlightened teachers will punish their students for daydreaming when, in fact, it is healthy.

This is important for adults as well. Regular daydreaming is a natural and beneficial activity for a person's growth and well-being.

In this lower CPS there is sometimes non-thought. Here the brain cycles around eight to twelve CPS.

3. Theta: In the early stages of sleep the brain slows down further. The mind naturally processes information from the day. Theta is also quickly passed through in morning on the way to waking up.

This rhythm is also associated with your creative and intuitive states. During dreams you will slip into theta. At four to seven CPS the right brain is most active.

4. Delta: In the delta brain rhythm you are in a deep, dreamless sleep. At this point the cycles slow down to one-half to three CPS.

THE AMAZING BRAIN

Tony Buzan, author of *Use Your Head*, writes, "Your brain is like a sleeping giant." Its size belies its immense power and untapped potential. In most ways, the amazing brain is only partially understood. Note the case of Leslie Lemke who at birth had cerebral palsy, was blind and severely mentally challenged.

Leslie is unable to do most simple motor skills like use a fork and knife, and can only repeat what is told to him in a monotone voice and needs constant care. Yet, at age fourteen, Leslie was listening to a record of Tchaikovsky's *Piano Concerto No. 1* for the first time. Immediately after this, he sat at a piano and astonished his parents by playing the concerto with complete accuracy.

Leslie has never had piano lessons, but can hear any piece and play it entirely and accurately. No matter the length and how complicated, he could play back anything he hears.

In clinical terms, Leslie Lemke is known as an idiot savant, much like what

We all have pockets of genius.

was portrayed by Dustin Hoffman in the 1989 Oscar-winning *Rainman*. Considered a clinically accurate portrayal of an autistic adult, Hoffman's character could instantly count the number of toothpicks dropped on the floor or know exactly which cards were dealt and which cards remained from a half-dozen stacks at a blackjack table. Yet, he could not add two plus two. His character in the movie displayed an uncanny ability for genius in one area and a severe mental handicap in another.

How can this happen?

We all have pockets of genius. Under deep relaxation and hypnosis people are known to recount minute details of a hidden memory long past. Even accounts of unexplained past lives have been recorded by some of the world's most respected physicians, psychiatrists and psychologists.

In 1955, Albert Einstein died and willed his vital organs to science. It was reported by clinical scientists that he only used a fraction of his cerebral cortex, the thinking part of his brain. In the research for this book I found that estimates show only between 10 and 0.5 percent of the brain is actually used—that means between 90 and 99.5 percent of the brain is untapped. What, then, can we do to tap this potential?

Riding the alpha waves

Unlocking the secrets of the brain involves a combination of a scientific, strategic approach along with a lifestyle, Zen-like convergence. By accessing the alpha you can balance your life with:

1. Activity and inactivity: Stress alone is a common killer. Activity and inactivity in balance, an approach to managed stress, gives the mind and body a chance to recoup. It is much like the regeneration of the muscles. Intense workouts must be followed by rest and regeneration—it is similar for the human brain.

Think of a time when a name escaped you. The harder you tried, the more elusive the name became. So, you said to yourself, "I'll put it aside for now. It will come to me." Then seconds, minutes, hours or, in some cases, days later… "click," the name comes to you. The brain serves up information as if a computer were sifting through millions of lines of code looking for a piece of information.

2. Intellectualizing and intuitive creativity: Ask any artist, athlete, salesperson or negotiation specialist about their best performance and they will tell you they stopped pushing. It's as if the second you start thinking, you're only half-capable. Balancing the process of intellectualization with natural creative energy will surface the answers you are looking for.

In attempting to unlock the DNA puzzle, Bernard Crick agonized over the numerous theories and postulations. Then, in a dream one night, he saw a double helix design in 3-D. He launched out of bed and recorded his idea. This turned out to be the missing piece of the puzzle in trying to explain what had remained a mystery to scientists for ages.

3. Fixed and flexible beliefs: Fixed beliefs are truths and a person's truth is their reality. A shift in your cognitive filter leads to new results. Since most of your source truths are subconscious, the key to the lock on your subconscious mind is using your alpha rhythms to your advantage. A twist on an old belief can release a cascade of opportunity. Quite simply, a change within produces change in your outer life.

THE PLACEBO EFFECT

In the 1920s, the French physician, Emile Coue coined the term, "the placebo effect." In his effort to improve the health of his patients, he gave them sugar pills professing that the medicine had extraordinary healing powers. In an amazing number of cases the patients got better. Coue deduced that the mind could heal, if it believed something to be true. In turn, Coue had his patients repeat these words, "Every day, in every way, I am getting better and better." Repeated affirmations resulted in a drastic increase in recovery of his patients.

Recently some studies indicate that placebos work just as effectively as morphine in 54 percent of the cases. In another study where patients were given fake or placebo chemotherapy, 33 percent of the patients actually lost their hair.

Everyone has experienced "flow."

FLOW

Read any book related to peak performance and you will see the word "flow," which was first coined by the professor and former chairman of the Department of Psychology at the University of Chicago, Mihaly Csikszentmihalyi (pronounced "zik-zent-mi-hall-ee"). He calls flow the psychology of optimal experience—self-consciousness disappears and the sense of time is distorted or lost.

Though athletes, musicians, painters and actors are best known for experiencing flow, people in all areas of life can experience flow. Watching a child learn a new skill can be flow for both the child and the parent. As you close a sale with a client, you innately connect with the state of flow where the deal just takes on a life of its own.

Many people relate to the feeling of flow with regard to sexual activity. During sex, a person will lose all concept of time and space. Nothing seems to matter except the experience itself. Dr. Csikszentmihalyi's flow activity provides "a sense of discovery, a creative feeling of transporting the person into a new reality." He also states that "it pushes the person to higher level of performance, and leads to previously undreamed-of states of consciousness. In short, it transforms the self by making it more complex. In this growth of the self lies the key to flow activities."

Dr. Csikszentmihalyi examined why the complexity of self increases as a result of flow experiences. Let's consider the following example, relating flow to the sport of skiing.

The two most important factors we will consider in examining learning to ski are the *challenges posed* compared to the *skills owned*. You, as novice, will experience four stages of relative enjoyment, flow or non-flow experiences.

At stage one you don't know what you are doing and you have no basis for the right way to do it. It is reasonably enjoyable. You are outdoors. You are with friends and more likely than not, you have fun. You slip into flow.

At stage two you find the bunny hill too easy. The others in your group are up the mountain. Your skill level has increased, but the challenges are few.

In stage three you then take the big chair-lift up and throw yourself into the unknown again. The challenge has jumped way up, yet your skill level is still at the bunny level. Plus, now you know more about what you don't know. Anxiety rises when you look down at the bottom of the mountain and start to imagine how many pieces of you would be found if you fell and started to slide down. But, you take on this next challenge. You ski to the right and take the green beginner run that clearly has a gentler slope. Eventually, and naturally, you move to a blue intermediate slope.

In stage 4 you slip into a more profound state of flow. You have increased the level of challenge and skill thereby increasing the complexity of consciousness. And, so it goes where stage four becomes stage one and you find yourself approaching stage two or three on the quest for another hit of that addictive flow experience.

Most people have experienced the feeling of flow. If you think back to a time when you were golfing, playing music or achieving some exceptional level of performance, could you identify how long you were there? Did a second in time seem like a second or could it be an immeasurable moment? Did you have any concept of space? Were you aware of anyone else at that moment? In effect, you went out of your conscious mind and performed at a higher level. What you did was spontaneous, automatic and natural.

FLOW AND RELIGION

Flow and religion have been connected from the earliest times. Religious expression was, and still is, often conveyed through music and/or dance. According to Dr. Csikszentmihalyi, "What we call religion is actually the oldest and most ambitious attempt to create order in consciousness. It therefore makes sense that religious rituals would be a profound source of enjoyment."

If we think of the conduit for the experience as the mind, the next question is, what feeds the conduit?

GOD AND THE MIND

Sir Isaac Newton believed that God created a perfect world with one exception—people. His understanding of science made for a world that was either/or—black or white. Two plus two, always equaled four. He identified the law of gravity and used mathematics to explain our universe. Yet people were the unknown factor. This is where God comes in.

How could you attempt to define God? God is neither static nor can God be interpreted in a rational fashion. As outlined in Principle 6, you cannot reason your way to faith. We are born perfect and then spend the rest of our lives undoing and searching for what was ours in the first place. In Newton's perfect world, everyone has faith in something. Even atheists have faith. They have faith that there is no God.

Therefore, I will not attempt any religious debate; nor will I attempt to contain as broad a topic as faith. But, I will attempt to combine and connect from God to our minds—to alpha—to more of what we want in our life through improved results. My intention is to provide information that will be useful to you, the reader. I trust that this information will strengthen your faith, whatever it may be.

In the Book of Genesis it is written, "Let us make man in our image, after our likeness: And let them have dominion over the fish of the sea, and over the fowl of the air, and over the cattle, and over all the earth, and over every creeping thing that creepeth upon the earth. So God created man in his own image, in the image of God created he him." This passage was the focus of one of the greatest works of art on the planet.

Pope Sixtus IV built the Sistine Chapel in 1480, as the pope's personal chapel and the place where the College of Cardinals would select the new pope. Twenty-three years later, Julius II became pope. He was the nephew of Sixtus IV.

Julius II was known for his energy, enthusiasm and vision. He wanted to paint the Sistine Chapel as a tribute to his uncle. Hence, in 1508 he summoned Michelangelo to the Vatican. Michelangelo was a thirty-three year-old sculptor known for his incredible works like the *Pieta* and *David*.

Michelangelo resisted, explaining he was a sculptor, not a painter. But, Renaissance artists of the time were commonly used as journeymen with talents in all areas of design be they architecture, new weapons for war, painting or sculpting.

Later that year, Michelangelo acquiesced and took on the daunting task.

The task was more than artistic. Michelangelo also had to find a way to paint sixty-seven feet off the floor on a barrel-shaped ceiling covering 5,800 square feet. In addition, he was to use the fresco style of painting.

This is a process where one first covers the area with a rough coat of plaster and then allows it to dry. Upon applying a second coat, smooth plaster is put over the area that will be worked on that day. Next, color is mixed into a thinned plaster mix and painted on the still-wet, smooth surface. Absolutely no corrections can be made to a dried section, so every application has to be perfect.

Four tumultuous years later, on October 31, 1512, Julius II and Michelangelo unveiled 343 figures to an astonished crowd. The painting presented a powerful story with the nine panels in the middle as the central theme from the book of Genesis.

Never before had God been portrayed in such a manner. In the panel *The Creation of Adam*, there is an interesting underlying story.

Michelangelo's understanding of the world was more profound than most knew. To improve his art and knowledge of the human body he would study anatomy in detail. Despite the death penalty for mutilating or studying a human cadaver, Michelangelo needed to know more. In secret he would study anatomy late at night in a hidden room lit only by candlelight.

He was quoted as saying, "The trouble with sculpture is, you have to know all the crafts... better than the craftsmen." Hence, he went to extraordinary lengths to perfect his craft. Michelangelo was fascinated by the brain. Five hundred years ago, Michelangelo discovered in his atypical pursuits that all functions appeared to lead to or end up in the brain.

Michelangelo's genius was profound. He solved the greatest architectural puzzle of the Renaissance, which required a freestanding dome to cover Saint Peter's Cathedral. Given his genius and understanding of human anatomy, look carefully at the *The Creation of Adam*, taken from the first panel.

Here you see God reaching out to man. God is portrayed as strong, powerful—omnipotent. Man, cast dramatically in the lower left corner, shows powerful potential. Yet, he lounges and barely lifts a finger during creation. To the uninformed, it appears that man is barely lifting a finger, as God, in

all His might, reaches back. Here, man almost connects with God, but doesn't. The figures of God and Adam seem to reach toward one another, but they fail to touch. "This is the most intense expression of man's tragic fate," according to historian Marc Le Bot, in his book *Michelangelo*.

Again, look carefully at the backdrop of God. The shape is a strikingly similar profile of the human brain. If the brain were taken out of a skull and laid on a table, it would have a practically identical shape to one that God overshadows in the first panel. Is this a coincidence … or is it a clue?

In the Bible Jesus is quoted, "…you are to be perfect, as your heavenly Father is perfect." This raises more questions about the potential of the brain. It is not this writer's intention to say that God is our brain, but there is a connection. In *Return to Love*, Marianne Williamson writes, "God isn't separate from us, because He's love inside our minds." The whole concept is intriguing, complex and virtually unfathomable.

As a result, we walk this earth and attempt to grow in the best ways we know how. Over thousands of generations we have explored our inner reaches. Our quest continues.

ALPHA ACCESS

Techniques to access the alpha rhythm have been used for thousands of years. Hypnosis and meditation are two that we will cover here.

There has historically been resistance to these techniques in Western society, where some people have dismissed hypnosis and meditaton as "the work of the devil." In days of old, heretical behavior was punished by hanging or burning at the stake. Today, a milder form of retribution is displayed with finger pointing and tongue wagging by "enlightened ones."

Hypnosis has become "entertainment" through people who take volunteers on stage and embarrass them by convincing them, for instance, that they are a monkey in a zoo or a famous striptease artist. Meditation is often associated with some non-Christian religions, and people in trances are instantly categorized with a primal association or as being within the realm of magic.

But it is a physiological and psychological fact that hypnosis and meditation access the alpha rhythms. Alpha rhythms are completely natural and absolutely do not need to be associated with the occult. There is an opportunity to use these techniques for obtaining alpha access for a greater good.

Through extensive research during my athletic training, I discovered the unutilized potential in accessing the alpha. I then applied performance-improvement mental training techniques like a form of hypnosis called deep relaxation techniques. In addition, I would access the use of a biofeedback unit produced by Thought Technology. Plus, in using a sensory deprivation floatation tank I found another means to the same end: accessing the alpha state to imprint the powerful subconscious mind with the perfect ski run.

I laboriously researched each strategy. In all methods, the idea was the same: Practice techniques using the imagination, and imprint most effectively while the brain cycles between eight and twelve CPS. In the hypnotic, deep relaxation state, I would listen to an audio tape that I designed after a hypnosis script called *Skiing with the Wind*. I revised the script to fit the exact scenario for a speed skiing race.

More research revealed that biofeedback was a method of reducing stress. Reduced stress means a window of opportunity when accessing the alpha rhythms. With a handheld galvanic skin response unit called a GSR II, I would train my mind and body to work more in unison.

Further research recommended use of a sensory-deprivation floatation tank. A tank is more like an enclosed, eight-foot Fiberglas pod. With ten inches of water and three hundred pounds of Epson salts, the water density would float a body at the surface. With the body resting just inches into the water level, you would recline comfortably on your back. The water, kept at the exact skin temperature of 93.3 degrees Fahrenheit, gives a feeling as if you are floating in outer space. The pod is totally enclosed, so you can't see anything and your ears are under water where you can't hear anything. You can't feel anything since the water is body temperature. Weight is taken off your joints and stress virtually vanishes.

After I used the sensory deprivation tank for a few weeks, I then used my speed skiing hypnosis tape in the underwater speakers to compound the effectiveness of my mental training strategy.

This collection of techniques to use visualization and imagery took me to top-ten ranking in the world on my first year on the World Cup circuit. I have since taken variations of these same techniques and applied them to creating wealth, strengthening relationships and maintaining healthy lifestyles. The results have been incredible.

THE NATURAL RHYTHM—BAROQUE MUSIC

In recent years new forms of accelerated learning techniques have sprung up. It's been discovered that adding music that is in sync with the alpha waves can completely change the traditional methods of learning. This method is also known as "super-learning."

The pace of Baroque music is similar to the alpha wavelength of relaxed alertness where there are sixty to seventy beats-to-the-minute. Therefore, as you read this book, you are activating the left brain. Add Baroque music and you activate the right brain. This creates a synergy of the two hemispheres establishing a resonance that stimulates the creative juices. (I listened to Baroque music while writing this book.)

Back when I was ski racing, I played Baroque music as I watched videos of top racers. I would imagine I was racing down the slopes, skiing the same lines they took. In addition, I have found that Reggae music stimulates a similar synergy, too, yet the lyrics may confuse the intention of focusing on a particular, directed thought.

At times, it is best to have complete silence when using the stabilizing and profound effects of meditation.

MEDITATION

I have found people who do not understand meditation so they reject it. Based on over twenty-four years of personal practice and extensive research conducted at hundreds of universities, it is clear to me there is no more profound and efficient method to access the innermost resources of your mind.

By quieting the mind through short, consistent sessions of silence and solitude, I think you will experience movement to a more profound and settled level of your own awareness. In addition to the psyche, your physiology is also positively affected. Through meditation you will discover treasures of the mind, strengthen foundations of the body and fortify your spiritual resolve. It is a feeling of a deep connection at all levels.

It is difficult for people to believe that one technique could do all that. I want you to be skeptical. You will not believe something unless you understand it, and you will not fully understand something unless you experience it. Let us explore my own experiences, back this up with research, and maybe you will relate to it better.

GROWING UP

Up until first grade I was an affable, creative type who loved to play, pretend and daydream. Everything that was said to me, I pondered and tried to figure out. Life was an adventure.

Then, I entered the second grade. My teacher, we'll call her Mrs. Lumpy, took exception to my style. I did not fit with the rest of the class and I was often singled out. I would be sharply reprimanded for daydreaming and was often criticized for not conforming.

The more I was criticized, the more I checked out mentally. It got to the point where Mrs. Lumpy was overheard saying in conversations with other teachers that I was "border-line retarded." She started to hint that I should be moved into a special needs class, since I was falling behind. In her efforts to "recondition" me, she would force me to sit beside her desk facing the whole class. If I did something right, I remember her saying, "Look class, Vince did something right." It was hell for me. I hated school.

Halfway through the year my parents caught wind of the "border-line retarded" comment and insisted I be changed to the other second grade class. After the Christmas holidays I was moved into a stricter environment. I walked into class a little nervous and shy. I had been given a foot-long Christmas pencil in my stocking and I brought it to school to use. It had a little plastic elf head on the end of the pencil. I loved it.

Seeing this, the first thing the new teacher did was to charge over to me announcing that school was a place for work, not toys and she yanked the pencil out of my hand. Then, to my horror, she started pulling on the head thinking it was some sort of pop-off toy. After a good deal of effort she ripped off the head and found the cloth packing spiraling out of the end. With a shrug she handed back the pencil with the elf head dangling by a strip of extended cloth.

From then on, school was a place of punishment. Despite the fact that learning is a natural instinct for a child, I despised it. Slowly, I just made sure I kept out of trouble and did what I was told. I virtually squelched my own creativity.

Over the years my parents tried to undo what was done in school. I ever-so-slowly inched my way out of my shell. Then, at the age of fourteen everything changed. This was in the early 1970s, when Transcendental Meditation (TM) was brought to North America and made famous by the Beatles and a number of Hollywood actors.

My mother has always been a seeker. Her curiosity led to research where she found out the numerous benefits of taking the TM course. She signed up our whole family and we learned the technique.

I practiced TM daily and found it an effortless and relaxing thing to do. I understood that if I kept it up, my marks would go up, too. What followed shocked everyone, and my parents were thrilled. One day I announced that I wanted to get involved in a project for bringing a teen center to our suburb community. I soon became president of the Strathcona Youth Association board and conducted public forums on the issue. I was repeatedly interviewed by the local press. I helped lead fundraising efforts with the local and provincial governments, while my marks consistently rose.

I even started up a political action committee of the Young PCs in the Pembina constituency. My involvement led me to delegate status at the national convention where Joe Clark was elected the leader of the Progressive Conservative party.

In music, I excelled as a concert clarinet player. I played in the prestigious clarinet choir that had the top young clarinet players in the Edmonton area. Over the summer between the eleventh and twelfth grades, I taught myself how to play the saxophone and made our school jazz band. I later became a soloist and finished the year by winning the John Philip Souza award as the most outstanding musician in the school.

To top off my high school experience I became the valedictorian for our graduating class of over six hundred students. My speech to a packed Jubilee Auditorium of over two thousand people was met with a standing ovation that I will *never* forget!

I entered college at the age of seventeen. I traveled around the world at age twenty-one. I was the 1984–85 president of the student body for our Department of Recreation Administration. I competed in the Alberta Winter Games in luge and was selected to attend a high performance luge camp in Lake Placid.

Following college, I was a delegate at the Olympic Academy of Canada, the International Olympic Academy, the Bulgarian Olympic Academy, a trainer with the IOC's Olympic Solidarity program for developing nations and founder of the Alberta Youth Olympic Symposium.

At the age of twenty-six I quit everything and took up ski racing. Four years later I was vying for a gold medal in the Olympic Winter Games in Albertville, France, in speed skiing while holding five national records and two national championships.

In retrospect, I owe a good deal of my accomplishments to the exceptional benefits gained from TM.

Yoga for Union of Mind and Body

TM has its basis in the Vedic science of consciousness from ancient India. It is from here that the simple stretching exercises of hatha yoga and the

> # I owe a good deal of my accomplishments to the exceptional benefits gained from TM.

Ayurvedic approach to natural medicine originated. In fact, the foundations of all health and consciousness-related arts originated in India over five thousand years ago. With a keen awareness of a mind-body connection, Ayurvedic medicine sprang out of this area. Over time this knowledge has been lost, but today it is being revitalized.

Various forms of meditation abound. There is breathing, open eyes and silent meditation. In Sanskrit, yoga means "union." The aim of yoga is to unite the mind, thoughts and body with pure awareness. The inner self is the most settled, expanded level of the mind; it is the source of thoughts. This is where there is silence and peace. This is a field of bliss that underlies thought.

This pure awareness is not obvious to most but can be uncovered through a variety of mental exercises and skills. Traditionally, there are eight components to move from the outer to the inner self. The first two involve ethical preparation and attitudes. The second two work toward physical preparation and heightened control of the senses. The fifth skill links preparation and the actual yogic techniques. The last three involve the quieting of consciousness through mental techniques.

1. *Yama* **means "restraint" from actions that may harm others.** For example, refraining from lying, stealing or abusive behavior.

2. *Niyama* **means "obedience" to cleanliness, study and God.** One follows routines as a natural order of life.

3. *Asana* **are the various physical "postures"** designed for flexibility and physical control.

4. *Pranayama* **means "breath" control** designed to oxygenate your physiology and relax the body.

5. *Pratyahara* **is learning to "withdraw" attention** from outer objects to heightened senses and control. This ultimately is the control over that which happens in the mind.

6. *Dharana* **means "holding on" to attention** to a single stimulus, like a sound, in contrast to Pratyahara, where there is a "withdrawal" of attention. This is the yin and yang of the mind to balance control and letting go.

7. *Dhyana* **is a virtual flow of concentration** where the stimuli in Dharana is more of an echo than a thought.

8. *Samadhi* **is a slip into "self-collectedness" or transcendence.** It involves non-thought. An actual flow experience where there is a liberation of self awareness into universal intelligence. As best as I can describe it, meditation is time spent with God. You don't become God, you simply come to a unified field of universal intelligence. It is as if the energy that is you, resonates with the energy that is available in the universe. Sound weird? Skeptical? Fine, keep reading.

TRANSCENDENTAL MEDITATION

In 1958, Maharishi Mahesh Yogi came to America for the first time to introduce Transcendental Meditation to North America. He came at a time when meditation was perceived as mystical, obtuse, complicated and for the recluse. Maharishi showed that meditating is simple, effortless, natural, requires no change in belief or lifestyle and can be easily practiced by anyone.

His message was simple: Life is bliss. Humankind is meant to enjoy an unlimited resource of energy, happiness and intelligence. In all my research, I discovered that each meditation technique is a different means to the same end. The end is less stress, better health and a raised level of awareness.

From hundreds of scientific studies on TM versus other forms of meditation and relaxation techniques, TM leads by a large margin in areas of reduction of stress, reduced anxiety, improved psychological health, increased happiness, improved creative intelligence, reduced substance abuse (including cigarettes) and increased self-actualization.

Self-actualization is realizing one's inner potential in everyday life. From forty-two independent studies, TM was found to be two to three times more effective than other meditation or relaxation techniques. This statistical meta-analysis was printed in the *Journal of Social Behaviour and Personality, 1991*.

In the past thirty years there have been over six hundred scientific studies researching the effects of Transcendental Meditation in over 210 independent universities in thirty-three countries. Results from across the board have shown that Transcendental Meditation increases or improves:

- energy
- creativity
- intelligence
- happiness
- memory
- ability to learn
- inner peace
- mental and physical health
- relationships
- self-esteem
- a reduction and reversal in the aging process

In addition these same findings reveal a reduction of:

- stress
- depression
- anxiety
- insomnia

THE ADVANTAGES OF TM

WORK

Judy Garvey, the principal of a school in San Jose, California, says, "Transcendental Meditation allows my mind to completely settle down for twenty minutes, and I find that extremely refreshing. As a result, I am able to do my job better with less stress. I am able to stay calm under pressure in a world of anxious people. The technique lends clarity to my thinking and allows me to prioritize better and know where to put my energy and focus."

Susan Snow, an associate judge for the Circuit Court of Cook County, Illinois, describes Transcendental Meditation as her strategy to reduce stress and the omnipresent fatigue from working twelve years of divorce court. She had extensive results at work. She has all but eliminated procrastination and now has more energy and enthusiasm for tasks she avoided in the past. TM has, in her words, "enhanced so many facets of my life."

FAMILY LIFE

Christine Reed, a new mom in Chapel Hill, North Carolina, credits Transcendental Meditation for giving her more energy despite the demands of a new baby and sleep deprivation. The relaxation that she receives translates into the calm experienced by her son and has other positive impacts on her family.

Margaret Mitchell, M.D., a doctor in Buffalo, New York, has practiced Transcendental Meditation for over sixteen years and is a mother of two children. Despite her long days of practicing medicine and teaching medical students, she says, "I feel completely refreshed and revitalized after Transcendental Meditation. I can't imagine how people live without it."

BIOLOGICAL AGE

The first major scientific study of meditation was conducted in 1968 by UCLA psychologist Robert Keith Wallace in his doctoral thesis on "The Physiological Effect of Transcendental Meditation: A Proposed Fourth State of Consciousness." His first findings on meditation uncovered exceptional effects on physiology (breathing, heartbeat and blood pressure). In addition, the nervous system seemed to go into "restful alertness" where the mind reaches an alpha state of alertness, while the body slips into a deep relaxation.

By 1978, Wallace's research explored the effects of meditation on aging. He used three standards that are measures of aging: blood pressure, vision and hearing (all of which deteriorate with age). He hypothesized that aging would be reversed through a reversal of these three indicators of age. In the study he found:

1. Meditators who had practiced TM for less than five years had a biological age five years younger than the norm.

2. People who practiced TM longer than five years had average biological ages of twelve years younger than the chronological norm.

In later research of two thousand meditators it was uncovered that the TM'ers had half the number of doctor and hospital visits, 80 percent less heart disease and 50 percent less cancer. In the sixty-five and older age group, the results were even more dramatic.

THE MIND-BODY CONNECTION

The purpose of Ayurvedic medicine is to unite the various parts of the body and then link in the power of consciousness. To attain peak physical performance one can access this through the potential of the mind.

John Douillard, author of *Body, Mind and Sport,* has a background as a world-class triathlete. Douillard found that he had capped out with his training and kept pushing himself to exhaustion. His frustration with training and a small injury forced him to step back. He met an Ayurvedic doctor and followed the recommendation to use relaxation principles to increase his physical performance.

As a trained chiropractor, Douillard also spent a year in India studying the traditional form of medicine. The tools he learned increased his results as one of the top triathletes in the U.S. He also took his findings and helped other athletes like Martina Navratilova and Billie Jean King. Both of these tennis stars gave Douillard high praise in a foreword to his book.

During an athletic event, or any other performance for that matter, the strategy is to put the mind in a relaxed state while the body is highly active. The analogy Douillard uses often is "a hurricane where there exists the calm eye within powerful winds all around."

Concerning the body-mind connection, Douillard associates mouth breathing as a trigger for stress response. Babies, whose job is bliss, naturally breathe through their nose. We were born that way. Nose breathing leads to less strain and activation of the parasympathetic system, which increases relaxation.

STRENGTHEN YOUR FAITH

Rev. Dr. Craig Overmyer, a pastoral counselor in Indianapolis, Indiana, with a Masters of Divinity in 1982, and Doctorate of Ministry in 1985, from the Christian Theological Seminary in Indianapolis, has been a TM practitioner for over twenty-five years.

> I've always felt that Transcendental Meditation was an aid to my Christian growth. It never replaced my Christian growth, but it was an aid to it. In fact, I decided to commit my life to Christ after I'd been practicing Transcendental Meditation for three months."
>
> "I would say to any Christian—or to anyone of any religion—that Transcendental Meditation would benefit your life. It's a technique, a simple process that requires no belief. It is not a religion. There are so many thoughts that clutter the mind, and Transcendental Meditation is like taking a bath—it's very cleansing and very refreshing.

Father Kevin Joyce is a pastor at a Catholic church in San Jose, California who has meditated for over twenty years. He describes Transcendental Meditation as a source of "inner calm, great energy, leading to more presence of mind with which to serve the people of God." He goes on to say that it "involves no faith or belief and may be practiced with confidence by any religious person."

In general, people fear that which they do not understand. Skepticism is good, but ignorance is not good and it's not bliss. It is far from bliss. Ignorance is abhorrent and a misuse of one's God-given potential. TM is not, however, practiced as an end in itself. It is practiced as a basis for successful, dynamic and fulfilling activity. It is like pulling an arrow back on a bow. It is a preparation for activity.

WHAT IS TM?

Transcendental Meditation is a simple mental technique that naturally quiets the mind. It is practiced twice each day; once in the morning can set you up for an energetic day. And, once in the late afternoon before dinner. It removes the stress from the day and is the basis for a good night's sleep.

WHAT DOES TM DO?

Anyone can do it. Five million people of all ages, religions, and educational backgrounds, have taken the opportunity to learn TM. There is no consecration or control of the mind. No complications. No suggestions, no manipulation of thought. It's like diving into a cool pond on a hot day. It is cool and refreshing.

TM does not involve a swami or posture. You don't need to cross your legs in an impossible position or lie on a bed of nails wearing a big cloth diaper. You can practice it anywhere you have a few minutes to close your eyes. On the plane, subway, in the office after work, or at home.

CONSIDER TM

Think of the mind as an ocean. Consider that most of the activity in the ocean is at a depth relatively near the surface. So, too, is your mind active on the surface. The deeper you go the less activity you will experience. TM takes you from the noisy and disorderly to the silent and orderly. From activity to calm. Given the depth of potential in the mind, TM is a simple technique to experience this potential rarely accessed, especially in today's hectic world.

I have meditated for over twenty-four years and I still can't fully describe what it is like to transcend. It is a unique yet very comfortable feeling. Like trying to describe ice cream to a hunter and gatherer in Papua, New Guinea—when you try it, you will discover what it's like.

TM is a chance to take a respite from the noise and many pressures we face every day. In Transcendental Meditation, EEG research shows you are in the "alpha" state of the mind—the state of pure wakefulness, pure potential. It is a profound sense of self. It is not giving up any control whatsoever. It is merely a state that is 100 percent natural to the mind. It appears unique only because we all have a million and one distractions every day and we would never know this place unless we had a technique to get there.

It also is not to be compared with any drug-like experience. Drugs mask, dull or distort certain senses. The mind is altered from its normal functions. Through a foundation of mental and physical rest, regeneration is allowed to prosper.

WHAT IS STRESS?

Think of your life experiences as a bed of springs. Each spring represents a past stress which varies in degrees of tension. Know that the brain records all information that is charged with a certain amount of stress. Some stresses are simple; you forgot where you left your keys. Medium stresses occur when you forget where you left your keys, and you need to pick up your kids. Big stresses are when you forgot where you left your kids. Picture a spring the size used in a Bic pen for the little stresses. For medium stresses, imagine a regular bedspring. For the big stresses, picture the spring used in a truck's suspension. Because of the deep physical rest that meditation provides, the technique releases some or all of the tension in these springs.

Through regular meditation there are times, sometimes frequently, when you will find yourself "spring-less" and *voix la*. You slip into the transcendental state. This is why sleep, relaxation or vacations don't accomplish the same thing as TM. While sleeping you are not accessing the source of thought, because you're in the delta and theta states beyond the reach of transcendence. In relaxation, you may daydream, but this method is the under-utilization of this ancient meditation technique. As for vacations... how often do you take a vacation and then need a vacation when you get home?

WHAT DOES THIS MEAN?

The net effect is a basis for better, more dynamic, satisfying and productive activity. It is not a religion, philosophy or lifestyle. It is simply a tool to access the potential that you have within. You do not follow any moral code or rule of conduct or method of worship. Your whole objective is to know yourself better by visiting the source of your potential.

You might think of it as mental floss. Ask your dentist and he'll tell you, "Floss twice a day." Find ways to make flossing a habit and it will pay dividends with healthy gums and teeth. TM follows the same general logic and can be leveraged to help you in many ways.

WHEN AND HOW?

Each person is different. We each have our own unique history, physical make-up, and intellectual and emotional intelligence. If I attempted to teach the exact technique that I use, it would be a disservice to you. The necessary personalization is best done by a trained teacher. I have learned that a casual undertaking to learn TM results in a casual, nonchalant approach to applying its vast benefit. As a result, I will only write in general terms about how to do it. I encourage you to follow through with the structured courses that are available around the world.

GENERAL CONCEPTS

TM is practiced in a quiet place. Sitting is best. Lying down makes you susceptible to falling off to sleep. It is practiced twice per day.

There is an exceptional difference in meditating twice per day versus only once. Once each day is only slightly noticeable in your energy level. But a dedicated routine of twice each day is instantly recognizable. It is like the difference between feeling better and feeling refreshed. Instead of a little boost of energy, you experience a broader level of enthusiasm. Twice per day is the difference between relaxation and peace of mind!

Each session should last twenty minutes, followed by a three-minute rest period. Many people react by saying they don't think they can afford the twenty minutes. When you truly realize the benefit, you find the time. TM becomes a priority.

TM has been the single greatest tool I have used for getting more out of life. I encourage you to check it out. Use TM to your own advantage and enjoy the numerous benefits.

PRAYER

Prayer is both faith-based, and a practical tool. Done consistently, prayer will contribute to your spiritual cultivation. In a society of instant gratification, progress is rarely apparent. Life is more like climbing a mountain; fall and you must get back on track to keep on climbing.

Prayer is a letting go. It is a conversation with God, where you leave things up to His will. Prayer also directs your thought. Earl Nightingale calls it the world's greatest secret—where you will gravitate to your current dominant thought. Directing prayer to pain and suffering may actually create more of that. Instead, the strategy should be that of gratitude. Prayer is faith in a higher power that can be communicated to at any time. Most important, it is a consistent, daily dedication to personal and spiritual clarity.

THE DIFFERENCE BETWEEN PRAYER AND MEDITATION

I believe prayer and meditation are the yin and yang of connection to pure potentiality. Think of God wanting you to let go and pursue at the same time. Take the prayer by Reinhold Neibuhr as an extension of this: "God, grant me the serenity to accept the things I cannot change, courage to change the things I can and the wisdom to know the difference."

If you subscribe to Principle 2, you can come up with the *application of a consistent strategy* that involves both prayer and meditation. The strategy of letting go is done through meditation and your pursuits are clarified through prayer.

The technique I like to use is what I call book-ending. Before I meditate I say a little prayer. After TM I pray again, adding a few words of thanks. I find that prayer accesses power beyond our consciousness. It reduces stress, improves awareness, keeps me healthier and clarifies my intent. I never pray during TM, since that is time completely reserved for letting go.

NATURE

There is a vibration of energy in nature. There is a special connection you can only find in nature. In many cases, a walk in nature will clear the mind and even provide answers to questions that you have been mulling over.

ANSWERS FROM NATURE

Nature is one of my sources of inspiration, companionship and comfort. It is a teacher, it's fun and is a place where God seems to be everywhere.

Our bodies are like a microcosm of nature. Your body is not a machine that you wait until it is broken to fix or replace parts. It is an ecosystem that requires constant nurturing and prevention from excessive imbalance.

The microcosm (body) and macrocosm (nature) belong with and to each other. The harmony of the two can be brought together. Get out of the

> # The strategy of letting go is done through meditation, and your pursuits are clarified through prayer.

concrete jungle each day, if you can. Try to connect with nature's way.

NATURE'S WAY

In Daniel Quinn's book *Ishmael,* he tells a story of a man disillusioned by the abuses society makes on the world and itself. The main character meets a teacher who helps him understand the world and how to save it.

This excellent book explains that humans are at war with nature. Ten thousand years ago, we shifted from hunters and gatherers to an agricultural society where we used nature to our advantage. Over time we continued to develop tools and technology that are increasingly divergent from nature's way or "natural law."

By living within natural law, humankind can be sustainable. By trying to control nature, nature will push back. Technology is now changing at an alarming rate. Exponentially, we are diverging further from natural law. According to Quinn, there will be a correction.

Ultimately, *Ishmael* is a fictional story for humankind to understand how to work with nature's way or natural law. We don't need to become hunters and gatherers again, but we must create a partnership with our natural environment.

This partnership starts with you. Decide how you can best behave with *respect* to nature. Surrender to the wonder of nature. Awaken yourself to a new appreciation of nature. Instead of using it, work with it to your advantage.

If you have ever sailed, you know the feeling of the water, the boat, the wind, and sail working all together. The energy courses through your hand as you guide the rudder. It permeates your senses as you feel the wind in your hair, smell the water and more than anything … it feels right.

IN SUMMARY

1. The physiological source of pure potential is held in the mind.
2. The alpha rhythm in the brain, a state of relaxed alertness, is the ideal learning state.
3. A change within produces a change in your outer life.
4. Find the state of flow and you will find peak performance.
5. The mind is our source of God-given potential.
6. Hypnosis or deep relaxation is a powerful tool to shift attitudes or improve performance.
7. Baroque music matches the alpha state in the brain thereby enhancing super-learning.
8. Transcendental meditation is a phenomenal tool for you to get improved health and more of what you want in life.
9. Cultivate your spirituality and clarify your focus through consistent prayer.
10. Partner with nature for answers and growth.

The intention of this chapter was to uncover practical applications to the potential that you hold within. It is important to recognize that all techniques are simply tools that I have researched and used to a meaningful end. Your goal from reading this book must be to check in with your current reality and know what you want to do differently.

Why would you do something that takes this much of your valuable time if you want to continue doing what you have always done? In an ever-changing world, the static will be mowed over. Proactive people look for the growth opportunities. The winners move with the changing environment.

Ultimately, as with flow, meditation or accessing the alpha, the answers always lead to the simplest common denominator. The next Invinceable Principle is the simplest of all ... have fun.

PRINCIPLE 11 ... HAVE FUN!

"I never worked a day in my life. It was all fun."
–Thomas Edison

Happiness: Aristotle said, "More than anything, men and women seek happiness." Twenty-five hundred years later, we are still searching for that same goal. In fact, with the complexities of today, we sometimes seem further than ever from that goal.

Happiness is what a parent wishes for their child. Happiness is what newly-weds hope to achieve. Happiness is what entertainers hope to deliver. (Note: Entertainers are the most highly paid people on the planet.)

Yet happiness is not the ultimate thing we seek. Fulfillment is. Pills can make people happy. Movies can make you happy. A gift can make you happy. But, these are all relatively short-term. Fulfillment is a profound sense of happiness that is lasting and intrinsically manifested.

Finding fulfillment is the ultimate quest. It applies to each chapter of this book. Through your commitments to your actions, you will find fulfillment in places related to your purpose. Hence, your commitments make up your starting point.

The single greatest commitment you can make that will contribute to all others is this: Decide to have fun! Decide that this moment will be fun. Decide this negotiation, task, conversation, challenge or day will be fun. Thus, you set the stage to have the opposite of fear. Fear is where everything can get messed up in the first place.

From fear to bliss

In her book, *Feel the Fear and Do It Anyway*, Susan Jeffers, Ph.D. relates that we will always have fear to deal with. Therefore, the challenge is to deal with it or we will never begin. Fear is the beginning of a continuum that sets up poor results.

If fear is high, then stress is mismanaged. If stress gets out of hand, confidence goes down. With poor confidence, performance is compromised and hence the results are poor.

FEAR ↑ → STRESS ↑ → CONFIDENCE ↓ → PERFORMANCE ↓ → RESULTS ↓

On the other hand, if fear is held in check, stress can be better managed and then confidence is allowed to flourish. Raised confidence feeds improved performance and results will then rise.

FEAR ↓ → STRESS ↓ → CONFIDENCE ↑ → PERFORMANCE ↑ → RESULTS ↑

What, then, is the exact opposite of fear?

The answer is bliss.

At birth, we are filled with bliss. Look into a baby's eyes and you will see bliss. There is no fear, not a speck. There is only purity, a sea of love. A baby's job, in fact, is bliss. They have no other responsibility, if you can call it that, than to exist in bliss.

Therefore, if you want better results, set up the opposite of fear. The next step is to set up the opposite of stress.

The opposite of stress is fun. Fun and bliss are intimately connected. Think of a time that you laughed so hard, you lost yourself in the moment. In this state, otherwise known as flow, you feed confidence, performance and results.

BLISS ON DEMAND?

Bliss on demand is virtually impossible. Instead, the best method to create bliss is only to hope and trust that what you are about to do will be fun. Viktor E. Frankl, in *Man's Search for Meaning*, writes that "…happiness

---

A baby's job is bliss.

---

cannot be pursued; it must ensue ... as the intended side-effect of one's personal dedication to a course greater than oneself." This ensuing state is elusive. But, as Frankl states, a dedication to something larger sets the stage.

Deciding to have fun doing something that is out-of-step with who you are makes it an onerous task. How could you expect to reach any fulfilled state by doing something away from your purpose? Some things are tasks that must be done, like paperwork. But, should this paperwork contribute to your mission to make a difference in the lives of others, the paperwork takes on a whole new meaning.

Give yourself the advantage of staying "on purpose." Open the door for happiness or fulfillment to walk in. Then, let go. J. S. Mill states, "Ask yourself whether you are happy and you cease to be so." The flow is broken when conscious thought steps in. Being in the moment means a raised, unencumbered level of consciousness. Happiness and fun, like bliss, cannot be manifested on demand. Neither is it happenstance or luck. It is a state from within that needs to be prepared for and cultivated. It needs to be nurtured and shared.

Since there is no "bliss switch," how do you manifest it?

VULNERABILITY

By being who you truly are, you open the opportunity for bliss to exist. A baby personifies this in their every waking moment. But, in real life, in this shark-infested world, do you doubt you will survive? How about women in business? Can they afford to show the least bit of vulnerability in certain male-dominated industries?

This is where one of the paradoxes of life exists. We spend a good deal of our lives trying to be accepted. We dress well, shower, comb our hair and put our best foot forward. We do *not* show anything of our weaker side. We don't reveal it all.

Now, think of a person that you are closest to in your life. They feel the same about you. Do they accept you? Yes. Do they know all your qualities, and all your faults? Yes.

Now, we want others to accept us in that job interview, negotiation, sale, cocktail party ... but we hide our true self at the same time. It just won't work that way. Thus, the paradox: We try to hide our human side yet it is the shortest distance between two people.

YOU CAN'T HAVE MY BUD LIGHT!

The Budweiser commercials make light of this exact scenario. The one character, in an effort to get the last Bud Light, says with a seemingly rubber face with all the fake emotion he can muster, "I love you, man!" The other character knows what he's up to and says, "You can't have my Bud Light."

Feigning vulnerability or openly weeping at the job interview, negotiation, sale or cocktail party would pretty much have the same effect. Vulnerability means showing who you truly are. It is not easy, especially if the act you put on has worked for you so well in the past.

This act is how we all make it through life. You, I and everyone else cannot and should not just eliminate our act. More important, if your act is the only thing you have, then that happens to be who you are. Live that fully. The goal then is to be grounded.

BEING GROUNDED

One of the most vulnerable places that you can stand is in front of a group of people. Talking on a subject you are not familiar with or passionate about will amplify your act ten-fold. People pick up on this. This is why public speaking can be hard for some.

Those with a great act are familiar with the topic; they perform and feel like they did well. The crowd knows the difference between an act and the real you. Therefore, the best place to practice vulnerability is from the platform.

In preparation for my speaking skills, I took a course from Context Associated called leadership skills. Its whole design was centered around learning to be grounded from the platform. On the speaking platform, you cannot hide. It was led by Peggy Merlin of Vancouver, B.C. Her adeptness in bringing the best out in other people is amazing. She is a gifted facilitator.

In the course, we each took a topic and presented it from the stage. At first,

I thought, "No problem." I had felt comfortable speaking in front of people my whole life. But, alas, the act was as obvious as a glowing, neon billboard. I finished my first go-round, sat down and thought, "Geez, this being real stuff is hard."

The course lasted three months with a weekend meeting each month. Its format uncovered the best ways to be authentic for each participant in the course. It was a valuable lesson not just for the speaking that I do now, but also for life in general.

A couple of years later I was speaking in a small town about real estate investments and my training paid off. As I was one-third into my one-hour presentation, a man toward the back of the room jumped up and said while pointing his finger, "I know about slick city people like you. You just come in here and want to take all our money."

There was a brief pause and I replied, "Sir, you sound skeptical." This broke the tension with a little chuckle from the audience.

"You're damn right I'm skeptical," the man shot back, ready for a verbal battle.

"That's good," I said with conviction. "I want you and everyone else here to be skeptical. If you don't have questions, you won't know the benefits this program has to offer. That's why I am here. It's great that you're skeptical, so that you will want to know more. You have been around a long enough time to know a good thing when you see it. So, stay skeptical, I like that."

You could feel the tension in the room just evaporate. The man actually smiled and said, "Thank you," as he sat down. I continued on with the presentation thinking the whole time, *"Where did that come from?"*

Had I not been comfortable on the topic, I would have faltered. More important, I was comfortable with being honest. I did not give the man a slick line to shut him up. I just told him how I would want to feel if I were listening to this kind of investment program. It became clear to me that believing in what you are talking about is the key to getting others to believe it also. Presenting with any kind of fake pretense only succeeds in delivering a fake you.

Fun is contagious.

Being who you are is fun. Fun is where it is at. Katherine Hepburn said it best: "I never lose sight of the fact that just being is fun." There you go. "Just being." Two words to guide your way to life mastery.

PEOPLE ARE ATTRACTED TO FUN

Fun is contagious. A few years ago I was traveling through Europe on a Eurail pass. I made no plans, I just hopped the next train and took off to another town. On one particular trip I arrived in Rome as the tourist season was in full swing. I visited one hotel after the other and finally arrived at the Pensione di Roma. I walked up to the reception desk at the same time as an American named Richard.

"I have one room left, but it has two beds," said the clerk. "How about the both of you sharing the room?" Richard and I looked at each other and agreed on the spot.

Before turning out the lights, I neglected to tell Richard that I talk in my sleep. In the middle of the night, he awoke to me well into a full belly laugh. A few seconds passed and I burst out laughing again. The more I laughed, the more Richard got the giggles. Pretty soon we were both laughing hysterically, but Richard didn't exactly know why he was laughing.

The next morning he told me about my nocturnal hysteria. We both had a laugh about it. Clearly, fun is contagious and people are attracted to fun. Walk by a room of people laughing and you practically can't help yourself being curious.

The laughter of children is universally attractive. There is no agenda. There is only pure joy and the sound of youthful mirth. It has a magical quality. Conversely, some laughter by adults is readily identifiable as mean spirited, jealous or unsure. It doesn't take an intuitive ear to pick out the difference between a laugh that is genuine and one with ill intent. Yet, as Richard will tell you, an authentic laugh is contagious.

The opportunity we have is to relive our childlike spirit. Also, along the way we can help our children grow with continued connection to pure joy.

The childlike spirit of joy has always been my objective when speaking to a group. A few months ago I spoke to ten thousand people in a sports arena. I had a ball and the audience picked up on that. The feeling was electrifying. The audience was drawn into the passion, the enthusiasm and the fun. The presentation was videotaped and since then their company offered the video for sale to their employees. At the time of writing, over eighteen thousand people have purchased that tape.

> *"The forcefulness of a good speaker—a politician or an evangelist, say—*
> *works to entrain the emotions of the audience. That is what we mean by,*
> *'He had them in the palm of his hand.'*
> *Emotional entertainment is the heart of influence."*
> *–Daniel Goleman*

AT WORK

As I mentioned earlier in this book, the unwritten rule at our office is: if this is not fun, we go home. Having fun permeates all our other actions. We know that fun will ultimately result in peak performance.

A few years ago, some old college friends of mine related a story that still brings a smile to my face. Sean and Debbie teamed up in Calgary and sold real estate the same time I was ski racing and trying to hold down a real estate business.

One day, they had a chance to make a proposal to a development group for an exclusive listing on an entire condominium complex. It was a big deal, and they were slightly nervous.

In a rush to get out the door, Sean and Debbie had all sorts of clothes in the laundry room, and it was havoc to get ready and off to the appointment on time. On the way to the appointment, Sean turned to Debbie and said, "You won't believe this."

"What did you forget?" said Debbie.

"Nothing, it's just…"

"What?" interrupted Debbie.

"Well I'm wearing your grandmother's underwear," said Sean. "I couldn't find mine so I had to wear hers."

Debbie burst out laughing. In fact, they had a difficult time collecting themselves in time for the proposal.

They got the contract and the jury is still out on whether or not Sean wears his lucky underwear for all his important presentations.

As you know, my brother also sold real estate. With Steven's background in stand-up comedy and his natural charming way, he would entertain his clients while they walked through the real estate transactions. Buying a house from Steven was fun.

Five months ago I decided to upgrade my fish tank and explore the possibility of buying a saltwater tank. I had no idea that the cost would shoot up into the thousands until I walked into the store. I made a decision to hold off, but while I was there, I talked to the owner about what was involved.

John met me at the counter and proceeded to bubble over with enthusiasm about fish. (We're talking fish here.) He scurried me over to one tank to show me how great one particular fish was. Then he took me over to another tank to see the live coral that would go great with them. Then it was over to another tank to see more fish. As time went on, I started to catch his enthusiasm.

By the time I walked out the door, I had given him my credit card deposit on a tank and we arranged a time for my $2,000-worth of fish and related products to be delivered. John didn't sell me anything other than his enthusiasm for fish. I now have a pretty cool-looking fish tank in my office and a reminder that people buy enthusiasm, passion and, most of all, fun.

Four years ago, my father was having the battle of his life. He had a brain tumor that applied too much pressure on his brain and the physicians recommended surgery to remove as much of the tumor as they could. My father agreed to the surgery and the date was set.

> **My dad knew a sense of humor was more important than anything. He wanted to make sure his doctors knew that, too.**

In typical fashion for my dad, on the morning of the operation he had my mom pin a Far Side cartoon to his hospital gown for the physicians to see. It had three doctors all around a patient's head on an operating table. The patient's leg was raised in the air as the caption read, "Look what happens when you press there..." My dad knew that a sense of humor was more important than anything. He wanted to make sure his doctors knew that too.

AT PLAY

You would think that fun while playing is an obvious statement, but go to a kid's soccer, baseball or hockey game and you'll be shocked. Some parents have forgotten that this is supposed to be fun. Some coaches will let young souls just sit on the bench, while the best players ensure the win. Kids just want to have fun.

To those parents and coaches I say, "Chill out!" Don't forget this is all about fun. If you want to teach your children good skills for life, lead by example.

Up until recently, I played hockey in a men's league. It was a great way to stay in shape and have some fun at the same time. During one particular game a fight broke out at center ice. There was all sorts of pushing and shoving. In a goofy sort of way I raised my voice and said, "Why can't we all just love each other?"

You should have seen the looks on the faces of some of the players. They thought I was off my rocker. But my words did manage to diffuse the situation and the referee was able to get control of the game again.

Later that same game, the puck appeared to cross the line but the referee called no goal. Since I was closest to the net, I argued with the referee. He looked at me and said, "Fine, do you want to settle this?" and he proceeded to play rock, paper, scissors with me. Now, that was funny. I chuckled and shrugged my shoulders.

"You win some, you lose some," I said and left it at that.

Ron Jones of San Francisco wanted to coach a high school basketball team but ended up on a career detour. He wound up at the San Francisco Center for the Specially Handicapped. He still intended to coach basketball so he organized a time and put out a notice for all interested parties to attend.

On the first day, only five showed up with one player in a wheelchair and a six-foot African-American woman who insisted on changing in the men's locker room. After Jones took forty-five minutes just to get the team to line up on one side of the court to face the basketball net, he discovered his well-prepared game plan was useless.

He then shifted his focus to fun and the results were shared by many. They eventually had cheerleaders, hot dogs and anywhere between five and a dozen people on the team at any time. They played music—sometimes the game would stop and everyone attending game was invited onto the court to dance.

Ron Jones will tell you fun is far more important than most things he could accomplish with his team.

Peak performance

At the Nagano, Japan, Olympic Winter Games in 1998, the importance of fun for peak performance was played out in the women's figure skating competition. The American team was strong that year and there was a three-way race for who would win. In the end the gold medal performance was delivered by the effervescent Tara Lipinski, while the pressure weighed heavily on Michelle Kwan and Nicole Bobek.

During the three rounds of competition, it was clear that fourteen-year-old Lipinski was having a ball. It was painfully obvious Nicole Bobek was not having any fun at all. Her attempted comeback ended in tears.

Bobek's Olympic performance started to crumble in the short program when she fell on her triple lutz. Stepping out of another jump and cutting short a third left her far behind. Going into the free skate, she was in seventeenth place and had no chance to reach the medal podium. What led to this was a chain of events that was anything but fun.

In 1995, she won the U.S. nationals and finished third in the Worlds, but then she started to self-sabotage. She first left her coach Richard Callaghan and stumbled into a number of delinquent off-ice incidents. Eleven months prior to the Olympics her coach, Carlo Fassi, died. Just days before the Olympics, she was recovering from bronchitis.

Michelle Kwan, the more proven skater, was expected to win the gold. The pressure she endured contributed nothing to her quest to win.

In the 1992 Olympic Winter Games in Albertville, France, Karin Lee Gartner shocked the world. To date, the highest this Canadian woman had accomplished in world points was tenth. Halfway through the Olympics, in the women's downhill, Karin Lee Gartner came out of the blue and won the gold. When asked in an interview what her race strategy was, she said, "Most of all, I just wanted to have fun."

HOW TO HAVE FUN WHEN THE PRESSURE IS ON

It is no small task to decide to have fun when the pressure is on. I never knew what to expect at the Olympics until I experienced it myself. The same can be said for any high-pressure situation.

Whether it is an important World Cup, the Olympics, negotiation or presentation, how do you just decide to "have fun?"

First—treat pressure situations as a process. Put yourself in pressure situations as much as you can. In Jim Loehr's book, *Stress for Success,* he recommends it. Attempt to stretch as often and as far as you can. Join Toastmasters, volunteer for things at work and put yourself out there.

Imagine what a child would do and copy that. Would a child think twice about doing something? Or would they just do it?

Second—prepare, prepare, prepare. Get as much practice as you can prior to the time when the demands are high. Your objective should be to make your performance second nature. Especially prepare for various scenarios of stressful situations. Build your confidence in this way.

Third—set up a pattern prior to every race run, negotiation or presentation you do. I use a six-step plan prior to every speech that I give. These same six steps were used prior to every ski run I took, too. The ultimate objective was to have fun. This is how it works!

SIX STEPS

1. Get there early. By arriving before you have to, stress is managed better. You are more aware of your surroundings, and you leave room for the unexpected to occur. By reducing stress, you set up better chances to have fun and have peak performance.

2. Breathe. It sounds basic but, remember, when you are in a stressful situation, what happens to your breathing? It becomes shallow and you signal to your brain that this is a fight or flight situation. Again, this is opposite of fun. Deep breathing reduces stress and maximizes the possibility of having fun. The key to breathing properly is the breath out. Breathe only through your nose and fill your lungs with oxygen. Then push all the air out gently with your diaphragm, the base of your stomach. Now, you will fill the lungs with a completely new quantity of oxygen. You succeed in doing the opposite of shallow breathing and further reduce stress.

3. Visualize. Visualizing is a great thing to do when stress is low. Now is not the time to practice. Visualize the outcomes that you want, integrate the five senses and imagine the emotional high from accomplishing your task at hand.

4. The Vortex Technique. This technique may seem odd to you, but I have personally used it to a great deal of benefit. I simply imagine collecting energy from the universe. I close my eyes and imagine a swirl of energy above my head. Soon the swirl becomes a vortex of powerful energy. Then I imagine this energy twisting into a point much like a tornado. The energy then funnels down through the top of my head and through my whole body. It is as if I fill up every part of my body. I feel the energy course through my veins. It is a very exhilarating feeling.

5. Anchoring. Anchoring is a technique that is used in Neuro-Linguistic Programming (language of the mind). Anchoring is accomplished through physical actions creating mental states. A natural anchor may be when you clench your teeth, narrow your eyes and tense your body. If you did this right now, you would manifest the feeling or sensation of anger. Anchoring involves a conditioned response from a set physical action. The anchor I use before speaking is vigorously rubbing my hands together. Each time I do this, I anchor that action to the feeling of energy, confidence and fun. This puts me instantly in that positive state, and I have primed the pump completely.

6. Have fun. This is where you simply decide to have fun. Rationalize to yourself that you have done everything in your power to prepare for this event. Trying any harder at this point will only get in the way. Now is the time to have fun and let loose. You know deep down what to do, so do it and have fun at the same time.

LET GO OF THE RESULTS

Fun happens only when you are in the moment, in the now. You don't arrive at fun. You either are having fun or you are not. Therefore, let go of the results.

The results will take care of themselves. Given a fun process, you will enjoy the trip a little more. Plus, as you know, peak performance happens while you are having fun. Let go and enjoy the ride.

IN SUMMARY

1. We all seek the most profound state of happiness, which is fulfillment.

2. Shift from fear and stress to bliss and fun.

3. Being who you truly are is vulnerable. People are more attracted to the real you.

4. Being grounded will see you through stressful situations.

5. Fun is contagious.

6. Seek a childlike spirit when approaching anything.

7. Find ways to have fun at work.

8. Stay "on purpose."

9. Don't forget to have fun at play, too. Lighten up, chill out and enjoy.

10. Use the six steps to peak performance to have fun: Get there early, breathe, visualize, use the vortex technique, use anchoring, decide to have fun!

All this business about fun and living "on purpose" is challenging to attain. What is your purpose and how will you get there? The last chapter will give you some answers and hopefully give you more questions, as you seek your own path through life.

PRINCIPLE 12 ... SERVE WITH LOVE AND LIVE IN BLISS

"Follow your bliss."
—Joseph Campbell

Life is a gift. Cherish it, nurture it, love it, participate in it and let it flow. Heck that sounds good... but first, what is life all about? Now that is a question that has confounded people from the beginning. I venture to say, it will be an eternal question.

During my first year of college I took a pre-medicine program of science and math courses. I hated it. It was sheer torture and toward the end of the year, I was ready to drop out. One night, frustrated, I went to my mom. I was all choked up.

"What is life all about?" I asked.

"Now there's a question people have been trying to figure out for ages," she said. I don't remember the answer she had, but it must have been good, because I felt better.

Yet, if you ask people that question, you'll rarely get an "I don't know." It is more likely that the answer you receive will be based on that person's own set of experiences. The truth is we are like the proverbial blind men who are touching a small piece of an elephant. We each claim to know the nature of the whole beast, but really don't have a clue.

How could a fish understand the ocean? How could birds understand the atmosphere? What does a worm know about the earth? What do we know about life? The largest difference between humans and other creatures of the earth is we can use our brains for reason. There are many things that we can create and most things we have no idea how we affect.

For the purpose of understanding, let's focus on that which we can create.

LOVE VERSUS FEAR

Our lives have been shaped by love and by love of others. Love has a meaning beyond any description. It is many things to many people. Its significance evolves differently for each person, as we make our way through life.

According to *A Course in Miracles*, "Love does not conquer all things, but it does set all things right." Love is a repeated message in the Bible and through the teachings of Jesus. His message directed people toward loving God. Then they would be in the position to love themselves and others. "Love God with all your heart and mind and soul and strength, and your neighbor as yourself."

TYPES OF LOVE IN A RELATIONSHIP

1. Behavioral love is a give and take of actions. Vince Lombardi, the famous Notre Dame football coach, said that one of the most important qualities of a leader is to love people. "Love is loyalty. Love is teamwork. Love respects the dignity of the individual."

2. Cognitive love means you love people for what they think and what they stand for. M. Scott Peck in *People of the Lie* says that "it is in the struggle between good and evil that life has its meaning—and in the hope that goodness can succeed... Evil can be conquered by love."

3. Values-based love means you love people at a deeper level. You love them for who they are. Here is where shared values strengthen partnerships and relationships of all kinds.

4. Spiritual love is a profound sense of connection with current love relationships, with lost loves and even self-love. The Greeks called this *agape*—a form of love that is so deep that it transcends all other forms of love.

We were born with a natural capacity for love. We expressed this love in all areas of life. As an infant everything is amazing and new. Later, we jump out of bed with enthusiasm and pure intent—to love life. It is a natural impulse that is extended to everyone and all things.

Over time, we learned "rules." We learned bad and good. We went to school and learned jealousy and deceit. We learned about teasing and the sting of ridicule. We learned to distrust and how to manipulate. Love was no longer pure intent.

The older we get, the more we seek to find that pure love again. As new parents, like most new parents, my wife and I are captivated by this "lost love" we see revealed in our children.

Wayne Dyer in his book, *Your Sacred Self*, writes, "You moved away from love, but now you are back and making the choice for love. You know deep within you that at your primal level you have been designed for love and happiness. You simply let that false self direct you away from the loving presence that is your essence."

LOVE IS THE ANTITHESIS OF FEAR

Fear-based thoughts will deliver poor results. Love-based thoughts will deliver improved results. Fear itself is a learned behavior. In fact, you were born with only two fears: the fear of falling and the fear of loud noises.

Over time you learned other fears. Fear of embarrassment, success, failure, letting others down, worthiness, loss, negative results and a host of others.

Command and control leadership strategies often use fear to motivate subordinates.

"You will be fired, if you do not work harder."

"You will not be promoted, if you do not work late."

"You will lose your raise, if this project is not completed in 30 days."

Sometimes fear can be used as a self-motivator to a degree of effectiveness. But fear ultimately wears at the psyche and destroys resolve.

The best results will come from love and bliss.

PSYCHOLOGY OF LOVE

Since both my wife and I own our businesses, the demands that we have on our time are great. In making a decision to hire a nanny, we had a good deal to consider. Who would be the best caregiver for our children? Most important, we wanted a good stand-in for the love and affection that infants crave, and that we would not be able to provide while we were at work.

We eventually hired a loving woman with a Hispanic background. Her English was nearly nonexistent, but she's raised five children and helped with four grandchildren. The way she adores our kids more than outweighs any early child development skills that another person might offer.

The psychology of love is simple. Love, attention and affection speak volumes to the healthy growth of a child.

THE MEANING OF LIFE

"As far as we can discern, the sole purpose of human existence
is to kindle a light in the darkness of mere being."
–Carl Jung

At first, this statement appears as a cynical expression from a frustrated psychologist. Yet life would be dark without some guiding light. We each have the responsibility to kindle that light, a light for ourselves and others. Being, living, then has purpose.

So what would that purpose be? The clue is hidden in your actions. What you do that makes you feel most alive is that spark that gives you light.

A great exercise is to pretend a reporter for *Life* magazine interviews you. Write an article about yourself. What would *Life* have to say about you? What did you do personally and professionally? Imagine the reporter asking you what you feel most proud of.

Imagine this reporter interviews others in your life. What would they say about you? What difference did you make in their world?

Now write another article based on the future when you hit your one-hundredth birthday. What would be added? What difference did you make in these remaining years?

MAKING A DIFFERENCE IN THIS WORLD

My original intention for going into pre-med was to get a career that would make a difference. I felt that medicine was as noble as any profession. Noble, or not, I did not have what it took to get through the mountains of academia.

From an early age on, I knew that I would ultimately go into politics. My experiences as a community-minded youth clearly pointed me in the direction of politics. The defining moment came when I saw Peter Lougheed give a passionate speech as he left a couple of decades of successful office. Peter Lougheed was one of Alberta's great premiers and he was an idol for me. I knew that one day I would be premier of Alberta too.

What I realize now is that it is what Peter Lougheed represented that moved me. I had no idea that there was such a profession as professional speaking. I had never imagined myself holed up in a room, typing away at a computer keyboard. All I knew was people listened to the premier, and they could be moved to take action.

Then, the speaking business appeared after my experiences in the Olympic games. In studying the lives of others, including my own, I find it fascinating how a random set of dots connect to make such perfect sense. The common denominator is always connected to the prospect of helping others in some way.

Judith Bardwick, the author of *Danger in the Comfort Zone*, says, "Significance is to do things that matter and create value." Alfred Nobel was a case in point.

ALFRED NOBEL

Alfred Nobel was a Swedish chemist who amassed a fortune inventing and marketing explosives for use in weapons. When his brother died, the local paper mistook the facts and identified Alfred as the deceased. As a result, they wrote an obituary on Alfred Nobel.

Alfred had a unique glimpse of how he would be remembered. The author of the obituary summed up Alfred's life as the inventor of explosives. His contributions spoke of how much killing power his inventions had and what war efforts he had helped. It covered the mass destruction that his explosives were able to accomplish that inferior bombs could not.

That night he was unable to sleep with visions of innocent victims being killed by his inventions. The next morning, he committed himself to a new direction. Like the transformation of a Dickens character in *A Christmas Carol*, he completely changed the direction of his life and what he would be known for. He used his wealth to establish the Nobel Prizes. The most famous being the Nobel Peace Prize.

Alfred Nobel wanted his obituary to read how he made a difference by improving future generations.

WHAT MOTIVATES PEOPLE?

As I speak to groups, I research a great deal prior to each event. My objective is not to give a canned presentation. Instead, I hope to weave the challenges, stresses and solutions within the structure of my talk.

As I meet more people in corporate North America, I realize there are three areas that motivate people in business and the business of life.

1. Responsibility: People seek out opportunities to put their own mark on the world. Through creativity and individual insight, they feel a sense of contribution to a greater cause.

2. Growth: People want to be challenged by their environment. They yearn to reach new levels personally and professionally. By growing, they feel more fulfilled.

3. Significance: People want to make a difference. By being a valuable contributor they feel as though they have made some improvement in their environment, in the lives of others and for the future in some way.

FINDING MEANING IN LIFE

By finding a meaning in life, you will be aware of your purpose in life. Meaning and purpose will be the fuel for all action. It is your source of all results and those to come. W. Clement Stone said, "When you discover your mission, you will feel its demand. It will fill you with enthusiasm and a burning desire to get to work on it."

(If you skipped the *Life* magazine exercise, you have cheated yourself. Put this book down now and do it!)

Part of the reason making a difference is so important is based on the adage, "You get what you give." Give love and you will get love. Make a difference in the world and a difference will be made in your life.

Look around at faces in a crowd when you get a chance. It is a sobering exercise. You will see all kinds, but the sad ones are the walking, breath-ing, living dead. There is no purpose in their life. Or, they have resigned themselves to their unfortunate lot in life and they are just putting in time.

Serving others and yourself with love is essential to breaking this downward pattern. Making life one that is blissful, not full of suffering, is the key.

SERVE WITH LOVE AND LIVE IN BLISS

Helping others feels good. You feel satisfied. You feel successful. In the end of the poem, "Success," Ralph Waldo Emerson says, "To leave the world a bit better, whether by a healthy child, a garden patch, or a redeemed social condition; To know one life has breathed easier because you have lived... This is to have succeeded."

Albert Schweitzer worded it this way: "I don't know what your destiny will be, but one thing I do know, the only ones among you who will be really happy are those who have sought and found how to serve."

Serving is a powerful word. It does not have to mean subservient or any-thing demeaning. More or less, it has to do with a more giving approach. Lao-tse, the profound Chinese philosopher, wrote twenty-five hundred years ago, "The reason why rivers and seas receive the homage of a hun-dred mountain streams is that they keep below them. Thus, they are able to reign over all the mountain streams. So the sage, wishing to be above men, putteth himself below them; wishing to be before them, he putteth himself behind them. Thus, though his place be above men, they do not feel his weight; though his place be before them, they do not count it an injury."

In an effort to be a great teacher or servant of the people the sage puts him-self at a place where he can make the greatest difference. Serving others and serving yourself with love is all that there is. Some people may have difficulty doing anything for others, much less loving themselves. It is not about being selfish, it is about love. Challenge oneself to pure intent and love is the only option.

Buddha's last words were to be a lamp unto ourselves. He, like Jung, knew the spark necessary to light the way was through service. Serving others is a mentality. It is a way of life.

If you are in sales or seek to influence someone else, you know that your knowledge and passion will take you only so far. It is a leadership philosophy toward value and opportunity that makes the difference. As important as serving yourself is, it is the service to others that completes the circle.

As the author and speaker Ian Percy puts it in *Going Deep:*

> When self-love is limited to love of self, the result is chaos and distortion in all our relationships. If it is focused on God and others, the result is harmony, creativity and meaning. Self-love is a sacred state and we cannot have ongoing influence as a corporate spiritual leader without it.

DEVELOPMENT OF SELF-ESTEEM

Self-love is an investment in self-esteem. When I watched my brother take courses and listen to tapes, I thought him weak and dependent. Now, I am a firm believer that the healthiest people on the planet are those completely dedicated to personal growth.

It takes a strong and courageous person to take the steps within. It is sometimes safer to stay stuck than to find out what is behind the unknown door. Development in self-esteem is an exploration in self-love.

In conversations with North American psychologists, the Dalai Lama noted his shock at the family dysfunction and low self-esteem that was extraordinarily prevalent in Western society. Rebuilding self-esteem is ultimately up to the individual and in direct proportion to the courage to explore within.

I have a friend who is financially successful. He has a list of two hundred things he wants to accomplish. Many of the things are dangerous or involve a certain degree of courage to perform. Over the years, I have watched him alienate people at every turn. It turns out that his list does not include the most courageous thing he could do—embarking on a revealing journey within.

This is *not* the place to say, "Oh, I'll think about things and figure it out." Working alone on yourself has its limitations and often takes much more time. It is about the importance of having a third-party perspective.

ANOTHER PERSPECTIVE

John Gray is the author of the bestseller *Men Are From Mars, Women Are From Venus*. What is not well known about Gray is the personal story of the time when his dad had been car-jacked, locked in a trunk and left to die. When John and the family heard the news they rushed back home to Texas.

Gray tells a story of how he and his brother stood by the car where his father died and imagined what it must have been like trapped in a trunk in the Texas heat. After a moment John Gray climbed into the trunk and told his brother to close it. John could see the evidence of where his father tried to pry his way out. He noticed where he broke a taillight to further try to escape.

Then, John reached his arm through the hole where the tail light cover was. He talked to his brother who told him to reach a little further up and to the right. Then John was able to reach the button to let himself out. Despite the tragic story, the intent behind telling it is clear. Another set of eyes, from an external perspective, can shed new light on a situation.

If you have not done so in the past, I encourage you to know the options available to you. Reading a book like this is valuable, but another perspective is priceless. There are trained therapists, self-development courses, support groups, organizations, mentors and business coaches. Ask around and find what would work best for you. Be proactive and do this for yourself. You will bring a better you to the world as a result.

It is essential to get the wisdom from someone skillful and wise. There are plenty of people out there wanting to give you advice. The challenge is to find the best perspective you can. We have all had the experience where the message is much like "Here, take my advice. I'm not using it." Shop around and then make a decision to invest time and money in yourself.

Most important, find others who do *not* come from a place of judgmentalism. Seeking advice from divorcees when considering a divorce is not your best choice. Choose wisely. Also, know that there are times when guilt and self-hate get in the way. These are times when a third party can help you. They will encourage you on your own path toward fulfillment. Seek to be a student of life and find teachers who will contribute compassion to your quest of growth and inner peace.

Learning through trial and error gets old after a while. Know that what you learn just might hurt. Know that the greatest lessons are the ones that hurt the most. Charge ahead and learn what you can.

YOUR PURPOSE, MISSION, VISION

In the movie, *Dances with Wolves*, Kevin Costner plays a character who is lost in life while serving in a war he doesn't understand. A key line in the movie happens after he discovers his Indian name, Dances with Wolves. He then says, "It was then that I knew my purpose in life." What did he mean by that?

"Dances," as used in this title, means freedom of expression. Wolves are pack- and family-oriented. From that point onward in the movie, Costner's life changed. He joins the Indian tribe and starts a family with the woman he loves. He broke from his conventional role and chose a life in keeping with what he connected with. He lived *on purpose.*

Neitzche explained purpose this way: "He who has a *why* to live can bear with almost any *how*." Businesses write mission statements every day. Why don't people explore their mission? Because it's scary.

Discovering your purpose, mission or life vision is like peeling an onion. You peel back a layer and you come upon another layer. Each layer brings you closer to the core. At the core is the essence of you.

At your core are those qualities that are non-negotiable. You discover what you would crawl across broken glass to preserve or experience. What that is for you will remain a mystery until you take the necessary steps to dedicate part of your time to personal growth.

What decisions will you make?

GRATITUDE

Being grateful for all things in life is liberating. It frees the mind from fear and takes it squarely on love and bliss. It springs a new awareness toward a higher plane of fulfillment. Ralph H. Blum wrote, "There is a calmness to a life lived in gratitude, a quiet joy."

If you come from a place of gratitude, all things can be appreciated.

The past is a place to be grateful for. From it you have been given gifts. You have grown from the challenges and opportunities.

The future is a place where instead of wanting and expecting, you allow. You gravitate toward your dominant thought. If your dominant thought is want, you will get just that—wanting. If your life is consumed with expectation, you will be more in the state of expectation.

The present is the place to be most grateful. You choose between the state of happiness versus wanting or waiting. Life is short. At any one time you have space for one thought. Why not make that thought a gift to your self? A gift of gratitude and joy.

SHARING GRATITUDE

A thank you is always appreciated. Express it to others. Saying thank you in special ways is often remembered. We often forget to say it at home. Take a moment and write a thank you card to someone you live with. Let them know you appreciate them and thank them for being who they are.

At Vince Poscente International we have little postcards that have a photo of me skiing with the caption, "Speaking from experience... Thank you." They cost little to send, but people enjoy receiving them. Numerous people have commented on how nice it is to get a handwritten note.

SCREEN SAVER

If you have a computer, put on your screen saver what you are grateful for. If you like, use the affirmation, "Thank you for my opportunity to serve with love and live in bliss." Make this affirmation more of a dominant thought in your life.

GRATITUDE JOURNAL

In recent years, Oprah Winfrey has made famous the usefulness of a gratitude journal. When I was going through my divorce, I found writing ten things I was grateful for in my day set the tone for a better tomorrow.

Keeping a gratitude journal during times of trouble is especially useful. But, you need not be going through an emotional challenge before you start one. They are useful and beneficial at any time. When trouble hits, and it will, it will be like water off a duck's back. You just move on to the next opportunity.

IN SUMMARY

1. Follow your bliss.
2. Love often.
3. Eliminate fear with a focus on love.
4. Be a light for others to find their way.
5. Do things that matter and create value.
6. Seek out opportunities to put your own mark in the world.
7. Yearn to reach new levels both personally and professionally.
8. Make a positive difference in the lives of others.
9. Seek out another perspective toward your own personal growth.
10. Be grateful for your past, your future and, especially, your present moment.

Now is the time to act. The time to live on purpose is *absolutely now.* It is never too late to start anew, and the choice to change is yours for the taking. How will things be different for you from today forward? What has been left undone that you can change right now?

Martin Luther King, Jr. said that "even if I knew the world would end tomorrow, I would plant a tree today." He knew the best time to plant an oak tree is twenty years ago. The next best time is right now.

Change is good—and you will make the choice between fear or love, between chaos or bliss.

Serve with love and live in bliss.

Afterword

*"The unhappiness, unease and unrest in the world today are
caused by people living far below their capacity."*
–Abraham Maslow

Each principle in this book can take you closer to fulfillment. You will discover the more you learn, the simpler life becomes. Life mastery is a process of learning, growing and learning some more. As your thirst for knowledge grows, you will come closer still to peace of mind.

Challenge yourself to grow every day. If you would like a laminated list of these Invinceable Principles, contact our office through our website at www.invinceability.com. Stay on track by notching up your growth, consistently and diligently. Before you know it, you will be looking at your days with a quiet calm and understanding.

God bless you on your journey!

the opportunity to dream

invincible **KIDS** FOUNDATION™

APPENDIX

The Invincible Kids Foundation was established in 1999 to create change in the next generation. IKF helps give kids the opportunity, through education and empowerment, to pursue their dreams. Without the support of creative, community-conscious people, this program would not be possible.

There are many areas where help is needed, please let us know how you would like to contribute. Mail a copy of this form to: The Invincible Kids Foundation, 2528 Elm Street #200, Dallas, TX 75226, USA.

For further information, please call: 800-791-2078.

Name:_____

Company:_____(if applicable)

Address:_____

City:_____

State/Prov:_____ Zip:_____

Phone:_____

Fax:_____ E:Mail:_____

[ ] Please find enclosed a donation of $_____ U.S.

[ ] Tax receipt required   [ ] Tax receipt not required

[ ] Please send information on becoming a corporate sponsor of Invincible Kids.

[ ] Please send information on becoming a volunteer for Invincible Kids

[ ] Please send information on grants available for kids.

[ ] Please send information on how Invincible Kids programs may be brought to my community.

BIBLIOGRAPHY

Bardwick, Judith M. *Danger in the Comfort Zone.* (American Management Association, 1991)

Brenden, Nathaniel. *The Six Pillars of Self-Esteem.* (New York: Bantam Books, 1995)

Breathnach, Sarah Ban. *Simple Abundance.* (New York: Warner Books, 1996)

Buzan, Tony. *The Mind Map Book.* (Plume, 1996)

Campolo, Tony. *Carpe Diem.* (Dallas: Word Publishing, 1995)

Carnegie, Dale. *How to Stop Worrying and Start Living.* (New York: Simon and Schuster, 1984)

Chopra, Deepak M.D. *Ageless Body, Timeless Mind.* (New York: Harmony Books, 1993)

Chopra, Deepak M.D. *Creating Affluence.* (San Raphael: New World Library, 1993)

Chopra, Deepak M.D. *The Seven Spiritual Laws of Success.* (Amber-Allen Publishing, 1994)

Collins, James C. and Jerry I. Porras. *Built to Last.* (New York: Harper Business, A Division of HarperCollins Publishers, 1994)

Coue, Emile. *Self Mastery through Conscious Autosuggestion.* (Santa Fe: Sun Publishing Company, 1988)

Csikszentmihalyi, Mihaly. *Flow, The Psychology of Optimal Experience.* (New York: Harper Perennial, A Division of HarperCollins Publishers, 1990)

DePree, Max. *Leadership Jazz.* (New York: Bantam Doubleday Dell Pub., 1992)

Dilts, Robert. *Changing Belief Systems with NLP.* (Meta Publications, 1990)

Dryden, Gordon and Dr. Jeannette Vos. *The Learning Revolution.* (Auckland: The Learning Web, 1997)

Dyer, Wayne N. *Your Sacred Self.* (New York: HarperCollins, 1994)

Gillett, Richard. *Change Your Mind, Change Your World.* (New York: Simon and Schuster, 1992)

Goleman, Daniel. *Emotional Intelligence.* (New York: Bantam Books, 1995)

Hoff, Benjamin. *The Tao of Pooh.* (New York: Penguin Books, 1982)

Jeffers, Susan, Ph.D. *Feel the Fear and Do It Anyway.* (New York: Fawcett Books, 1992)

Jones, Laurie Beth. *Jesus CEO.* (New York: Hyperion, 1995)

Kita, Joe. *"That's Mr. Rodney, to You." Men's Health Magazine* (1995)

Kornfield, John. *A Path with Heart.* (New York: Bantam Books, 1993)

Krakauer, John. *Into Thin Air.* (New York: Random House, 1998)

Loehr, James. *Stress for Success.* (New York: Random House, 1997)

McGrath, Alister E. *Christian Theology.* (Blackwell Publishers, 1997)

Peck, M. Scott M.D. *The Road Less Traveled.* (New York: Simon and Schuster, 1978)

Percy, Ian. *Going Deep.* (Toronto: MacMillan Canada, 1997)

Quebein, Nido R. *How To Get Anything You Want.* (Executive Press, 1998)

Roth, Robert. *Marharishi Mahesh Yogi's TM Transcendental Meditation.* (New York: Donal I. Fine, Inc., 1994)

Rubin, Theodore Isaac M.D. with Eleanor Rubin. *Compassion and Self-Hate.* (New York: Collier Books / Macmillan Publishing Company, 1975)

Sheard, Jim and Wally Armstrong. *In His Grip.* (Dallas: Word Publishing, 1997)

About the man...

Photo: Kristina Hahn-Eleniak

During the 1992 Olympic Winter Games in Albertville, France, Vince Poscente raced to a Canadian national record of 135 miles per hour (216.7 km/h) on skis. Even more astonishing, at the age of 26, Vince had never ski raced before! He went from a recreational skier to the Olympic finals in just four years.

Vince currently resides in Dallas, Texas with his wife Michelle and their two children. As a highly popular keynote speaker, Vince also provides a line of self-improvement products. Vince continues to write and produce inspirational books and audio programs. Honors include:

- Former vice president of North America's largest real estate investment firm
- Highly acclaimed resource for Young Presidents' Organization
- Founder of Invincible Kids Foundation
- Board: Olympic Hall of Fame – Canada
- Five-time national record holder – Skiing

INVINCEABLE PRINCIPLES

THE NEW BOOK FROM WORLD RENOWNED MOTIVATIONAL EXPERT AND OLYMPIC ATHLETE

VINCE POSCENTE

COVER DESIGN   Benson Design, Dallas
COVER PHOTO   Leslie Baker, VPI
BACK COVER PHOTOS   Marcus Irvin

in**vince**ability series order form

no.	description	qty.	retail	save 20%	subtotal
V057	A Journey from Ordinary to Extraordinary - Keynote Video		~~$43.75~~	**$35.00**	
A049	Accelerate to Your Objectives - Audio Album (4 cassettes)		~~$50.00~~	**$40.00**	
B006	In**vince**able Principles - Book (Hardcover)		~~$25.00~~	**$20.00**	
B073	In**vince**able Principles - Book (Paperback)		~~$18.50~~	**$15.00**	
B09X	Your In**vince**ability Performance Journal		~~$15.00~~	**$12.00**	
V012	In**vince**ability in Business - 12 Segment Video Subscription Series*		~~$80.00/mo~~	**$64.00/mo**	
A014	Creating Wealth - 2 audio cassettes		~~$25.00~~	**$20.00**	
A022	Creating Your Optimum Body - 2 audio cassettes		~~$25.00~~	**$20.00**	
A030	Creating Peace of Mind - 2 audio cassettes		~~$25.00~~	**$20.00**	
A081	Creating Balance - 2 audio cassettes		~~$25.00~~	**$20.00**	
M02M	Mouse Pad - High Impact Ski Image		~~$12.50~~	**$10.00**	
M01T	T-Shirt - 'Do What the Competition is Not Willing to Do' Size ☐L ☐XL		~~$18.95~~	**$15.00**	

b e s t   b u y s   s a v e   2 5 %

no.	description	qty.	retail	save 20%	subtotal
P010	**The Invinceable You Package** All 4 Creating programs *plus* Your In**vince**ability Performance Journal		~~$100.00~~	**$75.00**	
P018	**High Performance Invinceability Package** A Journey from Ordinary to Extraordinary, Accelerate to Your Objectives *plus* Your In**vince**ability Performance Journal		~~$100.00~~	**$75.00**	
P014	**Total Invinceability Package** 3 Creating Programs – Accelerate to Your Objectives, A Journey from Ordinary – *plus* Your In**vince**ability Performance Journal		~~$200.00~~	**$150.00**	
P100	**The Whole Enchilada** Includes all of the above. *does not include subscription series* T-Shirt Size ☐L ☐XL		~~$292.70~~	**$225.00**	

U.S. Shipping and Handling Charges: Under $50 = $5.50, $51-$100 = $7.50, Over $100 = $9.95 | **Shipping** |

fax order to: 214-752-7401

(U.S. Funds) **TOTAL**

Credit Card Number: _____

☐ VISA ☐ MC ☐ AMEX ☐ DISC   exp. date ____/____

Signature: _____

ship to:

_____
NAME

_____
ADDRESS

_____   _____   _____
CITY   STATE/PROV.   ZIP/POSTAL CODE

_____
COMPANY

_____
E-MAIL ADDRESS

_____
PHONE

_____
FAX

For more information: visit our web-site **www.invinceability.com** or Call 1-800-791-2078.